T0134951

Human-Harmonized Information Technology,
Volume 2

Toyoaki Nishida
Editor

Human-Harmonized Information Technology, Volume 2

Horizontal Expansion

 Springer

Editor
Toyoaki Nishida
Graduate School of Informatics
Kyoto University
Kyoto
Japan

ISBN 978-4-431-56815-5   ISBN 978-4-431-56535-2   (eBook)
DOI 10.1007/978-4-431-56535-2

Printed on acid-free paper

This Springer imprint is published by Springer Nature
The registered company is Springer Japan KK
The registered company address is: Chiyoda First Bldg. East, 3-8-1 Nishi-Kanda, Chiyoda-ku, Tokyo 101-0065, Japan

Dedicated to the late Prof. Yoh'ichi Tohkura

Foreword

The Japan Science and Technology Agency (JST) is a major organization in Japan to promote science and technology policies and to provide research funds to researchers mainly in academia in order to support innovative science and technology. CREST is one of the funding programs promoted by JST, and in the field of Information and Communications Technologies, eight research areas are ongoing, one of which is "Creation of Human-Harmonized Information Technology for Convivial Society." Under the Research Supervisor, Prof. Toyoaki Nishida, who took over from the late Prof. Yoh'ichi Tohkura, ten projects have been initiated. I have served as a research advisor for two different areas, one of which is this area. There are ten highly advanced projects selected in the area. I noted as an advisor that the important point of projects in this area is to focus on the technologies for "convivial society". There have been several element technologies studied up to now such as virtual reality, augmented reality, robotics, sensing technologies, and so on. These technologies have been rapidly progressing, but in order to realize a convivial society, these element technologies should be combined and harmonized based on the requirements for convivial societies. The chapters in this publication can contribute to the creation of new theories, new architecture, new systems and the invention of advanced applications to provide convivial societies. Those societies are required not only in the 2020s and 2030s, but in the 2040s, when "singularity of artificial intelligence" is envisaged to be reality.

Tomonori Aoyama, Professor Emeritus, the University of Tokyo
Visiting Professor, Keio University

A harmonization between human beings and machines is becoming a more important function in daily life. The human-harmonized information technology that can understand a human's internal intentions will be able to realize healthy and cultured living and good preparation for an aged society. Some interesting themes of the human–machine harmonization have been explored by Prof. Tohkura and researchers in a CREST project. Chapters appearing in this book are bringing fascinating results not only to the harmonized society but also to Cyber Physical Systems and the Internet of Things.

Kazuo Asakawa, Fujitsu Laboratories, Ltd.

When the late Yoh'ichi Tohkura, Ph.D., started a field of research with the theme of harmony between human beings and the information environment, "information circulation" was emphasized as a key word that must never be forgotten. It not only referred to the processing of information but also pointed out the importance of feedback of the processed results to human beings. It expresses the idea that we should consider comprehensively the nature of the information environment being created, including "how" is "what feedback" given and whether the results will be useful at all. This book is the first to discuss the information circulation from three perspectives—with regard to people, information, and machines. The research findings introduced here serve as a persuasive guide to the design of our information society.

Eisaku Maeda, Vice President, Head of NTT Communication
Science Laboratories

Technological singularity is widely considered as an Artificial Intelligence disaster triggered by highly advanced information technology. This idea of an exclusive relationship between human beings and machines is fascinating and seems to be a relationship inspired by the old story of Frankenstein's monster. The concept of human–machine harmonization, advocated by Prof. Tohkura, considers both human beings and machines as the necessary parts of the "information circulatory system" in human-harmonized information technology. This book predicts the future appearance of technological singularity that would not exclude humans; it will create a harmonious relationship between humans and machines in the information circulatory system. In the future, humanity will have its embodiment harmonized between humans and machines.

Taro Maeda, Professor, Graduate School of Information Science & Technology
Osaka University/Center for Information and Neural Networks, NICT

This book guides the reader through cutting-edge research trends anticipating the way in which humans will live their lives in the rich information environments of the near future, receiving intellectual assistance while they work, study, eat, and have fun. The book's chapters cover a wide range of topics, but the reader may find that they come together under a coherent idea of looking ahead into the future. The entirety of this book is related to a research field of JST CREST, one of the most prestigious research grant schemes in Japan. This fact alone, however, does not fully account for the impression the book strikes on its readers. I am fond of the late Prof. Tohkura's stance in which a JST CREST research area should virtually function as a national research institute, with the research supervisor acting as its director. This was undoubtedly his role as the first research supervisor of the "Creation of Human-Harmonized Information Technology for Convivial Society" research area. From the beginning, he clearly showed his views regarding the definition of a convivial society, as well as how human-harmonized information technologies should be in such societies. In this regard, he emphasized that an information environment should enhance humans' intellectual capabilities. He showed his strong and talented leadership and excellent discernment while selecting all the research directors, who are responsible for each of the chapters in this book now with the prominent research outcomes. Moreover, he, as well as his successor, Prof. Nishida, continuously encouraged the research directors to not only pursue their original research objectives, but also to actively seek the opportunity to discuss and collaborate in joint research projects with other colleagues, in particular those working in this research area. I can say that those stances resulted in a great success. I am sure the reader will enjoy going through every chapter.

Yôiti Suzuki, Professor, Research Institute of Electrical Communication
Tohoku University

Japan is becoming a super-aged society ahead of the rest of the world, and with it, the number of persons who have cognitive disabilities is sharply increasing. Moreover, persons who have developed visual or auditory function disorders or communication disorders in their youth must keep living in a society while burdened by a major handicap. Information technology (IT) compensates for weaknesses in human information processing, and the hope has been that IT will serve as a tool to assist those with language and/or communication disorders. While it is said that current artificial intelligence (AI) has functions that exceed human potential, we must wonder if it has become a technology that is beneficial to everyone. There is also the chance that globalization of useful IT will even lead to the homogenization of human thoughts and sensitiveness.

This project does not simply aim for IT that exceeds human ability of intelligence, but explores the underlying potential and diverse functions of humans while examining what IT should be, such as AI, for harnessing the potential and diverse functions of humans. Through my own research I have experienced how the underlying potential and diverse functions of humans can often surface for the first time after persons develop a physical disability. Persons who have developed language and/or communication disorders will try to converse through gestures or tactile means, while elderly persons who have developed cognitive impairments will increasingly try to convey something through facial expressions and gestures. However, that is insufficient to properly communicate with others and leads to social isolation, and society has yet to come up with a good approach for how to assist these people.

Fortunately, the researchers of the themes in this project have taken on the challenge of elucidating information on the processing function that lies deep within the brain; not just "intelligence", but also "emotion" and "consciousness" that lie in the background of intelligence. Furthermore, several of the themes feature highly creative approaches, such as discovering the possibilities of humans from new perspectives and helping to revive the esthetic sense and spiritual cry that lie deep within the brain during the course of evolution. I believe that these approaches will contribute greatly to revealing and fostering human creativity, which are major goals of the project.

This book summarizes the results to date of this project. For example, it describes IT that grasps meanings conveyed by tactile means or movements in addition to words, whereby a computer answers using expressions with universal understanding. Persons with cognitive impairments and those with language and/or communication disorders have been waiting for this technology, which will become highly useful as a tool to promote their social participation. Additionally, research that reveals and fosters human creativity could give rise to various arts, such as new and yet familiar-sounding music that crosses racial and ethnic boundaries. This will give the joy of creativity to humans and give new purpose to living. This book describes how AI and IT should be developed, so that humans can truly understand each other and share the joy of creativity, and describes many hints and approaches for realizing this.

Professor Yoh'ichi Tohkura, the program officer of this project until 2014, was a friend of mine for more than 40 years. We shared the same dream of creating IT that is truly useful to humans, the kind described in this book. I hope that those of you who also wish to realize the same dream will enjoy this book.

Tohru Ifukube, Professor Emeritus, Institute of Gerontology
The University of Tokyo

Preface

This is the second in a pair of collections describing the major outcomes of the JST-CREST research area on the creation of human-harmonized information technology (IT) for a convivial society, launched in 2009. Even in the short year following the publication of the first volume, we have witnessed much technological progress in information and communications technology, such as Uber's first real-world test of self-driving taxis in Pittsburgh in September 2016. Recent surges in artificial intelligence, however, have significantly increased society-wide concern over the risks of its use to humanity, as illustrated by shocking accidents of Google self-driving cars and Tesla autopilot. The more we hear about the role of artificial intelligence in human society, the more convinced we are of the rightness of the direction of our research, which the late Prof. Yoh'ichi Tohkura set out upon almost 8 years ago. Increasingly, people have come to think that technology should be carefully oriented not to weaken humanity but enhance it, if not challenge it.

We have become more confident than in our early days that we are on the right track in attempting to establish technology to enhance human and social potential. Human potential is the power of an individual that enables her or him to actively sustain the endeavor to reach goals in maintaining social relationships with other people. This involves vision, activity, sustainability, empathy, ethics, humor, and an esthetic sense. Social potential is the power that a society of people as a whole possesses. It encompasses generosity, support, conviviality, diversity, connectedness, and innovativeness. We believe that human and social potential complement each other to enable conviviality.

Professor Tohkura focused on human perception to research human-harmonized IT on the road toward a convivial society. Human-harmonized IT centers on understanding and enhancing cognitive dynamics resulting in an interaction between pathos based on embodied perception and logos based on modern civilization. It is evident that people will need to find a non-traditional style of self-actualization and society will aspire to a new principle of endorsing harmony. Even if the current development of artificial intelligence eventually releases us from our labor, whether physical or informational, individuals and society as a whole will need to find new styles and ways of living for wellness in a new technological world.

The preceding volume emphasized the vertical aspects of science and technology, in which basic theories on human perception and embodied behaviors form the core of human-harmonized IT, which in turn serves as a foundation for what may be called human-harmonized services in the convivial society we see before us. In this volume, we stress higher layers of human-harmonized IT oriented to a broader range of applications, including content creation, the human-harmonic information environment, health care, and learning support. This volume consists of eight chapters.

Chapter 1 addresses technology to help people not only consume musical content but also use it in a creative fashion. Toward this end, Goto and his colleagues have developed a suite of technologies for building a similarity-aware information environment. Songle is a web-based active music appreciation service that can automatically determine four types of musical descriptions: musical structure (chorus sections and repeated sections), hierarchical beat structure (musical beats and bar lines), melody line (fundamental frequency, f0, of the vocal melody), and chords (root note and chord type). Songle's web service permits anonymous users to correct errors in the musical archive, to cope with the incompleteness of the automated tool. Songle Widget is a web-based multimedia development framework that allows the control of computer-graphic animation and physical devices, such as robots, in synchronization with music publicly available on the web. Songrium is a music-browsing assistance service that allows the visualization and exploration of a large amount of user-generated music content. Goto and colleagues have also developed content-creation support technologies, such as TextAlive, which enables the creation of music-synchronized lyrics animation.

Chapter 2 addresses 3D sound-scene reproduction. Ise and his colleagues have succeeded in the world's first implementation of an immersive auditory display, named the Sound Cask, which implements the principle of boundary surface control (BoSC), a theory of 3D sound-field reproduction. BoSC features the ability to reproduce a sound field, not using points but in three dimensions. As a result, the system can provide high-performance spatial information reproduction, including sound localization and sound distance, even as the listener freely moves her or his head. The performance evaluation of the system is reported, which encompasses physical performance, localization, and the psychological and physiological evaluation of the feeling of reality in a 3D sound field. The Sound Cask system helps music professionals such as musicians, acoustic engineers, music educators, and music critics enhance their skills and further explore their creativity by providing them with the means to experience 3D sound in a telecommunications environment. Applications include a sound-field simulator, sound table tennis, and sound-field sharing.

Chapter 3 describes a framework for user-generated content creation. Tokuda and his colleagues created the MMDAgent toolkit to build voice-interaction systems by incorporating speech recognition, HMM-based flexible speech synthesis, embodied 3D agent rendering with simulated physics, and dialogue management based on a finite state transducer. MMDAgent was released as an open-source software toolkit. Tokuda and colleagues have constructed an all-in-one set of materials on the use of MMDAgent and the production of dialogue content, including guidebooks/tutorials, slides, reference manuals, and sample scripts. The results have been demonstrated in public installations, including the ones in front of the main gate of the Nagoya Institute of Technology and at City Hall in Handa City, Aichi, Japan.

Chapter 4 presents a project that enables a mobile social robot to adapt to an open public space in a city. Toward this end, Kanda and his colleagues developed a series of techniques to harmonize their robots in daily human contexts. They addressed common-sense problems in the domain of open public spaces, such as a shopping mall corridor where pedestrians walk. They focused on technologies for sensing pedestrians. Their pedestrian model includes collision avoidance and task-oriented human–robot interaction (HRI) encompassing such activities as shopping and observation. They also introduced high-level harmonized HRI features to avoid collision, prevent congestion, and escape "robot abuse"—the nasty treatment of robots, by children in particular. They conducted several field studies and found that they were able to harmonize mobile robots in daily human contexts, and they encouraged people to acquire information from them.

Chapter 5 focuses on the varieties of gait a person has to uncover the relation between gait variation and inertial states, i.e., attention (gaze direction), human relation (group segmentation), and cognitive level (assessment of dementia). For attention estimation, Yagi and his colleagues conducted numerous experiments studying the relationship between gaze and whole-body behaviors. They found similar eye–head coordination in different conditions, which suggests that head orientation is directly related to visual perception; the distribution of the eye position varies systematically with head orientation; the angles of the gaze, head, and chest have linear relationships, under non-walking and walking conditions; not only head but also arm and leg movements are related to the gaze locations; and so on. They also propose a method of determining whether two people belong to the same group, combining motion trajectory, chest orientation, and gesture. Researching dual-task analysis for cognitive-level estimation, they conducted data collection at an elder-care facility and at the National Museum of Emerging Science and Innovation, or Miraikan, in Tokyo. The data obtained from the latter are immense, with more than 95,000 participants. The analysis of these data is in progress.

Chapter 6 addresses the design and demonstration of the future of the information environment where people get together. Naemura and his colleagues focus on three issues: privacy control of display content for promoting discussion in groups, projection-based control of physical objects for suppressing the incompatibility between the physical and digital worlds, and spatial imaging for augmented reality among people without wearable displays. For the privacy-control issue, they propose a privacy-control method called SHelective for sharing displays and a group-work facilitation system called Inter-Personal Browsing for collaborative web search. For the projection-based augmentation issue, they propose the concept of a bit-data projection system called the Pixel-Level Visible Light Communication Projector and a chemical augmentation system called Hand-Rewriting for paper-based computing. These latter two are functional extensions of existing image projectors to create a more advanced augmentation of the physical world. For spatial imaging, they propose EnchanTable, which can display a vertically standing mid-air image on a table surface using reflection; MiragePrinter, for interactive fabrication on a 3D printer with a mid-air display; and fVisiOn, a glasses-free tabletop 3D display viewable from 360° to augment ordinary tabletop communications.

Chapter 7 describes a reading-life log technology to help people leverage characters to live an intellectual life. Kise and his colleagues, based on character detection, recognition, and generation, transfigure traditional character and document media into new active media, using technologies such as high-speed character recognition and document image retrieval. Their technology is comprehensive, including real-time character recognition for alphanumeric and Japanese characters, omnidirectional character recognition that allows recognition of all characters in a 360° scene image, and real-time document image retrieval based on basic character detectors and recognizers, a large-scale character dataset, and an automatic font generator. On this basis, Kise's group developed reading-life log technology, which not only builds a record for one's reading life: the time spent on, amount of, and attitude toward reading activities, but also analyzes the content of the reading to support the user's intellectual activities. Using reading-life log technology, Kise's group prototyped applications such as Wordometer, which counts the number of words one reads to diagnose one's reading life, a scene-text detector and generator, an automated text annotator, a system for recording texts together with the facial expressions of the reader, and an augmented narrative that uses bio-feedback in a text–body interaction.

Chapter 8 addresses pedagogical machines that can teach and be taught. Hiraki and his colleagues take a threefold approach: the development of cognitive science, machine intelligence, and field studies in an educational environment. In the first approach, they found that infants are very sensitive to temporal contiguity in interaction with their mothers. In particular, it became clear that nowness and responsiveness are very important for the design of a pedagogical machine. With the second approach, they developed a pedagogical agent with gaze interaction (PAGI) that is designed to teach Korean words to Japanese students, capable of simulating mutual gaze, gaze following, and joint attention. Experiments with PAGI showed that even adults are implicitly affected by nowness and responsiveness during word learning with artificial agents. As a result of the third approach, several novel findings have been obtained, e.g., interactions among children where the interactions seem to affect each child's learning and altruistic behaviors.

Chapter 9 is the epilog. I summarize the results obtained in research activities over the past 8 years. In a nutshell, what we have built can be called a perceptually rich common ground between humans and computers. As potential next challenges, I suggest companion agents and robotic apprentices with a more comprehensive common ground, ranging from perception to cognition, that can build and maintain longitudinal companionship with us to help explore larger information spaces.

Kyoto, Japan   Toyoaki Nishida
January 2017

Contents

Chapter 1
OngaCREST Project: Building a Similarity-Aware Information Environment for a Content-Symbiotic Society

Masataka Goto

Abstract The purpose of this project is to develop fundamental technologies for building a similarity-aware information environment in which people are able to know similarities among vast amounts of media content. This environment helps establish a *"content-symbiotic society"* in which media content such as music and video can be created and used in innovative, but ethical ways. Furthermore, by developing technologies for enhancing content appreciation and creation, we aim to promote a society in which people can actively engage in content appreciation and creation, and a content culture that respects past content and emphasizes experiencing emotion. We developed various types of technologies for supporting music appreciation and creation, such as *Songle*, *Songrium*, and *TextAlive* web services, and made those services open to the public.

Keywords Music information processing · Music-understanding technologies · Content-appreciation support technologies · Content-creation support technologies · Similarity and typicality

1.1 Introduction

The amount of digital content that can be accessed by people has been increasing and will continue to do so in the future. This is desirable since more people can enjoy more content. However, problems have arisen. For content creators, their own works become easily buried among huge amounts of past works. For listeners and viewers, it is becoming more difficult to find their favorite content. Furthermore, as content increases, the amount of similar content is also increasing. As a result, creators will be more concerned that their content might invite unwarranted suspicion of plagiarism. All kinds of works are influenced by existing content, and it is difficult to avoid the unconscious creation of content partly similar in some way to prior content.

M. Goto (✉)
National Institute of Advanced Industrial Science and Technology (AIST),
Tsukuba, Ibaraki, Japan
e-mail: m.goto@aist.go.jp

© Springer Japan KK 2017
T. Nishida (ed.), *Human-Harmonized Information Technology, Volume 2*,
DOI 10.1007/978-4-431-56535-2_1

It is therefore desirable to clarify to what extent content can be similar but still acceptable. However, the ability of human beings to judge such similarity is limited. Judging the similarity between two things in front of one's eyes or ears is possible. But the speed of this judging is slow. Searching for similar content among a million items cannot be done for all practical purposes. Moreover, while humans are able to make accurate judgments based on past experiences, their ability is limited when it comes to judging "*typicality*" (commonness)—determining what will happen probabilistically from an overall phenomenon. For example, when an uncommon event is frequently observed, people tend to wrongly assume that it is likely to occur. And when an event that is by its nature frequent is not encountered, people tend to wrongly assume that it is rare. Because it is not quantitatively possible to view and listen to all accessible content, it is not humanly possible to carry out appropriate judgment that encompasses all content.

Consequently, if there is a high risk that one's work will be denounced as being similar to someone else's as a result of the monotonic increase in content, this could lead to a society in which it is difficult for people to create and share content with peace of mind. This could happen with the coming of an "age of billions of creators" in which anyone can enjoy creating and sharing works. Content is made up of a variety of elements. However, despite the existence of common elements (elements with high probability of appearing), there is the problem of fruitless suspicion of plagiarism due to misunderstanding of "the question of originality" that arises simply when these elements resemble other content. In the first place, creative activities build upon past content. Highly common elements and expressions should be appropriately recognized, shared, and used between creators and consumers as knowledge common to humankind.

In light of the above, we started the *OngaCREST Project*, a five-year research project to build a technological foundation that not only specialists and but also general users can use to answers the questions "What is similar here?" and "How often does this occur?" With the spread of such a technological foundation in the future, people could continue creating and sharing content with peace of mind. Furthermore, by developing *content-appreciation support technologies*, we want to allow people to actively encounter content and appreciate them. We also want to make it easy for even non-specialists to easily enjoy the content creation process by developing *content-creation support technologies* that enable "highly typical" elements (such as chord progressions and conventional genre-dependent practices) to be used as knowledge common to humankind.

The OngaCREST Project is officially entitled "*Building a Similarity-aware Information Environment for a Content-Symbiotic Society.*" It was carried out as a fiscal year 2011-selected research project (Research Director: Masataka Goto; Group Leaders: Masataka Goto, Shigeo Morishima, Satoshi Nakamura, and Kazuyoshi Yoshii) in the research area of "*Creation of Human-Harmonized information Technology for Convivial Society*" of the CREST (Core Research for Evolutional Science and Technology) funding program provided by the JST (Japan Science and Technology Agency). The main types of media content targeted in the project are music and music-related videos, such as music videos and dance videos, which are representative and important media content. It carried out basic and applied research related to music-understanding technologies and enabled end users to use research results as web services so harmonious interactions between humans and the information environment could be extracted. In this chapter, I introduce main research achievements of this project.

1.2 Project Overview

The overview of the OngaCREST Project is shown in Fig. 1.1. We call a society in which relationships between humans and content and between past content and future content are rich and capable of sustained development a *"content-symbiotic society."* To realize such a society, this project aims to build a similarity-aware information environment that promotes an awareness of similarity—i.e., allows people to understand similarity—among a huge amount of media content. If a content-symbiotic society can be realized, media content can be richly and soundly created and used. In short, people will be able to continue to create and share content with peace of mind. Anyone will be able to actively encounter and appreciate content and, furthermore, enjoy creating content easily.

We hope to contribute to the creation of a culture that can co-exist and co-prosper with past content while paying appropriate respect to it. This will become possible by supporting a new music culture that enables creators to take delight in finding their content being reused in much the same way that academic researchers take delight in finding their articles being cited. We feel that the value of content cannot be measured by the extent to which it is not similar to other content—pursuing originality at all costs in content does not necessarily bring joy to people. Fundamentally, content has value by inducing an emotional and joyous response in people. We would like to make it a matter of common sense that content with emotional appeal and high-quality form has value. In addition, we would like to see conditions in which content

Fig. 1.1 Overview of OngaCREST Project

that explicitly refers to many existing works and was build on the basis of those works can be considered valuable, similar to the situation with academic papers. We can anticipate that our similarity-aware information environment will form a new content culture that respects past content and gives greater importance to emotionally touching experiences.

In our similarity-aware information environment, not only technologies that can estimate "similarity" and "typicality" but also *content ecosystem technologies* will play a critical role in fostering a rich content ecosystem. We therefore also conducted research and development of technologies that comprehensively support appreciation and creation of music content as content ecosystem technologies. In a content ecosystem that is achieved by these technologies, the aim is to sustainably expand *"content circulation"* to foster new content from past content in collaboration with end users. To accomplish this, we developed *"content ecosystem web services,"* which mainly targeted music-related content available on the web, and field-tested them by releasing the services to the public. If a single web service has too different purposes and too diverse functions, it is difficult for users to understand. We therefore implemented several separate web services so that each service can have a different function of content appreciation and creation. These services are organically linked to form the entire content ecosystem web services.

In Sect. 1.3 below I first introduce research achievements related to content-appreciation support technologies that were first pursued for research of content ecosystem technologies. Next, in Sect. 1.4 I introduce research achievements related to content-creation support technologies realized by using content-appreciation support technologies. Then, in Sect. 1.5 I introduce our achievements in researching similarity and typicality estimation technologies, which we tackled in parallel with the above efforts. Finally, in Sect. 1.6 I discuss some related topics and in Sect. 1.7 I conclude by summarizing this chapter and discussing future directions.

1.3 Content-Appreciation Support Technologies

For appreciation support functions of the content ecosystem web services, support to appreciate both the internal aspect and external aspect of songs—in short, appreciation support focused on the content within a single song and appreciation support focused on the relationships between multiple songs—is important. To accomplish the former goal of providing appreciation support for the content within a song, we developed *Songle* (http://songle.jp), an active music listening service that uses music-understanding technologies to enrich ways of listening to music on the web. Furthermore, on the basis of Songle, we developed *Songle Widget* (http://widget.songle.jp), a web-based multimedia development framework for music-synchronized control. For the latter goal of providing appreciation support targeting the relationships between multiple songs, we developed *Songrium* (http://songrium.jp), a music browsing support service that visualizes relationships between content with web mining technologies and music-understanding technologies. We have released these services to the general public for field-testing, and have continued to research and develop functional extensions. In this section I describe Songle, Songle Widget, and Songrium in detail.

Besides these services, we developed a wide range of music-appreciation support technologies. These include:

- LyricListPlayer, a consecutive-query-by-playback interface for retrieving similar word sequences from different song lyrics [32]
- PlaylistPlayer, an interface using multiple criteria to change the playback order of a music playlist [33]
- LyricsRadar, a lyrics retrieval system based on latent topics of lyrics, which are analyzed and visualized by using Latent Dirichlet Allocation (LDA) [39]
- A music retrieval system based on vocal timbre analysis using Latent Dirichlet Allocation (LDA) and cross-gender vocal timbre similarity [35]
- An active music listening system that allows users to enjoy music by using timbre replacement of harmonic and drum components [30]

We also developed the following music-video-appreciation support technologies:

- SmartVideoRanking, a music video search system by mining emotions from time-synchronized comments on a video-sharing service [43]
- ExploratoryVideoSearch, a music video search system based on coordinate terms and diversification [42]

With these achievements, various types of user-led search, recommendation, browsing, and content appreciation by making use of music-understanding technologies and similarity became possible. Users could not only more freely appreciate music content to encounter favorite songs from a huge amount of music content, but also enjoy music content by changing it to reflect their personality.

1.3.1 Songle

Songle (http://songle.jp) [13] is a web service that allows users to enjoy music by using *active music listening interfaces* [12]. Active music listening is a way of listening to music through active interactions. In this context the word *active* does not mean that the listeners create new music but means that they take control of their own listening experience. For example, an active music listening interface called *SmartMusicKIOSK* [11] (Fig. 1.2) has a chorus-search function that enables a user to directly access his or her favorite part of a song (and to skip other parts) while viewing a visual representation of its music structure. This facilitates deeper understanding of the music structure and is useful for trial listening, but before we developed Songle, the general public has not had the chance to use such research-level active music listening interfaces in their daily lives.

Toward the goal of enriching music listening experiences, Songle uses automatic music-understanding technologies to estimate (analyze) musical elements (music

Fig. 1.2 SmartMusicKIOSK [11]: A user can actively listen to various parts of a song while moving back and forth as desired. The upper window shows a graphical representation of the entire song structure that is estimated by a chorus-section detection method [11] and consists of chorus sections (the *top row*) and repeated sections (the five *lower rows*). On each row, colored sections indicate similar (repeated) sections. Clicking directly on a colored section plays that section. A user can jump and listen to the chorus with just a push of the next-chorus button in the lower window

scene descriptions [10]) of songs (audio files) publicly available on the web. A Songle user can enjoy playing back a musical piece while seeing the visualization of the estimated descriptions. Four major types of descriptions are automatically estimated and visualized for content-based music browsing: music structure (chorus sections and repeated sections), beat structure (musical beats and bar lines), melody line (fundamental frequency (F0) of the vocal melody), and chords (root note and chord type). Songle implements all functions that the interface of SmartMusicKIOSK had and lets a user jump and listen to the chorus by just pushing the next-chorus button. Songle thus makes it easier for a user to find desired parts of a piece.

With a focus on popular songs with vocals, Songle has already analyzed more than 1,050,000 songs on music-sharing services such as *SoundCloud* (http://soundcloud. com) and *Piapro* (http://piapro.jp), video-sharing services such as *YouTube* (http:// www.youtube.com) and *Niconico* (http://www.nicovideo.jp/video_top), and various web sites distributing MP3 files of music. The user's browser plays back music streamed directly from the original web site. Since Songle does not distribute any music, if a song is removed from the original web site, it is not possible to play back its song on Songle. In addition to contributing to the enrichment of music listening experiences, Songle serves as a showcase in which everybody can experience music-understanding technologies with a lot of songs and understand their nature: for example, what kinds of music or sound mixture are difficult for the technologies to handle. Because of the variety of music on the web and the complexity of sound mixtures, however, automatic music-understanding technologies cannot avoid making some errors.

Songle therefore provides a crowdsourcing error-correction interface that enables users to help improve its service by correcting music-understanding errors. As shown in Fig. 1.3, each user can see the music-understanding visualizations on a web browser, where a moving cursor indicates the audio playback position. A user who finds an error while listening can easily correct it by selecting from a list of candidate alternatives, or by providing an alternative description. The resulting corrections are then shared and used to immediately improve user experience with the corrected piece.

Songle supports three main functions: retrieving, browsing, and annotating songs. The retrieval and browsing functions facilitate deeper understanding of music, and the annotation (error correction) function allows users to contribute to the improvement of musical elements. The improved descriptions can lead to a better user experience of retrieving and browsing songs.

1.3.1.1 Retrieval Function

This function enables a user to retrieve a song by making a text search for the song title or artist name, by making a selection from a (recommended) list of songs or artists, or by making a chord-progression search in which a user can provide a favorite chord progression to find songs including its progression. Following the idea of an active music listening interface called *VocalFinder* [5], which finds songs with similar vocal timbres, Songle provides a similarity graph of songs so that a user can retrieve a song according to vocal timbre similarity. The graph is a radially connected network in which nodes (songs) of similar vocal timbre are connected to the center node (a user-specified song). By traversing a graph while listening to nodes, a user can find a song having the favorite vocal timbre.

By selecting a song, the user switches over to the within-song browsing function.

1.3.1.2 Within-Song Browsing Function

This function provides a content-based playback-control interface for within-song browsing by visualizing musical elements as a music map shown in Fig. 1.3 and the lower half of Fig. 1.7. In the music map, the upper window is the global view showing the entire song and the lower window is the local view magnifying the selected region. The music map consists of the following four types of musical elements:

1. *Music structure (chorus sections and repeated sections)*
   In the global view, the SmartMusicKIOSK interface [11] is shown below the playback controls including the buttons, time display, and playback slider. Just like SmartMusicKIOSK shown in Fig. 1.2, the music structure consists of chorus

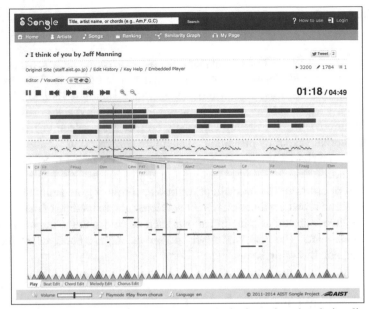

(a) When a music audio (MP3 file) on a web site is analyzed and visualized

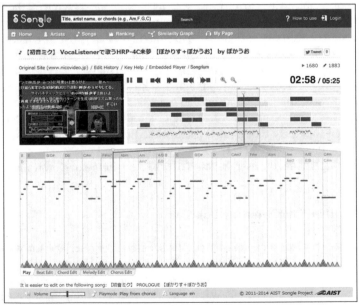

(b) When a music video on a video-sharing service (Niconico)
is analyzed and visualized

Fig. 1.3 Screen snapshots of Songle's main interface for music playback. This interface visualizes
the content of a song (musical elements) as a music map and allows the user to control playback
position freely. The horizontal axis represents time. The global view in the upper portion of the
screen presents the music structure of the entire song, and the local view in the lower portion shows
an enlarged display of the song interval selected in the global view

sections (the top row) and repeated sections (the five lower rows). On each row, colored sections indicate similar sections. A user can jump and listen to a chorus section with just a push of its section or the next-chorus button.

2. *Beat structure (musical beats and bar lines)*
   At the bottom of the local view, musical beats corresponding to quarter notes are visualized by using small triangles. The top of each triangle indicates its temporal position. Bar lines are marked by larger triangles.

3. *Melody line (F0 of the vocal melody)*
   The piano roll representation of the melody line is shown above the beat structure in the local view. It is also shown in the lower half of the global view. For simplicity, the fundamental frequency (F0) can be visualized after being quantized to the closest semitone.

4. *Chords (root note and chord type)*
   Chord names are written in the text at the top of the local view. Twelve different colors are used to represent twelve different root notes so that a user can notice the repetition of chord progressions without having to read chord names.

The music map makes it easy for a user without musical expertise to learn about the existence of the musical elements, the relationships between them, and their respective roles in the song. When a music audio (MP3 file) on a web site is played back, Songle can also visualize the music map in the four more attractive interactive display modes shown in Fig. 1.4.

1.3.1.3 Annotation Function (Crowdsourcing Error-correction Interface)

This function allows users to add annotations to correct any estimation errors. Here, annotation means describing the contents of a song, either by modifying the estimated descriptions or by selecting the correct candidate if it is available. In the local view, a user can switch between editors for four types of musical elements.

1. *Music structure* (Fig. 1.5a)
   The beginning and end points of every chorus or repeated section can be adjusted. It is also possible to add, move, and delete sections.

2. *Beat structure* (Fig. 1.5b)
   Several alternative candidates for the beat structure can be selected at the bottom of the local view. If none of the candidates are appropriate, each beat position or bar line can be changed directly. For fine adjustment, the audio can be played back with click tones at beats and bar lines.

3. *Melody line* (Fig. 1.5c)
   Note-level correction is possible on the piano-roll representation of the melody line. A user can specify a temporal region of a note and then adjust its F0 with semitone resolution. The synthesized melody line can be played back along with the original song to make it easier to check its correctness.

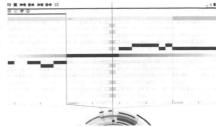

(a) Display of music content with broad movements linked to geometric patterns

(b) Display of melody line in piano-roll format

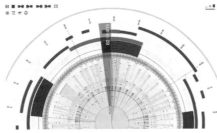

(c) Display of musical elements in semicircular format

(d) Disk-shaped "all-encompassing" display of musical elements

Fig. 1.4 Four interactive display modes of Songle's music visualizer for animating musical elements

4. *Chords* (Fig. 1.5d)

A user can correct chord names by choosing from candidates or by typing in chord names, and each chord boundary can be adjusted. As with beats and melody lines, it is possible to synthesize chords to be played along with the original song.

When the music-understanding results are corrected by users, the original automatically annotated values are visualized as trails with a different color (gray in Fig. 1.6) that can be distinguished by users. These trails are important to prevent excessive evaluation of the automatic music-understanding performance after the user corrections. Songle also makes a complete history of changes (corrections), and in this regard, functions are provided to enable any user to compare the musical elements before and after changes and to return to any point in the past. In this sense, we provided the "annotation version control" system. This has served as an effective deterrent to vandalism because even if some users should make inappropriate changes deliberately, annotations before the vandalism can easily be recovered.

Note that users can simply enjoy active music listening without correcting errors. We understand that it is too difficult for some users to correct the above descriptions (especially, chords). Moreover, users are not expected to correct all errors, only some according to each user's interests.

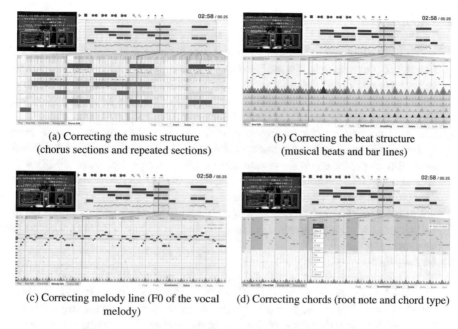

(a) Correcting the music structure (chorus sections and repeated sections)

(b) Correcting the beat structure (musical beats and bar lines)

(c) Correcting melody line (F0 of the vocal melody)

(d) Correcting chords (root note and chord type)

Fig. 1.5 Screen snapshots of Songle's annotation function (crowdsourcing error-correction interface) for correcting musical elements. This is an efficient, web-based annotation interface (editor) that allows the user to make corrections by candidate selection or direct editing

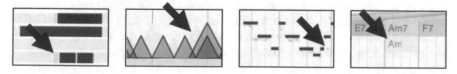

Fig. 1.6 Trails of original music-understanding results (colored in *gray*) remain visible after error corrections on Songle

1.3.1.4 Implementation of Music-Understanding Technologies for Songle

The four types of musical elements are estimated as follows.

1. *Music structure*

   This is estimated by using the chorus-section detection method *RefraiD* [11] which focuses on popular music. By analyzing relationships between various repeated sections, the RefraiD method tries to detect all the chorus sections in a song and estimate both ends of each section. It also has an advantage to detect modulated chorus sections.

2. *Beat structure*

The beats are estimated using a hidden Markov model (HMM) with 43 tempo states, each having 18 to 60 sub-states corresponding to the beat phase of different tempi. In each tempo a beat is modeled as a left-to-right HMM in which only some states have non-deterministic transition probabilities to allow for tempo fluctuations or tempo changes. The emission probability of a sub-state is calculated via the cosine similarity between a comb filter and an onset detection function.

The bar lines are estimated using harmonic cues. First, tatum-synchronous bass and treble chromagrams are extracted using NNLS Chroma [26]. Second, a chord detection model based on the chromagrams calculates posterior probabilities of chord changes. Using a sliding window, we compute the cosine similarity between the chord change probabilities and several different bar patterns that cover the 3/4, 4/4 and 6/8 meters and all possible bar phases. Then, the cosine similarities at each frame are normalized and used as emissions in another HMM similar to the beat-tracking model.

3. *Melody line*

This is estimated by using the F0 estimation method for the vocal melody [7], which is implemented by extending the predominant-F0 estimation method *PreFEst* [10]. This method focuses on the vocal melody by evaluating a GMM-based vocal probability for each F0 candidate estimated by PreFEst. Moreover, vocal activity detection was implemented by using a method described in [6].

4. *Chords*

Songle transcribes chords using 14 chord types: major, major 6th, major 7th, dominant 7th, minor, minor 7th, half-diminished, diminished, augmented, and five variants of major chords with different bass notes: /2, /3, /5, /b7, and /7. The resulting 14 types × 12 root notes = 168 chords and one 'no chord' label are estimated using an HMM approach on the same tatum-synchronous chromagram used for the bar-line estimation. Chord changes are allowed to happen only on beats.

We also include knowledge from the bar-line estimation and a key estimate. We model the key in a simple separate HMM with three different key scales: major, natural minor, and harmonic minor. Every key state has observation probabilities for all different chords, based on an expert function [27]. The posterior probability obtained from the HMM is then used to weight the chord probabilities for the chord HMM. During Viterbi decoding we use the bar-line estimates for dynamic transition probability weighting in order to encourage chord changes at bar lines.

1.3.2 Songle Widget

Songle Widget [14] is a web-based multimedia development framework that makes it possible to control computer-graphic animation and physical devices such as lighting devices and robots in synchronization with music publicly available on the web. As shown in Fig. 1.7, Songle Widget is implemented by using Songle

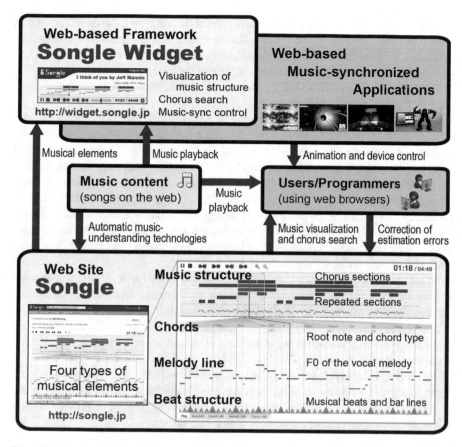

Fig. 1.7 Overview of Songle Widget framework (http://widget.songle.jp) using Songle web service (http://songle.jp)

(http://songle.jp) [13] described in Sect. 1.3.1. Songle Widget can use the four important types of musical elements (music structure, beat structure, melody line, and chords) to trigger changes in the motion and color of animation, or in the control of physical devices.

Since music can be easily and effectively combined with various types of content, it is often used when showing images, movies, and stories, and controlling physical devices such as robots and lighting devices. Synchronization is crucial when music is combined with other content, and to rigidly synchronize animation or physical devices with music, people usually have to annotate temporal positions of target events (musical elements related to the synchronization) in the music. This manual annotation is time-consuming, however.

Automatic music analysis is therefore useful for rigid synchronization. While there are music visualizers built into existing media players that can show music-synchronized (music-sync) animation of geometric patterns, their music analysis is usually based on the amplitude or spectrogram of audio signals. Such analysis is too basic to reflect various musical elements such as musical beats, bar lines (downbeats), chorus sections, and chord changes.

Songle Widget therefore makes it easy to develop web-based applications with such rigid music synchronization. Since Songle has already annotated the four types of musical elements for more than 1,050,000 songs on music- or video-sharing services, those songs can readily be used by music-synchronized applications. Since each musical element is represented as a series of time-stamped events (e.g., beat positions), Songle Widget can compare the time stamps with the current playback position to trigger a user program while playing back a music audio or video. To use a music video clip on video-sharing services for music-sync applications, Songle Widget uses the official embedded YouTube/Niconico player and its API to get the current playback position (elapsed time) as Songle does.

While playing back a music video clip on YouTube, for example, music-sync applications enable humanoid robot devices or animated human-like computer-graphic characters to dance to music, they control multiple lighting devices projecting various types of music-sync lighting patterns onto a stage-like space, and they show graphical objects whose changes in motion, size, and color are synchronized with changes in music.

For high-quality synchronization, we can take full advantage of the crowdsourcing error-correction interface on Songle. Any error corrections made to the musical elements can be instantly reflected on all applications using Songle Widget. This is effective when applications require error-free annotation.

1.3.2.1 Songle Widget Interface

Figure 1.8 shows the user interface of Songle Widget, which allows a compact dedicated player to be embedded in any web page for music-sync web applications. The outstanding features here are that it enables music-sync applications to instantly access the musical elements for more than 1,050,000 songs, which was hitherto difficult to achieve without music-understanding technologies.

To facilitate the development based on Songle Widget, we provide a template to write the JavaScript source code using the Songle Widget API so that programmers can simply add and modify codes for each event. For example, if a user code for showing a visual effect is written for the event corresponding to the bar line, its effect is automatically shown at the beginning of each bar. Programmers could also write an additional code to change all visual effects into more intense ones during chorus sections. Programmers without knowledge of music-related programming can thus achieve music-sync control quite easily.

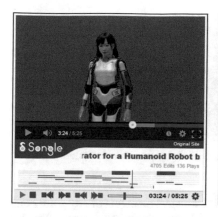 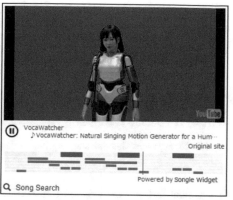

Fig. 1.8 Screenshots of Songle Widget user interface with different appearances, which should be embedded in a web page for music synchronization

1.3.2.2   Music-Synchronized Applications

Since we have made the Songle Widget framework open to the public, various music-sync applications using Songle Widget have been developed by us and by third parties. Seven of them are chosen to represent example applications.

1. **Two-dimensional Music-sync Animation**
   The Songle Widget framework has been used since August 2012 to draw music-sync animation in the background of various web pages including personal home-pages and blogs. We provide sample source codes for music-sync background animation in which each bar line (downbeat) generates a new expanding and dis-appearing pattern of geometric shapes (circles, triangles, or squares), the begin-ning of a chorus or repeated section generates several simultaneous expanding and disappearing patterns with different colors, and each chord change changes the background color of the embedding web page.
   In August 2012 Songle Widget was used by Crypton Future Media, Inc. to let visitors of their site watch a two-dimensional animated character dancing to music.
2. **Three-dimensional Animated Dancing Characters**
   In December 2012 Crypton Future Media, Inc. used Songle Widget to let visitors of their site watch three-dimensional computer-graphic characters dancing to music through WebGL rendering.
   This music-sync application also has a touchpad-like display with buttons labeled with the names of chords. These buttons light up in synchronization with the chord information from Songle Widget, and users can push any of these buttons to hear synthesized voices singing that chord.
3. **Music-sync Lighting**
   In 2013 we started using Songle Widget to link real-world physical devices—lighting devices—to music. This music-sync application supports the control of various lighting devices compatible with the DMX512 standard. It enables

Fig. 1.9 Photographs showing stage lighting linked to music by using Songle Widget

physical lighting devices to be linked to the musical elements of any song being played on Songle Widget and to be controlled accordingly. As shown in Fig. 1.9, various types of lighting linked to music were projected in a stage-like setting.

4. **Melvie: VJ Service for Coloring Music with Videos**
   A researcher *Makoto Nakajima* used Songle Widget in collaboration with us to develop the video jockey (VJ) web service *Melvie* (http://melvie.songle.jp/) that was opened to the public in June 2014. Melvie renders different sources of short video clips without audio after mixing them and applying various special effects such as overlaying, zooming, tiling, and color change in synchronization with the music playback.

5. **V-Sido x Songle: Real-time Control of Music-sync Robot Dancing**
   A roboticist *Wataru Yoshizaki* used Songle Widget in collaboration with us to develop a music-sync robot control system, called *V-Sido x Songle*, that automatically switches several different predefined dance motions according to the music structure and the beat structure of any song registered to Songle. By using a joystick or tablet, people can change motions on the fly while the robot is dancing. Such flexible music-sync robot control had not been achieved before. In January 2015 Asratec Corp. and AIST showed that this system can make three different types of robots dance in unison as shown in Fig. 1.10.

6. **Songrium3D: Music Visualizer Featuring Three-dimensional Music-sync Animation**
   Songle Widget has been used in an advanced music visualizer, called *Songrium3D* (http://songrium.jp/map/3d/) [17], that features three-dimensional music-sync animation through WebGL rendering. In this animation, visual effects and the

Fig. 1.10 Photographs of music-sync robot dancing controlled by V-Sido x Songle

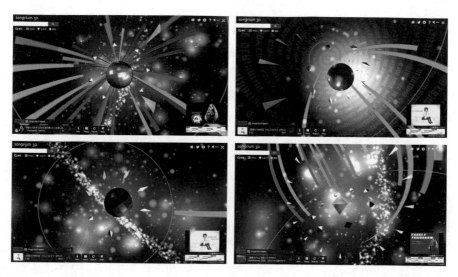

Fig. 1.11 Screenshots of Songrium3D, the music visualizer for generating three-dimensional music-sync animation in real time

motions of various objects are triggered by events in the music structure and the beat structure of a music video clip as shown in Fig. 1.11. Songrium3D is a function of Songrium web service described in Sect. 1.3.3.

7. **Photo x Songle: Music-sync Photo Slideshow**

   In December 2014 Songle Widget was used to develop a web service *Photo x Songle* (http://photo.songle.jp) that enables users to generate photo slideshows. A keyword or phrase entered by a user is used to retrieve relevant photos on the web. Those photos are then shown as animated slideshows during the playback of any song registered to Songle. A new photo usually appears at the beginning of each bar, but during chorus sections the new photos appear at every beat and with more vivid motion effects.

1.3.2.3 Implementation of Songle Widget

The implementation overview is shown in Fig. 1.12. Songle Widget was carefully designed and implemented so that it can be embedded into any web-based music-sync application without harmful side effects. We therefore chose an IFrame-based sandbox implementation that can execute our JavaScript code in a controlled environment isolated from the user application. For the sandbox implementation in JavaScript, we had to implement all necessary functions such as input sanitizer and DOM (Document Object Model) manipulation by ourselves without using external libraries such as jQuery and underscore.js.

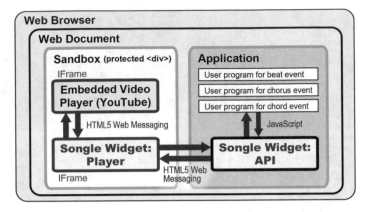

Fig. 1.12 Overview of Songle Widget implementation (in the case of using beat, chorus, and chord events with the YouTube embedded video player)

As shown in Fig. 1.12, Songle Widget consists of two components: player and API. The Songle Widget player generates the user interface shown in Fig. 1.8, manages user interactions on a web browser, and provides an encapsulation wrapper of different embedded video players and music players. On the other hand, the Songle Widget API serves as the programming interface for user applications and handles all events to trigger user programs. Those user programs should be registered and bound to events (musical elements) in advance by using this API. To achieve interdomain communication over the sandbox and IFrame, we use the *HTML5 Web Messaging* mechanism.

1.3.3 Songrium

Songrium (http://songrium.jp) [15–17] is a music browsing assistance service that enables visualization and exploration of large amounts of music content with the aim of enhancing user experiences in enjoying music. The main target content of Songrium is music video clips of original songs using a singing synthesis technology called *VOCALOID* [25] and their derivative works on the most popular Japanese video-sharing service, *Niconico* (http://www.nicovideo.jp/video_top). Songrium has analyzed more than 750,000 music video clips and revealed that over 610,000 derivative works such as covers and dance arrangements have been created from more than 140,000 original songs.

Figure 1.13 shows an overview of Songrium. Songrium allows people to understand various relations of music. It was difficult for people listening to original songs to notice that there exist various derivative works related to them, such as cover versions, singing or dancing video clips, and music video clips with 3D animations. By providing people with easy, intuitive access to those derivative works, Songrium

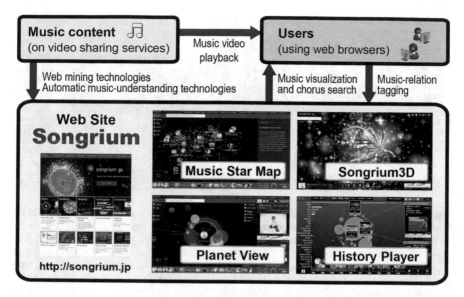

Fig. 1.13 Overview of Songrium web service (http://songrium.jp)

enables them not only to find interesting music video clips, but also to know and respect the creators of music and video clips. To visualize such relations, Songrium automatically gathers information related to original songs and their derivative works, which are expanding day-by-day. It then classifies them and estimates the relations between original songs and derivative works.

Songrium uses web mining and music-understanding technologies together with advanced data visualization techniques to achieve unique functions, such as a *Music Star Map* (Sect. 1.3.3.1), *Planet View* (Sect. 1.3.3.1), *Songrium3D* (Sect. 1.3.3.2), and *History Player* (Sect. 1.3.3.3), as shown in Fig. 1.13. These functions provide various bird's eye viewpoints about a huge amount of media content.

1.3.3.1 Music Star Map and Planet View

Music Star Map is a function that visualizes original songs. Figure 1.14a shows a screenshot of the Music Star Map function. The position of each original song is determined in a two-dimensional space of the Music Star Map so that similar songs can be closer to each other on the basis of audio-based music similarities among original songs.

When a user clicks an original song on the Music Star Map, its derivative works appear as colorful circular icons and orbit the selected original song. We designate this view as *Planet View*. Figure 1.14b shows a Planet View screenshot. Each circular icon denotes a derivative work with attributes represented by the icon orbit, size, color, and velocity. Table 1.1 shows how attributes of each derivative work are visually

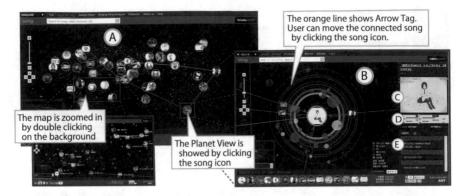

Fig. 1.14 Screenshots of the (**a**) *Music Star Map* and (**b**) *Planet View* interfaces of Songrium: the former visualizes original songs; the latter visualizes their derivative works. **a** All original songs are arranged in a two-dimensional space with similar songs positioned in proximity. Any area can be expanded for viewing by double clicking. It can then be scrolled to by dragging. **b** After selecting an original song on the Music Star Map, users can view its derivative works rotating around the selected song in the center. **c** Embedded video player of Niconico for video playback. **d** SmartMusicKIOSK interface provided by Songle Widget. **e** A list of *Arrow Tags* that represent annotated relations to and from this song instance

Table 1.1 Attributes of a derivative work represented by a circular icon on the Planet View of Songrium

Visual features	Attribues of derivative work
Radius of orbit	Publishing date
Icon size	Number of page views
Velocity	Proportion of "favorites" to page views
Color	Derivative category

represented by a circular icon. The official embedded video player of the Niconico service, shown at the upper-right corner, can play back a video clip of the selected song (Fig. 1.14c). Since this music-video playback interface is implemented by using the Songle Widget framework described in Sect. 1.3.2, Songrium also has all functions of the SmartMusicKIOSK interface, which is shown below the embedded video player (Fig. 1.14d). Songrium has an original social tagging framework called *Arrow Tag* that allows users to annotate various relations between music content. Figure 1.14e shows a list of Arrow Tags.

1.3.3.2 Songrium3D

Songrium3D is a visualization function based on the *Music Star Map* of Songrium. While the Music Star Map visualizes original songs and their derivative works in a two-dimensional space, Songrium3D visualizes them in a three-dimensional space.

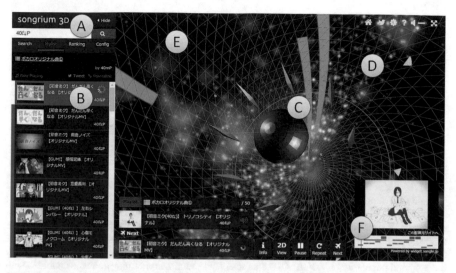

Fig. 1.15 Screenshot of the *Songrium3D* function. **a** A user can search songs using keywords. Similarly, a user can search playlists in Niconico using keywords or a URL. When the user chooses a playlist, it starts automatic playback of the playlist. **b** The lower-left panel shows a playlist. **c** The spherical object in the center represents an original song. Some objects and ribbons near the song are visual effects that are synchronized to a song. **d** A song is encompassed with many colorful particles that represent its derivative works. **e** Other original songs are apparent way out there. **f** The embedded video player of Niconico for video playback and the SmartMusicKIOSK interface provided by Songle Widget

Using three-dimensional visualization, it visualizes many original songs and derivative works together with their music structure simultaneously and seamlessly.

Figure 1.15 as well as Fig. 1.11 show screenshots of Songrium3D. The spherical object represents an original song in the center of the screen. When it plays a song, this object and peripheral objects move rhythmically in synchronization with the song. Just like the Music Star Map, the three-dimensional (x–y–z) position of a song is also determined so that similar songs can be closer to each other on the basis of audio-based music similarities among original songs. Many colorful circumjacent objects indicate derivative works of an original song. Color corresponds to the category of a derivative work in the same manner as the Planet View (Fig. 1.14b).

Three-dimensional animation of Songrium3D was used as a back-screen movie on the live stage of a virtual singer, *Hatsune Miku* [2], in the "SNOW MIKU 2015 LIVE!" concerts held four times in February 7–8, 2015. It was hosted by Crypton Future Media, Inc. for a total number of audiences of about 7,000. We generated a prerecorded animation of Songrium3D to avert problems deriving from internet connections or real-time rendering. Screenshots of Songrium3D are automatically

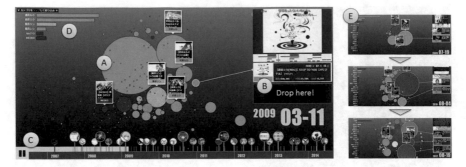

Fig. 1.16 Screenshot of the *History Player* function of Songrium. It visualizes the history of VOCALOID songs. **a** Each bubble represents a music video clip. Its size denotes the play counts; its color shows the VOCALOID character. When a user clicks a bubble, its thumbnail and metadata are shown. **b** If a user drags and drops a bubble, its song is added to the playlist. **c** The timeline at the bottom displays the current playback time and popular video clips in each period of the timeline. When a user clicks on the timeline, it jumps to the clicked period. **d** The bar chart shows the temporal popularity of VOCALOID characters (the summation of play counts of bubbles with the same color). **e** Along the playback timeline, new bubbles automatically appear in chronological order when those songs were published (uploaded)

generated and combined to produce a single movie. A movie of the live performance[1] and the animation of Songrium3D for the live[2] are available on the web.

1.3.3.3   History Player

History Player visualizes the history of VOCALOID songs on Niconico. Figure 1.16 portrays screenshots of the History Player. By automatically displaying songs in chronological order, it gives a user a full perspective on the trends and transitions of popular VOCALOID songs over time. Each song is represented as a "bubble" (a colored circle). New song bubbles appear in accordance with their respective published dates and congregate in an animation (Fig. 1.16a). The color of each bubble corresponds to the VOCALOID character, whereas the sizes of the bubbles indicate play counts on Niconico. On the left side of the screen, the bar chart presents a summation of play counts of bubbles for each VOCALOID character.

The interface exhibits growth in the music content creation community, arranged by published date, in an animated display. It automatically plays back music video clips of songs for which the play count is high in the period. Consequently, this feature enables a user to experience various popular songs in one continuous movie, providing a clear, intuitive picture of how trends on the Niconico video-sharing service change.

---

[1]https://youtu.be/GOano9x9cBY.

[2]https://youtu.be/71o8Jit1c4I.

A user can play back songs of interest with drag-and-drop operation if the user becomes curious about some displayed songs (Fig. 1.16b). In addition, the user can click on the timeline shown in Fig. 1.16c to jump from the current playback time to the clicked period (we called this function "time warp"), or click the bar corresponding to a VOCALOID character of interest on the left side shown in Fig. 1.16d to listen to songs of its character only. Furthermore, Songrium enables a user to easily play back the chorus section by using the SmartMusicKIOSK interface. This interactive function thus provides a bird's eye viewpoint about the history of a huge amount of media content; such historical viewpoint cannot be achieved on video sharing services in usual.

Furthermore, for users who particularly like singing or dancing derivative works, the History Player has two different versions: "Singing derivative works" version and "Dancing derivative works" version. They display specified derivative works with the same interface. The bubble colors correspond to their original songs and a bar chart shows a trend of original songs for derivative works.

1.3.3.4 Implementation of Web Mining Technologies for Songrium

Every music video clip on Songrium is automatically classified as an original song or a derivative work by using social tags of video clips and analyzing various related web sites. Derivative works can be identified when the description text of the video clip includes a hyperlink to the original video clip from which it was derived. These hyperlinks almost always exist on Niconico because users prefer to acknowledge the original video clip.

When a derivative work is incorporated, its relation to the original song is estimated automatically. The derivative works are classified into predefined categories. We defined six categories of derivative works: (a) Singing a song, (b) Dancing to a song, (c) Performing a song on musical instruments, (d) Featuring 3D characters in music video, (e) Creating a music video for a song, and (f) Others. The first three categories are derived from official categories used by Niconico; the other two categories are derived from our previous work [18, 19]. "Others" includes, for example, videos which review or rank existing videos, or which is karaoke version, or which use VOCALOID songs as the background music of other video clips. It also includes videos that are not classifiable. With the exception of category *Others*, all have their own unique social tags on Niconico. Using these tags, Songrium can produce a reliable classification of derivative works.

Moreover, Songrium provides a crowdsourcing error-correction interface that enables users to easily report an error in any of the above classification of video clips, extraction of links, or estimation of relations to improve the user experience further.

1.4   Content-Creation Support Technologies

For creation support functions of the content ecosystem web services, it is important
to realize technologies that support and complement human abilities of content creation by using automatic generation of music content as basic technologies. As an
example of such technologies, we developed *TextAlive* (http://textalive.jp), a lyrics
animation production support service that automatically synchronizes music and
lyrics to allow users to easily create music-synchronized lyrics animation. We have
released this service to the general public for field-testing, and have continued to
research and develop functional extensions. While this service is a content-creation
support technology, it is also a content-appreciation support technology that allows
users to enjoy creation results. It can also be used as a new method for discovering
(recommending) music through lyrics animation. In this section I describe TextAlive
in detail.

Besides TextAlive, we developed a wide range of content-creation support technologies applicable to songs. These include:

- Songmash (http://songmash.jp), a mash-up music production service that enables
  users to enjoy creating multi-song music mashups [3]
- AutoGuitarTab, a computer-aided composition system for rhythm and lead guitar
  parts in the tablature space [28]
- VocaRefiner, an interactive singing recording system with integration of multiple
  singing recordings [31]
- Song2Quartet: a system for generating string quartet cover songs from polyphonic
  audio of popular music [38]
- CrossSong Puzzle, a music game interface for generating and unscrambling music
  mashups with real-time interactivity [41]
- An interface that can edit the vocal F0 in existing songs by using F0 estimation
  and singing voice separation [21]
- A music performance assistance system based on vocal, harmonic, and percussive
  source separation and content visualization for music audio signals [4]

We also developed the following content-creation support technologies related to
music video:

- Songroid (http://songroid.jp), a dance animation creation/appreciation support service based on an automated choreography synthesis technology using Gaussian
  Process leveraging dance motion examples [8, 9]
- Dancing Snap Shot, a dancing character animation generation system that converts
  the user's face photo input into a three-dimensional computer graphics character
  model having a face similar to the user
- VRMixer, a music video mixing system that enables users to visually appear in
  existing music videos by using a video segmentation technology [20]
- A soundtrack generation system to synchronize the climax of a video clip with
  music [40]

Simple creation like easy customization by amateurs as well as advanced creation by professionals are important in the "age of billions of creators." With these achievements, users could enjoy casual content creation in a variety of forms even if expert knowledge is lacking.

1.4.1 TextAlive

TextAlive (http://textalive.jp) [22–24] is a lyrics animation production support service that enables users to animate lyrics in time to music. Due to the spread of music- and video-sharing services, many videos matched to music have been published (uploaded). Lyrics animations (kinetic typography videos) in particular can express the lyrics of music attractively, but production requires enormous effort, from installing and learning how to use video production tools to adjusting the timing of character movement.

Since TextAlive is based on music-understanding technologies and programming environment technologies, users can easily produce and share lyrics animations (Fig. 1.17). By choosing a song and specifying the video's style, novice users without expertise can quickly produce lyrics animations with various effects. In addition, users can choose "templates" of visual effects for each phrase, word, or character with an intuitive interface to express intended effects. Furthermore, advanced users (programmers) can program templates and their parameter tuning interfaces, then share the templates with other users on TextAlive. Using TextAlive, thus, allows people with diverse background to demonstrate their creativity and enjoy lyrics animation production without an enormous effort.

TextAlive uses a song and its lyrics on the web to create, edit, and share lyrics animations. It operates by the following mechanisms (Fig. 1.18).

(1) When a user registers the URL of a song and the URL of its lyrics, TextAlive analyzes the content of the song and estimates the timing of each word and character in music by using our lyrics synchronization technology.
(2) When a user selects music registered to TextAlive, the music streamed directly from the original web site is played back, and lyrics animation is rendered in synchrony, so the music and its lyrics can be enjoyed visually and acoustically.

Fig. 1.17 Overview of TextAlive web service (http://textalive.jp)

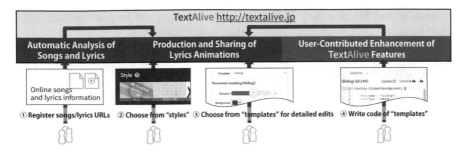

Fig. 1.18 TextAlive enables users to produce and share lyrics animation easily

Users can choose visual arrangements for the entire video from various "styles" and change instantly, easily producing lyrics animations which they prefer.

(3) Users can choose detailed visual effects from "templates" for each phrase, word, or character, arrange them as they like, and share lyrics animations online. Other users can add further edits to produce derivative works of shared lyrics animations.

(4) Users who have programming skills can edit and produce new "templates" and "parameter tuning interfaces for templates." Because these are shared on TextAlive, this enhances the expressivity of all users.

1.4.1.1 Three Features of TextAlive

TextAlive has the following three features:

1. Enables easy production of lyrics animations based on online music and lyrics information

   Users can view lyrics animations that change in time to music by entering the URL of a song (audio file in MP3 format or music content on a music- and video-sharing service) and the URL of its lyrics (text file) into TextAlive, or by selecting a pair of a song and its lyrics which has already been registered. The lyrics animation is synthesized automatically on the user's web browser, based on lyric utterance timing information (Fig. 1.19).

   Users can choose a style on the web browser to instantly change effects of the entire video, and produce lyrics animations to their preference. They can also choose effects from templates and adjust them for each phrase, word, and character, to perform even more detailed effects. This is achieved with programming environment technologies, which can execute and update programs that synthesize lyrics animations from lyric utterance timing (styles), and programs that control the shape changes and movement of characters (templates) on the web browser.

   Thus, even users who have never produced a lyrics animation can enjoy producing music-synchronized lyrics animations with effects of their preference.

Fig. 1.19 Procedure to create lyrics animations on TextAlive

Fig. 1.20 Screenshot of TextAlive's editing interface. Because lyrics animations are saved in the TextAlive web site, edited animations and programs can be shared with other users. Users not only can view lyrics animations, but can also enjoy producing derivative works to their preference

2. Supports people's creativity with intuitive interfaces and mechanisms that simplify production of derivative work

   TextAlive provides three editing interfaces with which users can easily produce lyrics animations. Because users can edit using lyrics animations produced automatically based on the chosen style, manual effort is greatly reduced even for advanced users with experience in production (Fig. 1.20).

   (a) Style selector panel: Using the simple interface for choosing styles, users can change effects for the entire lyrics animation instantly, and produce lyrics animations to their preference.

   (b) Timeline: Users can easily search for lyrics in any part they want to see by moving the timeline cursor left and right with the mouse. In addition, automati-

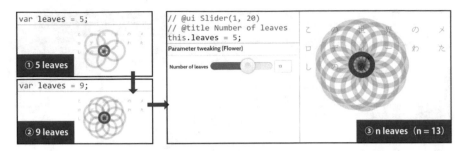

Fig. 1.21 Example of using the programming panel on TextAlive. Changing the default value of the leaf number of the template program from 5 to 9 changes the number of red circles displayed. The final screen shown has a slider for adjusting the number of leaves added to the editing panel. Thus, by programmers preparing interfaces, even users who do not program can set the desired number of leaves, and reflect their intended effect

cally analyzed lyric utterance timing is displayed in colored sections by phrase, word, and character, so that by stretching sections and moving sections left and right, users can edit lyric utterance timing for any group of characters or single character, and correct errors in automatic synchronization results. This is yet another crowdsourcing error-correction interface.

(c) Edit panel: This panel is displayed when the user clicks the edit button while viewing a lyrics animation. Users can choose the font, size, motion and transformation of phrases, words, and characters chosen on the timeline from a lot of templates. Visual effects of templates can be easily customized with the intuitive parameter tuning interface, such as sliders.

3. Enables enhancement of effects and editing features by web-based programming
   In TextAlive, when users are not satisfied with the templates prepared in advance, they can program their own new templates. The service realizes a new type of live programming, in which users can revise algorithms that determine the movement of characters while still playing a lyrics animation, without closing the editing interface. Since each edited program is immediately executed to update the lyrics animation, it is easier for novice users, who are new to the study of programming, to understand the program.
   The parameter tuning interface on the edit panel can be easily extended by adding text comments to a template program with a simple notation method. With the added interfaces, users can customize the visual effect of a template, (Fig. 1.21). Furthermore, TextAlive provides an web API that allows users to display lyrics animations on their own web pages.

1.4.1.2 Implementation of TextAlive

TextAlive generates lyrics animation in real time without using video clips that are rendered in advance: programs such as styles and templates written in JavaScript are safely executed on the user's web browser to display lyrics animations. On the other hand, all video-sharing services just distribute video clips that are displayed by rapidly changing multiple still images prepared in advance. Because of this, it was difficult to change the content of video clips after production. Since TextAlive does not rely on such prepared video clips, it is easy for TextAlive users to apply effects for existing videos to videos of other music, or edit just part of a video. This advantage could underpin a culture in which various users can create many derivative works from a single original work.

Each user-generated lyric animation on TextAlive consists of the following information: 1) URLs to the song and lyrics, 2) the structure of the lyrics, which is a tree of the text units (phrases, words, and characters), and 3) a list of assigned templates and their parameter values for each text unit. These set of information is represented by a JSON object and is version-controlled on the TextAlive web site. In fact, not only the created animation but also the estimated timing information, correction history, and template definitions are all version-controlled, enabling to fork derivative work and to rollback flawed edits.

Just like Songrium, TextAlive is also implemented by using Songle Widget that streams music directly from the original web site. Furthermore, all music-understanding technologies including the lyrics synchronization technology are internally executed on Songle, and TextAlive retrieves vocalized timing of lyric text and other music-analysis information from Songle.

1.5 Musical Similarity and Typicality Estimation Technologies

Musical similarity between songs refers to the degree to which a song is similar to a baseline song. We proposed to estimate the similarity by calculating the generative probability of musical elements in a song from a probabilistic generative model of the baseline song. Meanwhile, musical typicality refers to the degree to which an individual song is typical (common) in a baseline set of songs. We therefore proposed to estimate the typicality by calculating the generative probability of musical elements of an individual song from a probabilistic generative model of a set of songs. The probabilistic generative model here refers to a model that can calculate the probability (generative probability) of each musical element (musical feature, lyrics, chord progression, etc.) in terms of how likely it is for the element to appear. A key advantage of this approach is that a common unified framework based on probabilistic generative models can be used for calculating both similarity and typicality [34, 36, 37].

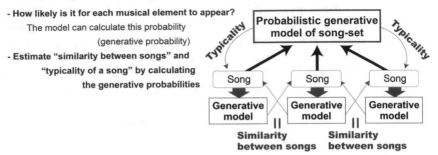

Probabilistic generative models of musical elements

Fig. 1.22 Estimation of musical similarity and typicality based on probabilistic generative models

1.5.1   Musical Similarity and Typicality Estimation Based on Probabilistic Generative Models

Since music contains multifaceted aspects, such different aspects should be taken into account when calculating musical similarity and typicality. We therefore developed a framework that can calculate the similarity and typicality for various aspects (musical elements) of music [34, 36, 37]. Our framework uses probabilistic generative models of five musical elements (vocal timbre, musical timbre, rhythm, lyrics, and chord progression) to estimate "similarity between songs" and "typicality of a song" by calculating the generative probabilities from these models. The five musical elements are estimated from music audio signals containing sounds of singing voices and various instruments.

As shown in Fig. 1.22, for each aspect of music (each musical element), estimation of the "similarity" between songs was made possible by building a probabilistic generative model of each song and then calculating the generative probability of the target musical element within a different song. Furthermore, the "typicality" of each song in a set of songs was estimated by building a probabilistic generative model of the entire set of songs and then calculating the generative probability of the target musical element within an individual song.

Of the five musical elements, the audio features representing vocal timbre, musical timbre, and rhythm were estimated for every frame (time-series unit). They were then discretized with vector quantization. Lyrics were broken down into symbols of Japanese morphemes and English words. Those discrete symbols of vocal timbre, musical timbre, rhythm, and lyrics were modeled using Latent Dirichlet Allocation (LDA) as shown in Fig. 1.23. With LDA analysis, the topic distribution in each song (distribution of topic mixture ratio) and symbol distribution in each topic (distribution of unigram probability of symbols) were obtained. These distributions can be estimated as posterior distributions by Bayesian estimation assuming Dirichlet distributions. The parameter of the posterior Dirichlet distribution can be interpreted as the number of observations of the corresponding topic or symbol. Using these

Latent Dirichlet Allocation (LDA)

- **Vocal timbre**: Liner Prediction Mel-Frequency Cepstral Coefficient (LPMCC), ΔF0
- **Musical timbre**: Mel-Frequency Cepstral Coefficient (MFCC), ΔMFCC, ΔPower
- **Rhythm**: Fluctuation Pattern (FP)
- **Lyrics**: Japanese Morphemes, English Words

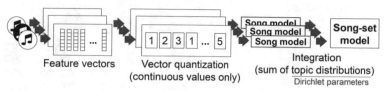

Fig. 1.23 Song modeling and song-set modeling with Latent Dirichlet Allocation (LDA)

parameters, the topic distribution of the song-set was estimated from the topic distributions of the songs in the song-set. Similarity and typicality were estimated by calculating the generative probability of a song from the model of each song and the model of the song-set obtained in this way.

Meanwhile, as for the chord progression, we used the chord estimation results from Songle described in Sect. 1.3.1, and modeled their chord progression by using a variable-order Markov process (up to a theoretically infinite order) called the variable-order Pitman-Yor language model (VPYLM) [29, 44]. By infinitizing n (length of chord progression) in the n-gram model, posterior distribution of the appropriate n for each chord could be estimated. The probabilistic generative model of the song-set was trained from chord progressions of all songs by using VPYLM. However, because the number of chords in each song is small, suitable training for the probabilistic generative model of each song could not be carried out with just a Bayesian model. We therefore dealt with this problem by first using maximum likelihood estimation to obtain a trigram (n = 3) model for each song, and then integrating it with VPYLM trained from the song-set. The perplexity of each song was calculated from the model trained on each song and the model trained on the song-set. The average generative probability of each chord in the song was calculated as the inverse of the perplexity to estimate similarity and typicality [36, 37].

However, when scrutinizing the above estimation results, we discovered the problem that the probability of unintended sequences became high with our initially-proposed generative probability (likelihood)-based calculation methods. For example, suppose for the sake of simplicity a music model that generates 0 with the probability of 60% and 1 with the probability of 40%. Under undesirable conditions in which 0 is 100% (e.g., "0 0 0 0 0" in a song), the problem of the generative probability becoming maximized occurs, regardless of the original importance of each proportion in the song. To resolve this issue, we introduced *type theory* from information theory [1], and defined the generative probability as the probability of a sequence sharing the *type* (unigram or multinomial distribution). We then calculated this probability by an exponential function of Kullback-Leibler divergence of the multinomial distribution that expresses the type of a song from the multinomial

Bayesian estimation of song-set model (integration of song models)

Assume a song-set has a Dirichlet distribution that generates type of each song

➡ Estimate prior distribution (Dirichlet distribution)

from types of all songs (set of multinomial distributions)

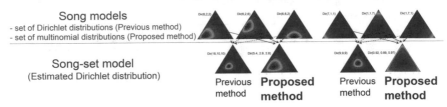

Song models
- set of Dirichlet distributions (Previous method)
- set of multinomial distributions (Proposed method)

Song-set model
(Estimated Dirichlet distribution)

Previous method   **Proposed method**   Previous method   **Proposed method**

Fig. 1.24 Bayesian estimation of song-set model from song models

distribution generated from the generative model (Latent Dirichlet Allocation). In this way, using the above example the generative probability under conditions that include probabilities 60% for 0 and 40% for 1 (e.g., "0 1 0 0 1" in a song) could be maximized [34].

Furthermore, with our initially proposed method, the song-set model is determined by summing the Dirichlet distribution parameters of individual LDA song models. However, as shown in Fig. 1.24, the problem that these individual song models (set of Dirichlet distributions) are not appropriately reflected in the song-set model arises. To resolve this problem, each song is expressed with multinomial distribution (topic distribution). By assuming that multinomial distributions of the songs in the song-set are generated from the Dirichlet distribution of the song-set, we used Bayesian estimation to estimate the generative model of the song-set [34].

The above methods are not limited to audio or music. We have already estimated the typicality of text data and developed an interface that uses its results. Specifically, to estimate the typicality of artists, we obtained categories on the artists' Wikipedia pages and important words (words found on the Wikipedia pages), and created an LDA-based artist-set model. Because an artist's history is written in Wikipedia, text-based relations that are different from audio-based relations obtained from musical features of songs could be found [33].

1.5.2 Evaluation of Typicality Estimation Results

We investigated how the results of estimating typicality should be evaluated and proposed original evaluation methods. In general, evaluation of similarity between songs is based on correlation with human judgment. However, because typicality is defined by the relations among songs in a huge song-set, which are difficult for human beings to grasp in the first place, typicality cannot be evaluated on the basis of human judgment criteria as in the case of similarity. Thus we proposed evaluation based on *central tendency* (the number of similar songs), one of the definitions of typicality in cognitive psychology. Specifically, we assume that typicality can be appropriately estimated if the correlation with "the number of highly similar songs" is high [36, 37].

However, it turned out that using only the above method was insufficient for showing the effectiveness of the methods for estimating typicality. This is because the absolute value of similarity and the estimation accuracy differ with different methods, so standards of "high similarity" also differ. We therefore tested the effectiveness of the proposed methods of calculating typicality by using the correlation between the ratio of songs making up the song-set and the estimated typicality, using song elements whose characteristics could be known in advance. For example, we focused on vocal timbre, namely the gender of the vocalist (male or female), and estimated the typicality provided by several of our proposed methods while changing the ratio of male and female vocals. This made it possible to conduct evaluation testing by comparing the correlations. With these steps, our contributions of calculating similarity and typicality and settling on overall criteria applicable to research on typicality in general are not limited to the domain of music, but useful for any domain in the future [34].

1.6 Discussion

In the future, everything can be digitally traceable and computable. This chapter has described various research achievements under this future vision. In the past, it was difficult to assume a huge amount of media content for research and provide various bird's eye viewpoints. Our project has explored the frontiers of dealing with such a huge amount of music content on the web and developed Songle for analyzing it, Songrium for providing such bird's eye viewpoints, and TextAlive for creating new values based on the accumulation of such content. In Sect. 1.6.1 below I discuss *"web-native music"* that is a word coined by us to emphasize such a future vision. Next, in Sect. 1.6.2, I introduce that Songrium started providing a new type of influence ranking verifiable by third parties. Then, in Sect. 1.6.3, I summarize how the above mentioned web services we developed form the entire content ecosystem web services.

1.6.1 Web-Native Music

By advancing research on music content available on the web, we investigated what is different about music on the web, which will become mainstream in the future, compared with previous music. We then realized that while the integration of music and the web gradually began with web-streaming of music previously distributed as packaged media, what is being born is "music content native to the web." This type of music could not have arisen without the web.

We call music that fulfills the following three conditions *"web-native music"* [16]:

(1) Original music people naturally think as being first released on the web
(2) Music whose derivative works can be created and released on the web without hesitation
(3) Music whose creators can publicly receive feedback that promotes further creation

With web-native music it is possible to identify works, release dates, and reactions of viewers and listeners (reviews, comments, number of playbacks, number of users who bookmarked, etc.) because it is released and played on the web. Web-native music also makes it possible to track original songs and their derivative works. As a result, phenomena that cannot previously be observed can be observed. Because everyone can refer to the original song by its permalink URL, every derivative work can reliably refer to the URL of the original song, and every introduction and acknowledgment can refer to the URL of the original song, attention to (the URLs of) original songs on the web encourages a chain of creation. Such music does not exist in the past.

An example of web-native music is VOCALOID music that uses the VOCALOID singing synthesis technology and is posted on the Niconico video-sharing service. By taking advantage of web-native music that can be digitally traceable and computable, we were able to develop a series of music web services. Such music is continuing to grow steadily. For example, the musical genre of Electronic Dance Music (EDM), which has surged in popularity in recent years in Europe and North America, has qualities similar to web-native music. We therefore started adding EDM music on SoundCloud to our services of Songle and Songrium.

In this way, web-native music will further spread in a variety of forms. Furthermore, I believe that every media content will eventually become *web-native content* in the future.

1.6.2 Influence Ranking Verifiable by Third Parties

The number of derivative works shows the power of influence of original songs. There is great value to songs from which many derivative works are created—in short, songs that are liked so much that many people create and release derivative works. Songrium made it possible to visualize that different songs could have different trends of derivation. For example, there are songs that people want to dance to and songs that they want to sing. When we first began our research of Songrium, this could not be realized at all. With Songrium, we are able to analyze and realize qualities and quantities about the derivation of content for the first time.

We therefore developed and released a new function of Songrium *"Influence Ranking"* to the general public as the world's first ranking based on the act of creating and releasing derivative works by users. This ranking represents a song's power to promote content generation (we call it *"content-generating power"*). With this ranking, songs for which many derivative works are created can be discovered for each type of derivation.

To improve the reliability of rankings with this function, we discovered that it was important to provide a list of Niconico URLs of derivative works on the web so third-party verification becomes possible. Actually, in widely used popularity rankings based on the number of playbacks, acts of individual playbacks do not have transparency due to the lack of third-party verification. Therefore, one must trust the ranking aggregator. If for some reason an error or improper operation occurs, there is no way of knowing. In contrast, the Influence Ranking system we developed has the unprecedented feature of enabling third parties to verify an original work's popularity in the form of individual derivative works on the web. So it is a highly transparent third-party verifiable ranking system. We believe that this philosophy will become essential and critical for media content of the future.

1.6.3   Content Ecosystem Web Services

Even if automatic analysis based on similarity calculation and music-understanding technologies becomes possible, and content-appreciation support technologies and content-creation support technologies are realized, they are insufficient as a similarity-aware information environment for a content-symbiotic society if they are not in conditions to be used by people. We therefore made it possible for people to directly use "content ecosystem web services" such as Songle, Songrium, and TextAlive as an information environment that accumulates automatic analysis results of music content and allows people to use those results for appreciation and creation.

In terms of an information environment, Songle allows people to access music-understanding results for more than one million pieces of music content, and similarity between content (similarity of vocal timbre and musical timbre). By leveraging Songle, Songle Widget serves as an information environment that promotes collaboration with external web services and applications, and contributes to delivering a music-synchronized world to people. Next, Songrium allows people to see user annotations on song relationships (Arrow Tags), relationships between original songs and derivative works, audio-based similarity between songs, the history of media content (History Player), and content-generating power (Influence Ranking). Those functions make possible user-led search, recommendation, and browsing and help people find their favorite content. Furthermore, TextAlive makes possible the content circulation that fosters new content from past content, and appropriate reference (citation) that respects past content.

When this OngaCREST Project initially began, we could not assume that use of these services could grow to their present state and synergistic effects between services and use cases could be obtained. However, already a variety of collaborations and applications have taken place with this series of web services. In particular, use of Songle has begun inside and outside the lab as a common foundational platform. Songle's music-understanding technologies are being used directly or indirectly by several content-appreciation support technologies and content-creation support technologies. In this way, provision of "content ecosystem web services" to end users and developers has already begun and they are being used.

1.7 Conclusion

This chapter introduces research achievements of the OngaCREST Project and describes content-appreciation support technologies that provide interfaces and services for actively enjoying music, content-creation support technologies that contribute to an "age of billions of creators," and musical similarity and typicality estimation that is important to build a similarity-aware information environment for the content-symbiotic society. In the digital content society, future content would be apt to be overwhelmed by a huge amount of ever-increasing past content but without being forgotten. The OngaCREST Project took up the challenge of creating the content-symbiotic society capable of rich, sustainable development in a "cannot-be-forgotten society" brought about through digitization. I hope that our research achievements could contribute to enable people to feel the symbiosis between past and future content and to create a society in which people can enjoy a huge amount of content through a symbiosis between people and content.

In the future, *uncopyable experiences* will become more important. A content industry has developed by advancing methods of copying experiences—-e.g., by reproducing appreciation of music performances with music CDs and DVDs. As the distribution cost of digital content will further approach zero, there is concern that the industrial value from copyable, passive experiences will be gradually lost. On the other hand, active experiences unique to each person have value because they are uncopyable experiences. For example, the activity of creating something is an uncopyable experience. Even if one looks at a creative work and imagines its process of creation, one cannot have the same experience and emotions as the work's creator.

Our technologies described in this chapter can thus contribute to create such uncopyable experiences. Even if we seek to create an "age of billions of creators," it is not easy to enable anyone to easily create high-quality music content from scratch by using content-creation support technologies. However, from the standpoint of creating "uncopyable experiences," no matter how simple a customization may be, this is an active experience that differs for each person. It has the possibility of providing sufficient value if it is uncopyable. Furthermore, content-appreciation support technologies for active music listening are also critical for creating uncopyable, active experiences. The experiences of deepening understanding through visualization during playback, customizing content through casual modification, and encountering content through interactive music search and browsing are the first steps toward "uncopyable experiences."

Although the digitization of content has progressed, the latent true value of the digital content has not yet been fully extracted. In the past, changes in content appreciation have centered on *quantitative changes* (changes in the number of content) in the huge amount of content that can be accessed passively. The next stage of changes is *qualitative changes* (changes in the quality of experiences) that bring about active "uncopyable experiences." I believe that this is the essence of digitization. We therefore seek to continue to contribute academically, industrially, socially, and culturally by researching and developing diverse content-appreciation and content-creation support technologies of achieving uncopyable, active experiences.

Acknowledgements This research was supported in part by CREST, JST. I would like to thank all those involved in the OngaCREST Project, especially co-researchers Shigeo Morishima, Satoshi Nakamura, and Kazuyoshi Yoshii, and the following who devoted their energies to developing the web services: Masahiro Hamasaki, Tomoyasu Nakano, Satoru Fukayama, Jun Kato, Kosetsu Tsukuda, Yuta Kawasaki, Keisuke Ishida, and Takahiro Inoue. I also would like to extend my appreciation to the Research Supervisor, Professor Toyoaki Nishida and Late Professor Yoh'ichi Tohkura, and Advisors of the research area of *"Creation of Human-Harmonized information Technology for Convivial Society"* of CREST, JST.

References

1. M.T. Cover, J.A. Thomas, *Elements of Information Theory* (Wiley, 2006)
2. Crypton Future Media. What is the HATSUNE MIKU movement? http://www.crypton.co.jp/download/pdf/info_miku_e.pdf, 2008
3. M.E.P. Davies, P. Hamel, K. Yoshii, M. Goto, AutoMashUpper: Automatic creation of multi-song music mashups. IEEE/ACM Trans. Audio Speech Lang. Process. **22**(12), 1726–1737 (2014)
4. A. Dobashi, Y. Ikemiya, K. Itoyama, K. Yoshii, A music performance assistance system based on vocal, harmonic, and percussive source separation and content visualization for music audio signals, in *Proceedings of SMC*, pp. 99–104, 2015
5. H. Fujihara, M. Goto, T. Kitahara, H.G. Okuno, A modeling of singing voice robust to accompaniment sounds and its application to singer identification and vocal-timbre-similarity-based music information retrieval. IEEE Trans. Audio Speech Lang. Process. **18**(3), 638–648 (2010)
6. H. Fujihara, M. Goto, J. Ogata, K. Komatani, T. Ogata, H.G. Okuno, Automatic synchronization between lyrics and music CD recordings based on Viterbi alignment of segregated vocal signals, in *Proceedings of ISM*, pp. 257–264, 2006
7. H. Fujihara, T. Kitahara, M. Goto, K. Komatani, T. Ogata, H.G. Okuno, F0 estimation method for singing voice in polyphonic audio signal based on statistical vocal model and Viterbi search, in *Proceedings of ICASSP 2006*, pp. V–253–256, 2006
8. S. Fukayama, M. Goto, Automated choreography synthesis using a gaussian process leveraging consumer-generated dance motions, in *Proceedings of ACE, 2014*
9. S. Fukayama, M. Goto, Music content driven automated choreography with beat-wise motion connectivity constraints, in *Proceedings of SMC*, pp. 177–183, 2015
10. M. Goto, A real-time music scene description system: predominant-F0 estimation for detecting melody and bass lines in real-world audio signals. Speech Commun. **43**(4), 311–329 (2004)
11. M. Goto, A chorus-section detection method for musical audio signals and its application to a music listening station. IEEE Trans. Audio Speech Lang. Process. **14**(5), 1783–1794 (2006)
12. M. Goto, Active music listening interfaces based on signal processing, in *Proceedings of ICASSP*, 2007

13. M. Goto, K. Yoshii, H. Fujihara, M. Mauch, T. Nakano, Songle: A web service for active music listening improved by user contributions, in *Proceedings of ISMIR*, pp. 311–316, 2011
14. M. Goto, K. Yoshii, T. Nakano, S. Widget, Making animation and physical devices synchronized with music videos on the web, in *Proceedings of IEEE ISM*, pp. 85–88, 2015
15. M. Hamasaki, M. Goto, Songrium: A music browsing assistance service based on visualization of massive open collaboration within music content creation community, in *Proc. of the 9th International Symposium on Open Collaboration (WikiSym + OpenSym 2013)*, pp. 1–10, 2013
16. M. Hamasaki, M. Goto, T. Nakano, Songrium: A music browsing assistance service with interactive visualization and exploration of a web of music, in *Proceedings of the 23rd International World Wide Web Conference (WWW 2014)*, pp. 523–528, 2014
17. M. Hamasaki, M. Goto, T. Nakano, Songrium: browsing and listening environment for music content creation community, in *Proceedings of SMC*, pp. 23–30, 2015
18. M. Hamasaki, H. Takeda, T. Hope, T. Nishimura, Network analysis of an emergent massively collaborative creation community: How can people create videos collaboratively without collaboration?, in *Proceedings of ICWSM*, pp. 222–225, 2009
19. M. Hamasaki, H. Takeda, T. Nishimura, Network analysis of massively collaborative creation of multimedia contents—case study of Hatsune Miku videos on Nico Nico Douga, in *Proceedings of uxTV*, pp. 165–168, 2008
20. T. Hirai, S. Nakamura, T. Yumura, S. Morishima, VRMixer: Mixing video and real world with video segmentation, in Proceedings of ACE, 2014
21. Y. Ikemiya, K. Yoshii, K. Itoyama, Singing voice analysis and editing based on mutually dependent f0 estimation and source separation, in *Proceedings of IEEE ICASSP*, pp. 574–578, 2015
22. J. Kato, T. Igarashi, M. Goto, Programming with examples to develop data-intensive user interfaces. IEEE Comput. **49**(7), 34–42 (2016)
23. J. Kato, T. Nakano, M. Goto, TextAlive: Integrated design environment for kinetic typography, in *Proceedings of ACM CHI*, pp. 3403–3412, 2015
24. J. Kato, T. Nakano, M. Goto, TextAlive Online: Live programming of kinetic typography videos with online music, in *Proceedings of ICLC*, pp. 199–205, 2015
25. H. Kenmochi, H. Ohshita, Vocaloid—commercial singing synthesizer based on sample concatenation, in *Proceedings of Interspeech*, pp. 4010–4011, 2007
26. M. Mauch, S. Dixon, Approximate note transcription for the improved identification of difficult chords, in *Proceedings of ISMIR*, pp. 135–140, 2010
27. M. Mauch, S. Dixon, Simultaneous estimation of chords and musical context from audio. IEEE Trans. ASLP **18**(6), 1280–1289 (2010)
28. M. McVicar, S. Fukayama, M. Goto, AutoGuitarTab: computer-aided composition of rhythm and lead guitar parts in the tablature space. IEEE/ACM Trans. Audio Speech Lang. Process. **23**(7), 1105–1117 (2015)
29. D. Mochihashi, E. Sumita, The infinite Markov model, in *Proceedings of Advances in Neural Information Processing Systems 20 (NIPS 2007)*, pp. 1017–1024, 2007
30. T. Nakamura, H. Kameoka, K. Yoshii, M. Goto, Timbre replacement of harmonic and drum components for music audio signals, in *Proceedings of IEEE ICASSP*, pp. 7520–7524, 2014
31. T. Nakano, M. Goto, VocaRefiner: an interactive singing recording system with integration of multiple singing recordings, in *Proceedings of SMC*, pp. 115–122, 2013
32. T. Nakano, M. Goto, LyricListPlayer: a consecutive-query-by-playback interface for retrieving similar word sequences from different song lyrics, in *Proceedings of SMC*, pp. 344–349, 2016
33. T. Nakano, J. Kato, M. Hamasaki, M. Goto, PlaylistPlayer: An interface using multiple criteria to change the playback order of a music playlist, in *Proceedings of ACM IUI*, pp. 186–190, 2016
34. T. Nakano, D. Mochihashi, K. Yoshii, M. Goto, Musical typicality: how many similar songs exist?, in *Proceedings of ISMIR*, pp. 695–701, 2016
35. T. Nakano, K. Yoshii, M. Goto, Vocal timbre analysis using latent dirichlet allocation and cross-gender vocal timbre similarity, in *Proceedings of IEEE ICASSP*, pp. 5239–5343, 2014

36. T. Nakano, K. Yoshii, M. Goto, Musical similarity and commonness estimation based on probabilistic generative models, in *Proceedings of IEEE ISM*, pp. 197–204, 2015
37. T. Nakano, K. Yoshii, M. Goto, Musical similarity and commonness estimation based on probabilistic generative models of musical elements. Int. J. Semant. Comput. (IJSC) **10**(1), 27–52 (2016)
38. G. Percival, S. Fukayama, M. Goto, Song2Quartet: a system for generating string quartet cover songs from polyphonic audio of popular music, in *Proceedings of ISMIR*, pp. 114–120, 2015
39. S. Sasaki, K. Yoshii, T. Nakano, M. Goto, S. Morisihima, LyricsRadar: a lyrics retrieval system based on latent topics of lyrics, *Proceedings of ISMIR*, pp. 585–590, 2014
40. H. Sato, T. Hirai, T. Nakano, M. Goto, S. Morishima, A soundtrack generation system to synchronize the climax of a video clip with music, in *Proceedings of IEEE ICME*, 2016
41. J.B.L. Smith, G. Percival, J. Kato, M. Goto, S. Fukayama, Generating and unscrambling music mashups with real-time interactivity. CrossSong Puzzle, in *Proceedings of SMC*, pp. 61–67, 2015
42. K. Tsukuda, M. Goto, ExploratoryVideoSearch: a music video search system based on coordinate terms and diversification, in *Proceedings of IEEE ISM*, pp. 221–224, 2015
43. K. Tsukuda, M. Hamasaki, M. Goto, SmartVideoRanking: video search by mining emotions from time-synchronized comments, in *Proceedings of IEEE ICDMW*, 2016
44. K. Yoshii, M. Goto, A vocabulary-free infinity-gram model for nonparametric bayesian chord progression analysis, in *Proceedings of ISMIR*, pp. 645–650, 2011

Chapter 2
Development of a Sound Field Sharing System for Creating and Exchanging Music

Shiro Ise

Abstract Many interactions in modern society have become virtual. To form deep bonds between people in our highly connected society, a mechanism for sharing one's true feelings is required. Sound is one of the strongest tools that can be used to emulate an in-person experience, making 3D auditory interface technology a necessary area of exploration. There are several reasons for such a simple solution, realistic sound, not yet being realized. First, development of visual technology has been prioritized owing to its clarity and ease of understanding. Second, text-based technology has rapidly grown because of commercial requirements. Finally, the conventional theoretical basis of sound field reproduction is not sufficiently realizable. However, the principle of boundary surface control (BoSC) was proposed during the 1990s as a new theoretical basis of 3D sound field reproduction. After several trials of developing the sound field reproduction system based on the BoSC principle, this project started to clarify the applicability of the BoSC principle. As a result of this project over five years, we succeeded in being the first in the world to develop an immersive auditory display, which is named "sound cask" from its cask-shaped appearance. Since producing sound and listening to sound has been important to human interaction since early humanity, the sound cask will be an invaluable tool.

Keywords Immersive auditory display · Stereophonics · Virtual reality · 3D sound technology · Sound sharing system

2.1 Prologue

While bodily cues, especially emotions, are lost as soon as speech is transformed into text, text simultaneously ensures longevity and reproducibility. Sound emanating from the vocal chords vibrating reverberates through the air and dissipates in an instant. The listener reacts accordingly, interpreting each little sound wave one after another. On the other hand, written words will remain largely static regard-

S. Ise (✉)
Tokyo Denki University, Chiba, Japan
e-mail: iseshiro@mail.dendai.ac.jp

© Springer Japan KK 2017
T. Nishida (ed.), *Human-Harmonized Information Technology, Volume 2*,
DOI 10.1007/978-4-431-56535-2_2

less of passing time and, furthermore, allows for duplication and proliferation of the contents to other places. Furthermore, if the written word reveals new and useful knowledge, it tends to be proliferated even more. The development of informational technology in recent years has dramatically increased the possibility of distributing written words compared to prior printing technology. Text put on the internet forms a digital medium that can be reproduced and viewable from any connected device in the world. Although unwritten knowledge is everywhere, written-down partial truths, due to being easily proliferated on a large scale, have a significant effect on our physical environment as momentary social phenomena.

Modern humans have lost a significant number of opportunities to be physically active and create sound, by passing time interacting with others across virtualized worlds using mobile devices. Even in the office, instead of talking to one's neighbor, email, SNS, or the like are quite often used. Since communication that does not involve the exchange of emotions does not enhance feelings of unity, anxieties about social life cannot be expunged very easily. No matter how much superficial information is exchanged, the deep interpersonal communication that is necessary cannot be formed. Therein lies the root of what ails modern society.

As a start to solving this problem, we now focus on the interface between individuals and this information environment. Specifically, I suggest a sound interface that is able to sufficiently handle the means by which people create and broadcast sound in information space. A classic example of using sound in a physical space is the skill of performing with a musical instrument in a concert hall. The audience in the concert hall can then appreciate the musical arts, as a result of the musical group acting in coordination on stage. Modern-day rock music, theater, and other such various performances endure under a single cultural and economic value. Therefore, the fundamental position of this research project is that, while humanity's natural inclination involves the gathering of people into a shared space for such activities, the ideal for a society with harmony of information is for the same to take place for such activities in virtual space.

2.2 Theoretical Basis

Currently, several types of sound field reproducing systems are known to be in use. A 5.1 surround [1] is an example of a system in general use, and a 22.2-channel system [2] is a well-known example of an ideal reproduction environment. More academic or exact methods include various binaural reproduction methods, wave field synthesis (WFS) [3–7], and, more recently, the 6-channel system [8, 9] and higher-order ambisonics [10–12]. The boundary surface control (BoSC) technique proposed in 1993 by Ise is an academically important reproduction method [13–15]. Because the actual construction of a reproduction system using 62-channel loudspeakers is at an early stage, development has not only been a function of sound field reproduction, but the system has also been investigated as a function of sound field sharing at a remote location [16–21]. The experimental results indicate the

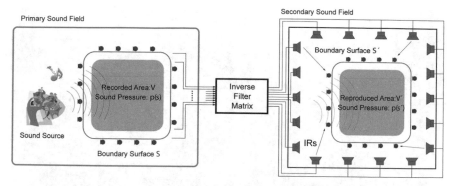

Fig. 2.1 Concept of the boundary surface control principle with an inverse filter matrix. The sound pressures at surface S are reproduced at surface S' in the secondary sound field. The inverse filter matrix, which is calculated from impulse responses from all possible combinations of loudspeakers and microphones, is introduced to reproduce the sound pressures at S'

validity of the system. The boundary surface control principle is described using the Kirchhoff-Helmholtz integral equation and the inverse system [15]. Figure 2.1 shows its basic concept.

We are considering the reproduction of a sound field within a recorded area V in the primary field into a reproduction area V' in the secondary field. Given that V is congruent with V', the following equation holds:

$$|\mathbf{r}' - \mathbf{s}'| = |\mathbf{r} - \mathbf{s}| \qquad (\mathbf{s} \in V, \mathbf{r} \in S, \mathbf{s}' \in V', \mathbf{r}' \in S') \qquad (2.1)$$

where S and S' denote the boundary of the recorded area and the boundary of the reproduction area respectively. If we denote the sound pressure in V and V' as $p(\mathbf{s})$ and $p(\mathbf{s}')$ respectively, $p(\mathbf{s})$ and $p(\mathbf{s}')$ are denoted by the following equations

$$p(\mathbf{s}) = \iint_S G(\mathbf{r}|\mathbf{s}) \frac{\partial p(\mathbf{r})}{\partial n} - p(\mathbf{r}) \frac{\partial G(\mathbf{r}|\mathbf{s})}{\partial n} \delta S, \qquad (\mathbf{s} \in V) \qquad (2.2)$$

$$p(\mathbf{s}') = \iint_{S'} G(\mathbf{r}'|\mathbf{s}') \frac{\partial p(\mathbf{r}')'}{\partial n} - p(\mathbf{r}') \frac{\partial G(\mathbf{r}'|\mathbf{s}')'}{\partial n} \delta S', \qquad (\mathbf{s}' \in V') \qquad (2.3)$$

where n and n' denote normal vectors on S and S' respectively. By applying Eq. 2.1, we obtain the following relationships of Green's function and its gradient:

$$G(\mathbf{r}|\mathbf{s}) = G(\mathbf{r}'|\mathbf{s}') \qquad (2.4)$$

$$\frac{\partial G(\mathbf{r}|\mathbf{s})}{\partial n} = \frac{\partial G(\mathbf{r}'|\mathbf{s}')}{\partial n'} \qquad (2.5)$$

Hence, it follows that if the sound pressure and its gradient on each boundary are equal to each other, then the sound pressures in each area are also equal to each other from Eqs. 2.2 and 2.3. This is expressed as

Fig. 2.2 3D sound field recording in a concert hall using a C80 fullerene microphone

$$\forall \mathbf{r} \in S \quad \forall \mathbf{r}' \in S'$$
$$p(\mathbf{r}) = p(\mathbf{r}') \quad \frac{\partial p(\mathbf{r})}{\partial n} = \frac{\partial p(\mathbf{r}')}{\partial n'}$$
$$\implies \quad \forall \mathbf{s} \in V \quad \forall \mathbf{s}' \in V' \quad p(\mathbf{s}) = p(\mathbf{s}'). \tag{2.6}$$

Considering this as a boundary value problem, the uniqueness of the solution follows in that either the sound pressure value or its gradient value are sufficient to determine the value for both [22]. To construct the recorded and reproduction areas, a microphone array is generally used. As shown in Fig. 2.2 the C80-shaped fullerene microphone array was adopted in our project. One additional feature of the BoSC principle is the introduction of the inverse filter matrix. Impulse responses between all possible combinations of loudspeakers and microphones in the secondary sound field (IRs in Fig. 2.1) are measured in advance, and the inverse filter matrix is calculated [15]. These filters are applied to the signals for reproducing the sound pressures of surface S at the target surface of S'. Another well-known sound reproduction method using the Kirchhoff-Helmholtz integral equation is wave field synthesis (WFS) [3–7]. However, a characteristic of the boundary surface control principle is that the configuration of the closed surface is not restricted because of the introduction of the inverse system. In addition to WFS, several stereophonic systems exist, e.g., 6-channel system [8, 9] and ambisonics system [10–12]. However, the sound cask has practical advantages compared with other systems in the following points:

• Sound image along the depth direction can be controlled even in the vicinity of the head of the listener;

- The whole system can be easily moved into any place.
- A theoretically assured combination with a recording system, an 80-channel fullerene-shaped microphone array in our case, can be constructed.

2.3   Sound Cask

The main characteristic of the BoSC system is its ability to reproduce a sound field, not by points but in three dimensions. A listener can freely move his head, and the system can provide high performance of spatial information reproduction such as conveying sound localization and sound distance [17]. Based on these system features, as an example of a more effective application of the BoSC system, we propose the design of a sound cask. In the design process of the sound field reproduction system based on the BoSC principle, space design, which is suitable for inverse filter calculation, will be important, since the quality of these filters directly affect the total performance of the system. The previous system [17] consisted of 62 loudspeakers mounted on a dome-shaped wooden frame arranged inside the music practice chamber whose floor space was around 2 m × 2 m. Several experiments indicated that the following items inevitably and adversely affected the performance of the inverse filter:

- reflection from the wooden frame,
- strong normal modes of the outer rectangular chamber,
- uneven distribution of loudspeakers, with dense location only at positions higher than the listener's head.

Measures against these items are:

- no parallel planes inside the enclosure except for ceiling and floor to suppress dominant acoustic modes;
- no reflective material inside the enclosure, e.g., loudspeakers are mounted directly on the walls with surrounding absorbing material;
- evenly distributed loudspeakers covering the whole body of the listener.

Additional design guidelines are summarized as follows:

- To increase opportunities to have many people experience the sound field reproduction system, easy disassembly, transportation, and assembly should be ensured.
- Smaller-scale hardware is also preferred for easy transportation.
- A completely enclosed space is aimed for in order to realize an immersive environment.
- The inner space must be large enough to play musical instruments.
- The basic performance of sound acquiring and reproducing devices, such as the microphone and loudspeaker, should be higher, to the extent possible, to achieve so-called Hi-Fi reproduction.

Fig. 2.3 Sound cask

- The space density of reproducing loudspeakers should also be higher, to the extent possible, to achieve higher resolution of sound localization. At the same time, a larger dimension of the loudspeaker unit would be preferred for better response in the low frequency range.
- The numbers of channels should be practically controllable from a commonly available computer and digital audio workstation (DAW).

As a practical and reasonable compromise of the conditions above, 96 loudspeakers are allocated inside the sound cask. Figure 2.3 shows a picture of the practically designed sound cask. In particular, a higher-grade loudspeaker unit (FOSTEX FX120) was adopted in the current version of the sound cask after several listening tests.

The horizontal cross section of the sound cask is the shape of a regular nonagonal cask. Hence, except for the floor and ceiling planes, the sound cask has no parallel sides. This shape has the effect of suppressing any dominant acoustic mode inside the sound cask. With internal dimensions of a diameter of 1950 mm in the central horizontal plane and a height of 2150 mm, the sound cask has a sufficiently large internal space to play wind and string instruments. Ninety-six full-range loudspeakers are installed on the walls and ceiling but not the floor plane. Six loudspeakers are installed on the ceiling plane. The speaker is installed on the wall surface at six heights. Nine loudspeakers are allotted to the top and bottom heights, and 18 loudspeakers are allotted to each of the remaining heights. The average interval between the adjoining heights is around 350 mm. The average interval between adjoining loudspeakers in the horizontal direction is around 540 mm for the top and bottom heights, and around 330 mm for all other heights. In our previous BoSC system, 62 loudspeakers were installed around the upper body of the listener. However, in the sound cask, loudspeakers were installed to cover the whole body of the listener. Therefore, this is expected to improve the sound reproduction performance in the vertical direction. In addition, the wall parts of the sound cask are modularized and can be dismantled when transporting the system. The system is divisible into nine parts horizontally with each part forming a side of a regular nonagon. The walls of the sound cask are divisible into three: top, middle, and bottom in the vertical direction. Each wall of this sound cask can be disassembled within around 30 to 40 min, and can be assembled within around two hours by several workers. For a sound-absorbing material, poly-wool, recycled material from plastic bottles (thickness 120 mm, density 32 kg/m^3), is used to achieve adequate absorption. The sound insulation performance of the wall of the cask is Dr-20. We also considered the ease of inverse system design by shortening the reverberation time.

The loudspeakers in the sound cask are driven by the newly designed digital amplifiers (Fig. 2.4). Ninety-six channels of audio signals are transmitted from the PC through only two MADI (multichannel audio digital interface) optical lines as shown in Fig. 2.5. The 128 channels of data, which consist of 124 channels of audio signals and 4 channels of control signals, are distributed to the 12 serially connected digital amplifiers using an optical MADI cable. Each 8ch D-class amplifier extracts appropriate 8ch audio signals from the MADI optical lines, and creates amplified PWM signals. After PWM signals pass through LPF, loudspeakers are driven in at 76 W at 10% THD+N 8Ω. In total, 12 D-class amplifiers, 12 third-order passive

Fig. 2.4 Newly designed 8ch digital amplifiers with a MADI interface

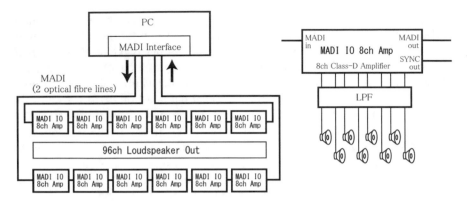

Fig. 2.5 Structure of the 96ch digital amplifier network

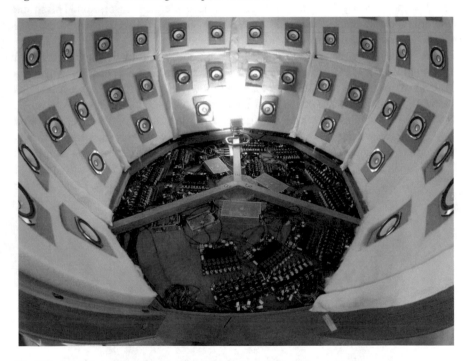

Fig. 2.6 Amplifiers and power supplies at the bottom of the cask

LPFs, 4 stabilized power supplies of 36 V (6.7 A), a 12 V (13 A) power supply, and a 5 V (15 A) power supply are installed at the bottom of the sound cask as shown in Fig. 2.6.

2.4 Performance Evaluation of the System

2.4.1 *Physical Performance*

In order to visualize the sound field reproduction, a microphone traverse system is located inside the sound cask as shown in Fig. 2.7. By moving a microphone, it can measure the sound pressure of the cylindrical region having a diameter of 1 m and a height of about 2 m. As the primary sound field, a loudspeaker and fullerene microphone were located in a soundproof room at a distance of 1.5 m. The loudspeaker was driven from five directions: front direction; right direction horizontal +30 and +120°; and left direction horizontal −30 and −120° by pulse signals with limited frequencies lower than 1 kHz. In the reproduced sound field in the sound cask, the sound pressure signals were measured iteratively at the moving point at each 4 cm distance and 4°. As depicted in Fig. 2.8, the wave front in the circle of 1 m in diameter can be seen, in order from the top, 30° left direction (L), 30° right direction (R), front direction (C), 120° left direction (Ls), and 120° right direction (Rs). In Fig. 2.8, the left-to-right change indicates the passage of time. It was found that the wave front was reproduced in a wider region than the fullerene microphone diameter (45 cm) [23].

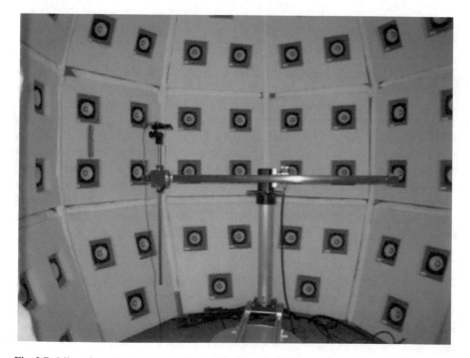

Fig. 2.7 Microphone traverse system located in the sound cask

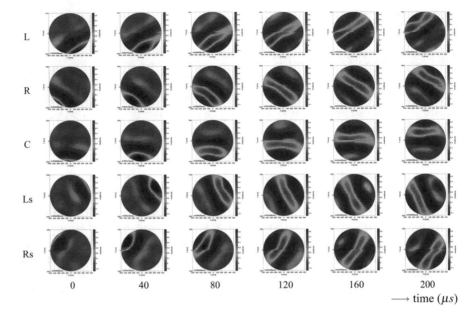

Fig. 2.8 Measured reproduced sound field

2.4.2 Localization Test

To verify the principal performance of the sound cask and the recording system, a simple localization test was carried out. Eight adults with normal hearing (age 20–22, four females) participated in this experiment. Informed consent was obtained after the nature and possible consequences of the studies were explained. Auditory stimuli were pink noise (1 s on-time and 0.4 s off-time, three bursts). Each stimulus was convoluted with each impulse response, in order to simulate the signals at each control point at the primary boundary surface in free space. The impulse responses were calculated assuming a point source was located at a distance of 2 m from the center of the microphone array and at the angle of each direction. The A-weighted sound pressure level of stimulus was adjusted to 60 dB at the center of a head to eliminate the level differences between directions or distances.

2.4.2.1 Procedures

Testing was conducted in the sound cask. The participants sat down in the chair and listened to the auditory stimuli. The experiment was divided into three sessions: horizontal, vertical, and distance sessions. In the horizontal session, stimuli were presented from angles of 0–345° with 15° intervals. In the vertical session, the stimuli were presented from angles of 0–90° each with 15° intervals. In both sessions, the distance was 2 m. The participants were asked to illustrate on the answer sheets their perceived direction after listening to the stimuli. In the distance session, we used the magnitude estimation method [24]. The standard stimulus was at a 100 cm distance and was given a numerical value of 100. For subsequent stimuli, participants were asked to report numerically their perceived distance relative to the standard so as to preserve the ratio between the sensations and numerical estimates. We set seven conditions: 30, 60, 90, 120, 150, 180, and 240 cm. In this session, the horizontal angle was 0° and the vertical angle was 0°. As the perceived distance for each participant, we calculated the geometric average across repeated trials for each distance condition. The session order was the horizontal, the vertical, and the distance session for all participants. The trial was repeated 10 times for each condition, and the presentation order was randomized in each session. The participants were permitted to move their heads and bodies during the stimulus presentation. The participants took part in a practice session, which was followed by the experimental session. Intervals between the trials were 5 s.

2.4.2.2   Results and Discussion

Horizontal session: Fig. 2.9a shows the mean perceived location versus actual locations in the horizontal session across all participants. The mean error angle was 7°, the minimum error angle was almost 3° and the maximum error angle was 14°. Previous studies showed that the minimum error angle was 2° and the maximum error angle was almost 15° in the horizontal localization with real sources [26]. These results indicate that the listeners can perceive the sound image at the presented locations in the horizontal plane.

Vertical session: Fig. 2.9b shows the mean perceived location versus actual locations in the vertical session. The mean error angle was ±3° across participants, the maximum error angle was 30° in the 0° condition, and the minimum error angle was 15° in the 45° condition. Previous studies showed that the minimum error angle was 3° and the maximum error angle was 15° in vertical localization with real sources [26]. It is difficult for the listeners to localize the sound image into the presented locations in the vertical plane at this time.

Distance session: Fig. 2.9c shows the mean perceived distance versus actual distance across all participants. It is clear that the listeners tended to overestimate the distance to the sound image within 100 cm in the sound cask. At more than 100 cm, the participants could not discriminate the difference in distances. In this study, we used auditory stimuli that simulate the impulse responses of the free field, and set the same sound pressure level across all conditions. Under these conditions, it is considered that the participants used the cue of HRTFs to estimate the distance from the stimuli. However, the HRTFs lost validity at a distance of more than 100 cm [27]. Thus, participants could not estimate the distance at more than 100 cm. In addition, previous studies also showed that listeners tend to overestimate the distance of the sound image within 100 cm in the front direction [28]. From these results, we

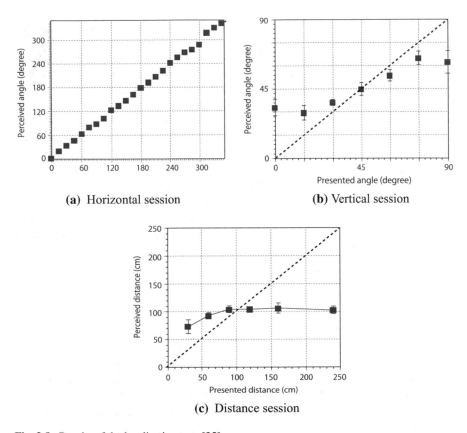

(a) Horizontal session

(b) Vertical session

(c) Distance session

Fig. 2.9 Results of the localization tests [25]

consider that the sound cask can provide reasonable reproduction performance to perceive the distance from the apparent source.

2.4.3 Psychological and Physiological Evaluation of Feeling of Reality in a 3D Sound Field

In order to be confident that others are present in the same space, sound is an essential element. Rather, it has been found that humans have the potential ability to feel the presence from a trace of someone's existence using auditory sensation. This means that it is possible that some physiological phenomenon occurs when you understand the atmosphere of the space. Therefore, three psychological and physiological experiments were carried out focusing on the "presence of the speaker (pronounced body)" changing the experimental conditions of the 3D sound field. From these results, reproducing a 3D sound field with high accuracy can create a feeling of extremely high reality of the speaker (pronounced body). At the same time, the psychological and physiological method is effective for evaluating the performance of recreating the atmosphere of the space using a 3D sound field system.

2.4.3.1 Autonomic Responses Caused by Acoustic Information of the Speaker's Tiny Movements

Many engineers have created communication systems that enhance the sense of presence or reality to realize natural communication with those in remote locations. However, there are very few methods by which a sense of presence or reality can be quantitatively evaluated. Here, we describe a quantitative evaluation of the acoustic sensation of presence by measuring autonomic responses. We examined the effects of acoustic information about speakers' movements on the sense of presence in personal communication by using a three-dimensional sound field reproduction system based on the boundary surface control principle, by which listeners can experience a highly realistic sensation of speakers. We prepared two types of speech stimuli, "dynamic" and "static." In the dynamic condition, the speakers' speech was recorded along with their subtle unconscious movements. In the static condition, the speech stimulus in the dynamic condition presented from a mouth simulator was recorded to remove any information about the speakers' movements. The sense of the speakers' presence and friendliness was assessed subjectively by the participants. In physiological experiments, we evaluated the autonomic responses by measuring blood volume pulse amplitude and the skin conductance response during the speakers' voice presentation. We found that a higher sense of presence was observed in the dynamic condition than in the static condition, and that the participants expressed greater friendliness towards speakers in the dynamic condition. Moreover, there were differences in the autonomic nervous system activities between the dynamic and the static conditions. These findings suggest that a sense of presence is influenced by acoustic information about speakers' unconscious subtle movements and that the existence or non-existence of speakers' movements can be detected from the autonomic responses [29, 30].

2.4.3.2 Physiological Response Due to the Approach of Moving Sound Sources

By observing time variation of activity of the autonomic nervous system and subjective assessment due to the approach of moving sound sources, we confirmed that the accuracy of 3D sound field reproduction affects the feeling of reality of human presence. In the experimental result, by listening to the approach of moving sound sources with high accuracy of 3D sound field reproduction, the activity of the sympathetic nervous system of the listener increases. Because this phenomenon occurs

in the case of invasion of personal space, it is indicated that personal space can also
be invaded by a sound in a virtual space [31].

2.4.3.3   Activity of the Mirror Neuron System Caused by Action-Related Sound

The motor cortical area is often activated in the presence of auditory stimuli in the
human brain. In this section, we examine whether the motor area shows differential
activation for action-related and non-action-related sounds and whether it is suscep-
tible to the quality of the sounds. A three-dimensional sound field recording and
reproduction system based on the boundary surface control principle (BoSC system)
was used for this purpose. We measured brain activity while hearing action-related or
non-action-related sounds with electroencephalography using μ rhythm suppression
(μ-suppression) as an index of motor cortical activation. The results showed that
μ-suppression was observed when the participant heard action-related sounds, but it
was not evident when hearing non-action-related sounds. Moreover, this suppression
was significantly larger in the 3D sound field (BoSC reproduction), which generates
a more realistic sound field, than in the single-loudspeaker condition. These results
indicate that the motor area is indeed activated for action-related sounds and that its
activation is enhanced with a 3D realistic sound field. It is indicated that the mirror
neuron system is related to the subjective sense of reality, not only in real space but
also in virtual space (Fig. 2.10) [32–34].

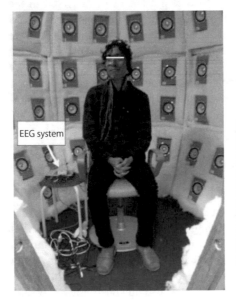
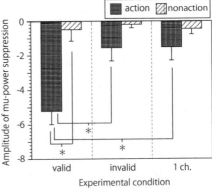

Fig. 2.10 Experimental setup of brain activity in the sound cask and the result of μ-suppression [35]

2.5 Application of the Sound Cask

2.5.1 Sound Field Simulator

As shown in Fig. 2.11, the source signal U generated from a loudspeaker, assumed an instrument of a player on a concert hall stage in the primary field, passes through the transfer functions $[F_j]$. The BoSC microphone is located at the position of the player. The transfer function is given by $[F_j] = [D_j + R_j](\in \mathbf{C}^{1 \times M})$, where $[D_j]$ is the direct sound and $[R_j]$ is the reverberant sound. In the simulated field, as in the primary field, after the source signal U is picked up by a microphone for the musical instrument, the output signal $\widehat{X}$ of the microphone is convolved using the FIR filter $[Q_i](\in \mathbf{C}^{1 \times N})$ in real time. Driving the loudspeakers in the sound cask with the filter output $[S_i](\in \mathbf{C}^{1 \times N})$ reproduces the same sound field as the primary field in the region surrounding the head of the listener (Fig. 2.12). From these conditions, FIR filter $[Q_i]$ is obtained as follows,

$$[Q_i] = \frac{[R_j][G_{ij}]^{-1}}{\widehat{D}_0 + [R_j][G_{ij}]^{-1}[G_{i0}]} e^{j\omega\tau_1}. \tag{2.7}$$

Fig. 2.11 Impulse response measurement in the primary sound field

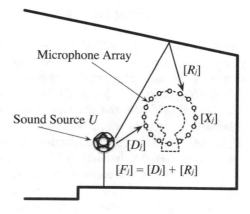

Fig. 2.12 Structure of the sound field simulator system using the sound cask

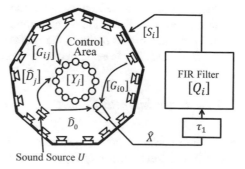

where τ_1 is the delay time of real-time computing of the FIR filter $[Q_i]$. Assuming that the microphone for the musical instrument is located near the sound source, we obtain $\widehat{D}_0 >> [R_j][G_{ij}]^{-1}[G_{i0}]$. Furthermore, the transfer function from the source to the microphone for the musical instrument is just the delay τ_2, i.e., $\widehat{D}_0 = e^{-j\tau_2\omega}$. Then, the FIR filter $[Q_i]$ is expressed as

$$[Q_i] \simeq [R_j][G_{ij}]^{-1}e^{j\omega(\tau_1+\tau_2)} \tag{2.8}$$

where $[G_{ij}](\in \mathbf{C}^{N \times M})$ is the transfer function matrix from i-th loudspeaker in the reproduced sound field to j-th microphone on the surface S'. By considering the causality of the inverse system, we need to assume the delay time τ_h caused by the inverse system. Instead, the reflective sound $[R_j]$ can be shifted τ_r earlier, i.e., $[R'_j] = [R_j]e^{j\omega\tau_r}$. Therefore, actual FIR system $[Q'_i]$ is given as

$$[Q'_i] = [R'_j][H_{ji}] = [R_j][G_{ij}]^{-1}e^{j\omega(\tau_r-\tau_h)} \tag{2.9}$$

where $[H_{ji}](\in \mathbf{C}^{M \times N})$ is the inverse system of the transfer function $[G_{ij}]$ considering the causality mentioned above. $[Q_i] = [Q'_i]$ in Eqs. 2.8 and 2.9 holds when $\tau_1 + \tau_2 = \tau_r - \tau_h$.

2.5.1.1 Experimental Condition

As the primary sound field, the impulse responses in a multi-purpose hall with a reverberation time of 1.5 s are measured, and the reverberant filter is calculated by assuming the starting time of the reflective component of the impulse response to be 25 ms. $[H_{ji}]$ in Eq. 2.9 is designed using the regularization parameter method with an FIR tap length of 4096 and a latency of 2048 points (about 42.7 ms) after truncating the impulse response with 2048 points and converting it into a frequency domain signal by discrete Fourier transformation with 8192 points. Figure 2.13 shows the experimental setup of the sound field simulator. A small omnidirectional microphone (DPA-4060) as the instrument microphone is located on the wall inside the sound cask at a height of 145 cm. A BoSC microphone located at the center in the sound cask at a height of 120 cm is used to obtain the indicator of room acoustics. As a feedback suppression method we adopt the inverse design method so that the sound at the instrumental microphone in the sound cask is canceled [36]. In order to confirm the effectiveness of this method, the performance of the sound field simulator with the feedback canceler is evaluated using parameters of room acoustics.

2.5.2 Experimental Result

From the impulse response measured in the sound field simulator (Fig. 2.13), the reverberation time in the frequencies of each octave band, early reflection energy L_{er}, and late reflection energy L_{rev} were calculated. In these calculations, the direct sound

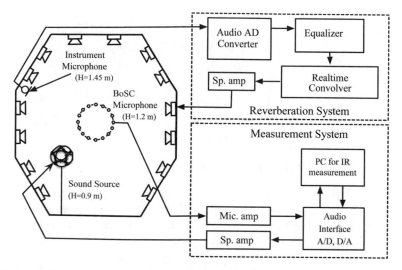

Fig. 2.13 Experimental setup of the sound field simulator

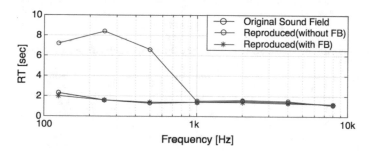

Fig. 2.14 Reverberation time in the frequencies of each octave band

energy of the impulse response is calculated from the energy within the time span of the direct sound arrival time to 10 ms after. The early reflection energy and the late reflection energy are calculated from the proportion of energy of 25 ms to 100 ms and after 100 ms, respectively, to the direct sound energy. The reverberation time is shown in Fig. 2.14. As shown in Fig. 2.14, without the feedback cancellation system, large error can be seen in the frequency range below 500 Hz between the primary sound field and the simulated sound field. However, with the feedback cancellation system, these errors become small. The early reflection energy and the late reflection energy are depicted in Figs. 2.15 and 2.16, respectively. Unlike the case of the reverberation time, large error can be seen in the frequency range below 2 kHz between the primary sound field and the simulated sound field regardless of whether or not feedback cancellation is employed. This is thought to be caused by the assumption that the frequency response of $\widehat{D}_0$ is flat in the formulation previously described. Therefore, we correct the frequency characteristic of the instrumental microphone using a one-

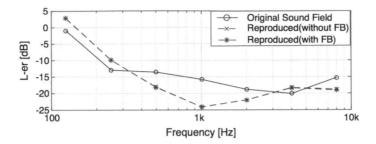

Fig. 2.15 Comparison of the reflection energy (before correction): early reflection energy

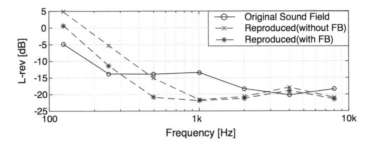

Fig. 2.16 Comparison of the reflection energy (before correction): late reflection energy

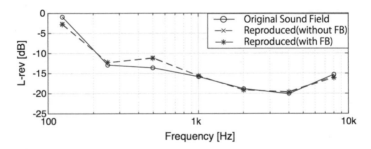

Fig. 2.17 Comparison of the reflection energy (after correction): early reflection energy

third-octave band equalizer so that the sum of the early reflection energy and the late reflection energy in the simulated sound field become equal to that in the primary field. The early reflection energy and the late reflection energy corrected in the manner mentioned above are depicted in Figs. 2.17 and 2.18, respectively. We can see that both the early reflection energy and the late reflection energy in the simulated sound field basically correspond to those in the primary field.

As described above, the sound field simulator can be realized by using the immersive auditory display, the sound cask. In the formulation to design the sound field simulator, the frequency characteristic of the instrumental microphone is not flat because of the frequency characteristic inside the sound cask. To improve the per-

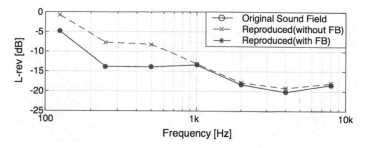

Fig. 2.18 Comparison of the reflection energy (after correction): late reflection energy

formance of the sound field simulator, it was found that the equalizer is required to correct the frequency response of the instrument microphone input.

2.5.2.1 Evaluation of Instrument and Musical Performance

In order to reveal the applicability of the sound cask to music players and instrument makers, we investigated the auditory impression of a music performance with flutes in a concert hall using the sound cask regarding whether there is a feeling of near-field sonority and far-field sonority (Fig. 2.19). In the experiment, sounds produced by eight flutes, recorded on the stage and the audience seats of a concert hall, were presented to the participants; they were asked to evaluate both the near-field sonority and the far-field sonority of each flute. In addition, we interviewed them about the definition of near-/far-field sonority and its evaluation points. The results showed that the definition conforms to the general definition in that the clarity of sounds in the audience seats is an important factor while determining the near-/far-field sonority of the instrument. Moreover, the sonority was not similarly evaluated by all participants, whereas several other instruments have been similarly, and highly, evaluated. Acoustic analyses of the sounds produced by flutes showed the possibility that their evaluation was related to the physical characteristics of the sound level and overtone spectrum [37].

2.5.3 Sound Table Tennis

A virtual sound table-tennis system was developed using the sound cask. Sound table tennis is a modified table tennis for visually impaired people, in which players need to roll a ball from one end of the table to the other, instead of hitting the ball over a net. And by using a sound-ball and a special racket, the player may hit the ball by listening for the direction in which the ball is rolling [38] (Fig. 2.20).

Fig. 2.19 Recording of flute performance and listening test [37]

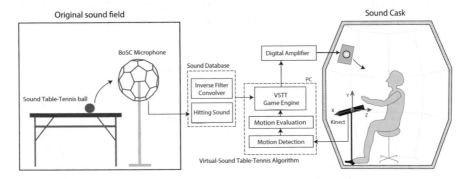

Fig. 2.20 Sound table tennis system

2.5.4 Sound Field Sharing

As an application of the BoSC system, the concept of a sound field sharing system using more than one system has been introduced. This system is a distant communication system that allows us to communicate with each other as if we were in the same room. A similar sharing system has already been designed and tried as shown in [39]. In this reference, the concept and the practical scheme, and examples of distant field sharing, are shown. However, the methods of sound field capture and re-construction are quite basic; e.g., a conventional recording technique with several microphones was used and reverberation sounds were reproduced from the loudspeakers located in the direction of incidence (details of the reproduction method are unclear). The advantageous of our proposed system can be summarized as follows:

- capability of capturing directional information with high accuracy by the microphone array;
- theoretically proved reproduction method;
- capability of moving sources;
- real immersive environment by enclosed space, the cask.

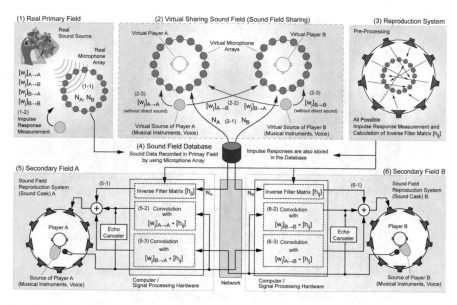

Fig. 2.21 Sound field sharing system

Figure 2.21 shows a conceptual diagram of the sound field sharing system, in which Player A and B share a sense of being in the same primary field. Space (1) in the figure is the existing real primary field (Fig. 2.22) and is the sound field that a subject aims to share. In this primary field, for example, music performances are recorded using a microphone array as (1-1). The array is installed in places in which it is assumed that Player A and B stand and recorded signal N_A or N_B can be played back by a reproducing system. In addition, impulse responses between sound sources and the adjacent microphone array in this real space are measured as indicated (1-2). These are necessary for yielding musical sounds or voices, which can be recognized as if they are being played in the primary sound field by the experiment participants, the players. For example, the impulse response from the instrument position of Player A to the j-th microphone at Player B is indicated as $[w_j]_{A \to B}$ in the figure. Space (2) in the figure is a virtual sound sharing field, and a sharing space for the players. Players A and B listen to music in the same primary sound field with a high degree of presence by using a reproduction system based on the BoSC principle. Recorded signals N_A and N_B are played back as (2-1). In addition, they feel as if they are playing as an ensemble in the same primary field. The sound played by Player A is transmitted to Player B after passing through the impulse responses between the source position of A and the listening position of B measured in the primary field. This is the signal flow shown as $[w_j]_{A \to B}$ in the figure. The reverse process is the same, too, and expressed as $[w_j]_{B \to A}$ as indicated at (2-2). Furthermore, the played signals are also transmitted to themselves after passing through the impulse responses of their own source position and listening position. These are shown as (2-3) $[w_j]_{A \to A}$

Fig. 2.22 Concert hall measurement for the ensemble experiment

Fig. 2.23 Appearance of the ensemble test with two casks located side by side

and $\left[w_j\right]_{B \to B}$. Space (3) in the figure is the sound field reproducing system. This consists of a sound cask and a C80 fullerene-type microphone array. The impulse responses between all possible combinations of loudspeakers and microphones are measured at the preliminary stage and used to calculate the inverse filter matrix necessary for the BoSC principle. The inverse filter matrix is indicated as $[h_{ij}]$ in the figure. The recorded signals and impulse responses are stored in the database. These are transmitted via a network or dedicated line, on demand. The sound fields, where Players A and B exist, are indicated as Space (5), Secondary Field A; and Space (6), Secondary Field B, respectively. More precisely, these are the inner space of the sound field reproduction system, the sound cask, in this case. Real and detailed signal flows are provided in the lower part of the figure. The recorded signals in the primary field are played back after passing through the inverse filter matrix $[h_{ij}]$ and these are the signals of (5-1) and (6-1). In addition, the musical sound or voice of Player A is transmitted back after passing through the impulse responses $[w_j]_{A \to A}$ and inverse filter matrix $[h_{ij}]$, and to Player B with filters $[w_j]_{A \to B}$ and $[h_{ij}]$. These are indicated as (5-2) and (6-3), respectively. A similar process for Player B is indicated as (6-2) and (5-3). In the autoregression filters $[w_j]_{A \to A}$ and $[w_j]_{B \to B}$, direct sound should be removed and an echo canceler introduced in the regression process. A sound from the real primary field (1), which is added to the sound, is heard by Players A and B and expected to evoke the environment in which they exist and play in the same sound field and playing ensemble. In previous studies, a sound field sharing system using the BoSC system with 62-channel loudspeakers was developed [18, 19]. The BoSC system enables perception of the direction of the reproduced voice. The system transmits voice direction in a three-person conversation by changing the transfer functions in accordance with the angle the speaker is facing [20]. Only 24 loudspeakers were used to reproduce voices between the systems to avoid a large amount of calculation [21]. Basic experiments on communication between separate casks with necessary convolutions of signals in real time have been started recently as shown in Fig. 2.23. At the current stage, two casks are located side by side and players inside the casks have tried an ensemble while hearing the other play, which is reproduced by the necessary convolutions ((5-3) and (6-3) in Fig. 2.21). The possibility of a remote ensemble with high presence has been confirmed. For further improvement of performance, continuous experimental examinations are conducted.

2.5.4.1 Latency Reduction

In the case of playing in an orchestra, players on the stage of a concert hall listen to other players' sounds with delay caused by sound propagation. For example, if players are positioned at a distance of 10 m, sound from other players is delayed by 34 ms because of the sound propagation speed of 340 m/s. Therefore, the conductor is required to synchronize and control the orchestra's performance. When there is no conductor, such as in an ensemble performance, a delay of 20 ms is the maximum limit to play music naturally [40]. Thus, this sound field sharing system aims to suppress delay to less than 20 ms. In the sound field sharing system, delay is caused in the telecommunication system, the inverse system, and the audio input/output system. To reduce the latency of the audio input/output system, we developed an FPGA board, which can convolve 96ch data from two MADI input signals with 1071 FIR coefficients in real time. The impulse response after 1071 points is convolved using a PC and is added to the FPGA results. Then, 96ch impulse responses longer than 4 s can be convolved in real time with almost no latency [41].

2.5.4.2 Feedback Cancellation

In the sound field sharing system, the voice or musical performance is first recorded in one of the sound casks, and it is transmitted and reproduced in others. At the same time, the same recording and reproduction procedure is implemented for one of the other sound casks, providing the listener with a feeling of a shared-sound field. In this case, two types of acoustic feedback occur owing to the installation of microphones inside the sound cask. This feedback causes an echo and leads to instability of the system, thereby degrading the accuracy of the reproduced sound field. In this section, we introduce an acoustic feedback suppression method by manipulating the inverse system design algorithm, in which we introduce an additional control point, called a "null space," where summation of all signals fed from the speakers is equal to zero. Figure 2.24 shows the results of an octave band analysis at the reference microphone using the musical signal. The signal can be suppressed over all ranges of frequency bands. Specifically, the suppression level of the center frequency of 500 Hz is about 30 dB in both measurement signals. However, the suppression level is low in the higher frequency band [36, 42].

2.5.4.3 Ensemble Experiment

In order to confirm the performance of the system, an ensemble experiment of the sound field sharing system using two sound casks was performed. Generous cooperation was given by five ensemble groups (10 players in total). As a result, we found that the time delay of the system caused by transferring and calculating data

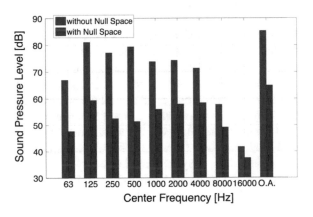

Fig. 2.24 Octave analysis of the observed signal at the microphone when using the orchestra as the primary signal. [43]

can be entirely ignored, and we received the favorable comment that the sound field sharing system using two sound casks can realize a stage in a virtual concert hall. Furthermore, we received constructive comments concerning another application, for example, "This system can be used for remote music education." On the other hand, it is pointed out that the directivity of musical instruments is nearly imperceptible and the visual monitor should be larger if the system is to be used for music education.

2.6 Further Improvement

We outline two topics for future work. First, we propose a method to include information on the body movement of the source in the primary sound field of the sound sharing system, which can increase the presence of the source (e.g. music players in an ensemble performance or speakers in a conversation) in the receiver's sound field. Second, two other types of sound field reproduction rooms are introduced: an open system and a small system. Long-term perspectives of the immersive auditory display based on BoSC principle are also described focusing on cost reduction, increase in the internal space and enhancement of the sound quality, smaller and lighter equipment and practical application.

2.6.1 Reproduction of Sound Source Directivity

One of the features of the BoSC system is that it allows a listener to move his/her head. In addition, the players and speakers can move their bodies during the communication process as well. It is possible that the minor changes in the sound caused by the speaker's body movements stimulate the sense of the presence of the other party [30]. A change in the sound directivity is specified as one of the physical changes caused by the players' or speakers' movements. In this section, we propose a sound directivity reproduction method that estimates the radiation from a sound source by solving an inverse problem between the secondary sound sources enclosing the sound source and a microphone array outside the secondary sound sources. We demonstrate the effectiveness of this method by simulations and measurements made in an anechoic chamber.

Figure 2.25 shows the concept of the proposed method of sound directivity reproduction. First, we consider the radiation from sound sources inside a three-dimensional volume, V_1, that is bounded by surface S_1. On the basis of the external Helmholtz integral equation (HIE) [44], the sound pressures of volume V_O outside of V_1 are

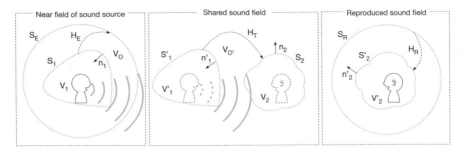

Fig. 2.25 Concept of sound directivity reproduction

$$p\left(r'_1\right) = \iint_{S_1} \left(G\frac{\partial p\left(r_1\right)}{\partial n_1} - p\left(r_1\right)\frac{\partial G}{\partial n_1}\right)dS_1 \qquad (2.10)$$

$$\left(r_1 \in S_1, r'_1 \in V_O\right),$$

where G is a Green's function, and n_1 is a normal vector to surface S_1. This equation implies that the radiation of sound sources is expressed by the sound pressures and particle velocities on closed surface S_1.

Now we consider observation surface S_E that is outside of surface S_1. Because $S_E \subset V_O$, the sound pressures on S_E are also given by Eq. 2.10. We discretize surfaces S_1 and S_E into N_1 and M_1 small elements of areas $\Delta S_{1,k}(k = 1, \ldots, N_1)$ and $\Delta S_{E,j}(j = 1, \ldots, M_1)$, respectively. From Eq. 2.10, the sound pressure in area $\Delta S_{E,j}$ is

$$p_E(j) = \sum_{k=1}^{N_1} \left(G_{j,k}\frac{\partial p_1(k)}{\partial n_1} - p_1(k)\frac{\partial G_{j,k}}{\partial n_1}\right)\Delta S_{1,k}, \qquad (2.11)$$

where $p_1(k)$ is the sound pressure in $\Delta S_{1,k}$, and $G_{j,k}$ is the Green's function between areas $\Delta S_{E,j}$ and $\Delta S_{1,k}$.

Let $\Delta S_{IN,1,k}$ and $\Delta S_{OUT,1,k}$ be small elements of the areas that are inside and outside of $\Delta S_{1,k}$, respectively, in the direction normal to S_1 and at distance h from its surface. When distance h is short enough, the sound pressures and particle velocities in small area $\Delta S_{1,k}$ are

$$p_1(k) \cong \frac{p_{IN,1}(k) + p_{OUT,1}(k)}{2}, \qquad (2.12)$$

$$\frac{\partial p_1(k)}{\partial n_1} \cong \frac{p_{IN,1}(k) - p_{OUT,1}(k)}{2h}, \qquad (2.13)$$

where $p_{IN,1}(k)$ and $p_{OUT,1}(k)$ are the sound pressures in $\Delta S_{IN,1,k}$ and $\Delta S_{OUT,1,k}$ respectively.

Inserting Eqs. 2.12 and 2.13 into Eq. 2.11 yields

$$
\begin{aligned}
p_E\,(j) = \frac{1}{2} \sum_{k=1}^{N_1} & \left(\left(\frac{G_{j,k}}{h} - \frac{\partial G_{j,k}}{\partial n_1} \right) p_{\mathrm{IN},1}\,(k) \right. \\
& \left. - \left(\frac{G_{j,k}}{h} + \frac{\partial G_{j,k}}{\partial n_1} \right) p_{\mathrm{OUT},1}\,(k) \right) \Delta S_{1,k}.
\end{aligned} \tag{2.14}
$$

Therefore, we obtain a matrix form of Eq. 2.14:

$$
\mathbf{p}_E = \mathbf{H}_E \mathbf{p}_1, \tag{2.15}
$$

where

$$
\begin{aligned}
\mathbf{p}_1 &= \left[p_{\mathrm{IN},1}\,(1), \ldots, p_{\mathrm{IN},1}\,(N_1), \right. \\
& \qquad \left. p_{\mathrm{OUT},1}\,(1), \ldots, p_{\mathrm{OUT},1}\,(N_1) \right]^T, \\
\mathbf{H}_E &= \frac{1}{2}\mathbf{G}\mathbf{S}, \\
\mathbf{G} &= [\mathbf{G}_1 \ \ \mathbf{G}_2], \quad \mathbf{S} = \begin{pmatrix} \mathbf{S}_d & 0 \\ 0 & \mathbf{S}_d \end{pmatrix}, \\
\mathbf{G}_1\,(j,k) &= \frac{G_{j,k}}{h} - \frac{\partial G_{j,k}}{\partial n_1}, \ \mathbf{G}_2\,(j,k) = \frac{G_{j,k}}{h} + \frac{\partial G_{j,k}}{\partial n_1}, \\
& (j = 1, \ldots, M_1, \quad k = 1, \ldots, N_1).
\end{aligned}
$$

Here, $\mathbf{p}_E$ is the column vector of the sound pressures in all small areas $\Delta S_{E,j}$, $\mathbf{H}_E$ is an $M_1 \times 2N_1$ matrix, $\mathbf{S}_d$ is a diagonal matrix $diag(\Delta S_{1,1}, \ldots, \Delta S_{1,N})$, and $[\cdot]^T$ denotes the transpose.

According to Eq. 2.15, the sound pressure vector of surface S_1 is represented by the following Eq. using the inverse matrix of $\mathbf{H}_E$:

$$
\mathbf{p}_1 = \mathbf{H}_E^{-1} \mathbf{p}_E. \tag{2.16}
$$

Equation 2.16 implies that we can obtain the sound pressures and particle velocities on surface S_1 from the sound pressures on surface S_E by solving the inverse problem. From Eq. 2.11, we also find that the radiation from the sound source is obtained through Eq. 2.15.

Next, we consider the reproduction of the sound source radiation in a shared sound field. Let V_1' and S_1' be the volume and surface in the shared sound field that are congruent with V_1 and S_1, respectively. On the basis of the external HIE, the sound pressures in a volume $V_{O'}$ which is outside of V_1' are given by an equation similar to Eq. 2.10 using the sound pressures and particle velocities on surface S_1'. Considering the congruency, we find that the radiation from the sound source in V_1 is reproduced in $V_{O'}$ when the sound pressures and particle velocities on S_1' correspond to those on S_1: $\mathbf{p}_1 = \mathbf{p}'_1$, where $\mathbf{p}'_1$ is the column vector of the sound pressures on S'_1. That is, when this Eq. is satisfied, there is a virtual sound source in V'_1 in the shared sound field.

In the shared sound field, we consider volume V_2 where a virtual listener is located and which is bounded by surface S_2. In the reproduced sound field, we also consider a volume V'_2 and surface S'_2 that are congruent with V_2 and S_2, respectively. On the basis of BoSC, the sound pressures in V'_2 correspond to those in V_2 when the sound pressures on S'_2 are matched with those on S_2 using secondary sources located on a surface S_R outside of S'_2: $\mathbf{p}_2 = \mathbf{p}'_2$ where $\mathbf{p}_2$ and $\mathbf{p}'_2$ are the vectors of the sound pressure in the small areas obtained by discretizing surfaces S_2 and S'_2 into N_2, respectively.

The relationship between the sound pressures at the secondary sources and those on surface S'_2 is

$$\mathbf{p}'_2 = \mathbf{H}_R \mathbf{p}_R, \tag{2.17}$$

where $\mathbf{p}_R$ is the column vector of the sound pressures in the small areas obtained by discretizing surface S_R into M_2, and $\mathbf{H}_R$ is an $N_2 \times M_2$ matrix corresponding to the transfer matrix between the two surfaces.

Finally, we consider the relationship between the sound pressures on surfaces S'_1 and S_2 to reproduce the virtual sound source for the virtual listener. This relationship can be derived in the same way as Eq. 2.15, and the column vector of the sound pressures on surface S_2 is

$$\mathbf{p}_2 = \mathbf{H}_T \mathbf{p}'_1, \tag{2.18}$$

where $\mathbf{H}_T$ is an $N_1 \times N_2$ matrix.

Therefore, from Eqs. 2.16–2.18, we can obtain

$$\mathbf{p}_R = \mathbf{H}_R^{-1} \mathbf{H}_T \mathbf{H}_E^{-1} \mathbf{p}_E. \tag{2.19}$$

That is, when we control the sound pressures at the secondary sources on surface S_R to satisfy Eq. 2.19, the radiation of the sound source in volume V_1 is reproduced in volume V'_1 and then reproduced in volume V'_2 after propagating in the shared sound field.

Well-known methods that trace the sound radiation back by solving the inverse problem are acoustical holography [45] and near-field acoustical holography [44]. In this paper, an inverse problem that traces back to the sound source is applied to a telecommunication system using an immersive sound reproduction system based on BoSC. To apply it to a telecommunication system, we install secondary sources between the measurement surface and the sound source and solve the inverse problem using the measured impulse response matrix. Note that solving the inverse problem makes it easier to remove the effect of the characteristic features of the loudspeakers, microphones, and room acoustics.

We consider a telecommunication system based on the concept described in the preceding section. Figure 2.26 shows the system, which reproduces a speaker's or player's original sound directivity into the other party's system.

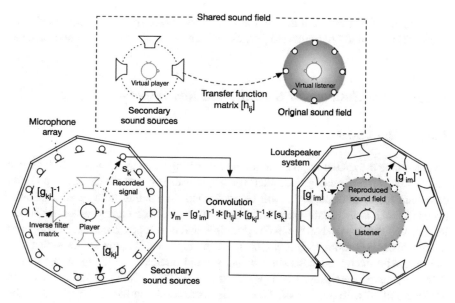

Fig. 2.26 Sound directivity reproduction system for use in telecommunication

The sounds produced by the player are recorded with a microphone array that is installed so as to enclose the player. Let the signal recorded by the k-th microphone of the array be $s_k (k = 1, \ldots, N_1)$ in the time domain. First, signals $[s_k]$ are convolved with inverse matrix $[g_{kj}]^{-1}$ to estimate the radiation from the sound source. This inverse matrix is derived from an impulse response matrix $[g_{kj}](j = 1, \ldots, M_1)$, which is measured using the microphone array, and M_1 secondary sound sources, which are placed so as to enclose the position of the original sound source. By this convolution, we obtain the signals of secondary sources to reproduce the radiation of the sound source.

Next, in the shared sound field, a loudspeaker array and a microphone array for BoSC sound reproduction are installed so as to enclose the position of a virtual player and a virtual listener, respectively. We measure impulse response matrix $[h_{ij}](i = 1, \ldots, N_2)$ from the loudspeaker array to the microphone array. On the basis of BoSC, we reproduce the sound field at the virtual listener into the area where a real listener is. Therefore, the reproduction of the sound field using the inverse system $[g'_{im}]^{-1}$ requires loudspeaker system signals $y_m (m = 1, \ldots, M_2)$ in the reproduction area to form the following equation:

$$y_m = [g'_{im}]^{-1} * [h_{ij}] * [g_{kj}]^{-1} * [s_k]. \tag{2.20}$$

Considering that the system is time invariant, and that secondary sources for the reproduction of the sound source's radiation are used only to measure impulse responses, the loudspeaker array can be replaced by a single loudspeaker that is moved to achieve the same result. The configuration of the secondary sources must be determined so as to control the sound pressures and particle velocities on the specific closed surface.

2.6.2 Other Systems for Sound Field Reproduction

2.6.2.1 Open System

To reproduce the spatial impression including feeling of distance with a high degree of accuracy, an enclosed environment for single user is required. However, an open environment for multiple users will be convenient in a sound field requiring lower accuracy, such as in a sound-surrounding environment. So, an open system for sound field reproduction based on the BoSC principle was developed. Figure 2.27 shows an octagonal-shaped room with a height of 1.8 m, eight walls (opposite-side distance is 3 m), with each wall consisting of six cuboid enclosures (1.5 m × 0.15 m × 0.15 m) stacked vertically. Loudspeaker unit FOSTEX FX120 is mounted on an enclosure filled with poly-wool. Though listeners can be in the area wider than the sound cask, the actual sweet spot of the listening area is the same size as the sound cask because, theoretically, the sound reproduction area is limited to inside of the BoSC microphone based on the boundary surface control principle. Compared with the sound cask, the open system has high portability and users can listen to the sound without an oppressive feeling.

Fig. 2.27 Open-type BoSC system

Fig. 2.28 Small-type BoSC system

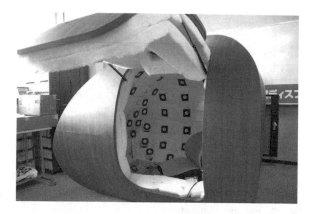

2.6.2.2 Small System

The sound cask is designed so that musicians can play instruments inside it. If the purpose is just to listen to the sound, a more compact BoSC reproduction room can be built. Therefore, we designed the small-size BoSC reproduction room shown in Fig. 2.28. Some people say that the small-size BoSC reproduction room can create a more composed space than the "Sound Cask".

2.6.3 Long-Term Perspectives

The immersive auditory display developed in this research constitutes a new medium that expands the interface between humans and information technology. That is, it represents a new means of using sound, which is a classical human communication method, and also of creating content with new value in the information society. Developing the technology to record and reproduce 3D sound has been a dream in the field of acoustics since the invention of the loudspeaker about a hundred years ago, far before the advent of "Virtual Reality". Recently, multichannel digital signal processing technology finally broke through. As a next step, we can consider the following improvements:

1. Cost reduction,
2. Increase in the internal space and enhancement of the sound quality,
3. Smaller and lighter equipment,
4. Practical application of the sound cask.

2.6.3.1   Cost Reduction

In this project, we used a C80-shaped fullerene microphone array, which consists of 80 omnidirectional microphones, for the BoSC recording system. Because each microphone costs tens of thousands of yen, the total cost is very high. On the other hand, the acoustic performance of the MEMS microphones used in smartphones is increasing year by year. If MEMS microphones could be used in the BoSC recording system, a significant cost reduction could be achieved. Regarding the sound field reproduction system, costs could be cut by lowering the performance of the loudspeaker unit and also by using a rectangular parallelepiped outer shape (like commercially available soundproof chambers) rather than a cask shape. However, in both cases, it is necessary to take into account that designing a stable inverse system would become difficult.

2.6.3.2   Increase in the Internal Space and Enhancement of the Sound Quality

By increasing the size of the microphone array while keeping the density of microphones constant, it is possible to enlarge the region where the sound field is reproduced, for example, to surround multiple listeners. Conversely, by increasing the density of microphones while keeping the size of the microphone array constant, the frequency range of the reproduced sound field can be extended, which will enhance the sound quality. Since the number of microphones increases in both cases, it would be necessary to increase the number of loudspeakers in the reproduction system in order to design a stable inverse system.

2.6.3.3   Smaller and Lighter Equipment

Regarding the size of the recording system, connecting 80 microphones to an 80-channel audio recorder requires an enormous amount of wiring, so there is much room for improvement. Its dimensions could be reduced if, instead of transmitting the microphone output as a weak electric analog signal using a huge cable, we convert it to a digital signal and transmit it through an optical cable. As for the sound field reproduction system, its size and weight could be reduced by using a smaller and lighter loudspeaker unit. In this case, however, it is necessary to consider the associated shortage of low frequencies—although this may be compensated for by drastically increasing the number of loudspeakers. Since the performance of electromagnetic loudspeakers built in smartphones has significantly improved, it is worth to try to develop a more reasonably sized immersive auditory display using small and light loudspeaker units.

2.6.3.4   Practical Application of the Sound Cask

Using the sound cask, it is possible to practically realize an acoustic virtual space, such as a high-end audio room precisely tuned by an audio expert, a music practice room where players can confirm their performance at the listener's position in a concert hall or a church, or a recording studio for 22.2ch audio where recording engineers can confirm the 22.2ch sound created by their mix-down signal.

2.7   Conclusion

The newly developed immersive sound field reproduction system, named "sound cask," was introduced. The system, which has 96-channel reproducing loudspeakers, realizes precise sound field reproduction by combination with an 80-channel microphone array and the principle of boundary surface control. The results of the basic test indicate that the sound cask has excellent performance for localization of reproduced sound sources in the horizontal plane. However, there is room for improvement in the performance of the vertical direction and recognition at distance. Further examinations for improvement, e.g., with various types of inverse filter, are currently being conducted. At the present stage of the project, four casks have been constructed at Kyushu, Kyoto, and Tokyo in Japan. Several hundred people have experienced the performance of sound field reproduction in the sound cask. A series of psychological experiments is shown. Including recordings in concert halls, many types of content such as environmental sound outdoors are being continuously accumulated and stored in a database for reproduction [46]. In order to make the sound cask commercially viable, the principal members of this project started a company called Cask Acoustics Co. Ltd. We are currently focusing on sound engineers for 3D sound creation, musicians for education and audiophiles for listening to high-end audio as target users of the sound cask.

References

1. ITU-R BS.775.1, Multichannel stereophonic sound system with and without accompanying picture, 1992–1994
2. SMPTE 2036-2-2008, Ultra high definition television–Audio characteristics and audio channel mapping for program production, 2008
3. A.J. Berkhout, D. de Vries, P. Vogel, Acoustic control by wave field synthesis. J. Acoust. Soc. Am. **93**(5), 2764–2778 (1993)
4. P.A. Gauthier, A. Berry, Adaptive wave field synthesis with independent radiation mode control for active sound field reproduction: Theory. J. Acoust. Soc. Am. **119**(5), 2721–2737 (2006)
5. P.A. Gauthier, A. Berry, Adaptive wave field synthesis for sound field reproduction: theory, experiments and future perspectives. J. Audio Eng. Soc. **55**(12), 1107–1124 (2007)
6. P.A. Gauthier, A. Berry, Adaptive wave field synthesis for active sound field reproduction: experimental results. J. Acoust. Soc. Am. **123**(4), 1991–2002 (2008)

7. G. Theile, H. Wittek, Wave field synthesis: a promising spatial audio rendering concept. Acoust. Sci. Tech. **25**(6), 393–399 (2004)
8. K. Ueno, K. Yasuda, H. Tachibana, T. Ono, Sound field simulation for stage acoustics using 6-channel system. Acoust. Sci. Tech. **22**(4), 307–309 (2001)
9. S. Yokoyama, K. Ueno, S. Sakamoto, H. Tachibana, 6-channel recording/reproduction system for 3-dimensional auralization of sound fields. Acoust. Sci. Tech. **23**(2), 93–103 (2002)
10. D.H. Cooper, T. Shiga, Discrete-matrix multichannel stereo. J. Audio Eng. Soc. **20**(5), 346–360 (1972)
11. M.A. Gerzon, Hierarchical system of surround sound transmission for HDTV, in *Proc. AES 92nd Convention, Preprint 3339* (1992)
12. M.A. Poletti, Three-dimensional surround sound systems based on spherical harmonics. J. Audio Eng. Soc. **53**, 1004–1025 (2005)
13. S. Ise, A study on the sound field reproduction in a wide area(1)–based on Kirchhoff-Helmholtz integral equation–(in Japanese), in *Proc. of Mtg. of Acoust. Soc. Japan* (1993), pp. 479–480
14. S. Ise, A principle of active control of sound based on the Kirchhoff-Helmholtz integral equation and the inverse system theory (in Japanese). J. Acoust. Soc. Jpn. **53**(9), 706–713 (1997)
15. S. Ise, A principle of sound field control based on the Kirchhoff-Helmholtz integral equation and the theory of inverse systems. Acustica **85**, 78–87 (1999)
16. S. Ise, M. Toyodaet, S. Enomoto, S. Nakamura, An attempt of sound field sharing system for profound communication–concept and basic stance of the project–(in Japanese), in *Proc. Mtg. Acoust. Soc. Japan* (2007), pp. 585–586
17. S. Enomoto, Y. Ikeda, S. Ise, S. Nakamura, Three dimensional sound field reproduction and recording system based on boundary surface control principle, in *ICAD 2008—14th International Conference on Auditory Displays* (June 2008)
18. S. Enomoto, 3D sound field recording/reproduction system for telecommunication (in Japanese). Arch. Acoust. Noise Cont. **38**(4), 37–42 (2009)
19. S. Enomoto, Y. Ikeda, S. Ise, S. Nakamura, 3D sound field reproduction system for the sound field shared communication based on the boundary surface control principle (in Japanese), in *Proc. Mtg. Acoust. Soc. Japan* (2009), pp. 1411–1414
20. Y. Ikeda, S. Enomoto, S. Ise, S. Nakamura, Three-party sound field sharing system based on the boundary surface control principle, in *ICA 2010—20th International Congress on Acoustics* (2010)
21. S. Enomoto, Y. Ikeda, S. Ise, S. Nakamura, Optimization of loudspeaker and microphone configurations for sound reproduction system based on boundary surface control principle, in *ICA 2010—20th International Congress on Acoustics* (August 2010)
22. R. Kleinman, G. Roach, Boundary integral equations for the three dimensional Helmholtz equation. SIAM Rev. **16**, 214–236 (1974)
23. S. Enomoto, Measurements of synthesized sound eld in vertical plane for sound reproduction system based on boundary surface control (in Japanese), in *Proc. of Mtg. of Acoust. Soc. Japan* (2014), pp. 841–842
24. S.S. Stevens, Problems and method of psychophysics. Psychol. Bull. **55**, 177–196 (1958)
25. M. Yamashita, H. Nakajima, M. Kobayashi, Y. Ikeda, S. Enomoto, K. Ueno, S. Ise, Sound localization experiment of "sound cask"–Comparison between 62-channel and 96-channel sound field reproduction system based on the BoSC principle (in Japanese), in *Proc. of Mtg. of Acoust. Soc. Japan* (March 2013)
26. J.C. Makous, J.C. Middlebrooks, Two-dimensional sound localization by human listeners. J. Acoust. Soc. Am. **87**(5), 2188–200 (1990)
27. P. Zahorik, Assessing auditory distance perception using virtual acoustics. J. Acoust. Soc. Am. **111**(4), 1832–1846 (1990)
28. D.S. Brungart, N.I. Durlach, W.M. Rabinowitz, Auditory localization of nearby source. II. Localization of a broadband source. J. Acoust. Soc. Am. **106**(4), 1956–1968 (1999)
29. M. Kobayashi, K. Ueno, M. Yamashita, S. Ise, S. Enomoto, Subjective evaluation of a virtual acoustic system: trials with three-dimensional sound field reproduced by the 'Sound Cask', in *ICA 2013—21st International Congress on Acoustics* (June 2013)

30. M. Kobayashi, Y. Ooishi, S. Enomoto, N. Kitagawa, K. Ueno, S. Ise, M. Kashino, Effects of the movement of speakers on the sense of presence Study by using the three-dimensional sound field reproduction system. in *Proceedings of the Auditory Research Meeting sponsored by the Technical Committee of Psychological and Physiological Acoustics*, vol. 42, (Feburary 2012), pp. 41–46
31. M. Kobayashi, K. Ueno, S. Ise, The effects of spatialized sounds on the sense of presence in auditory virtual environments: a psychological and physiological study. Presence **24**(2), 163–174 (2015)
32. K. Tsuchida, K. Ueno, S. Shimada, Motor area activity for action-related and nonaction-related sounds in a three-dimensional sound field reproduction system. NeuroReport **26**(5), 291–295 (2015)
33. K. Tsuchida, K. Ueno, S. Shimada, Brain activity to action- and non-action-related sounds in a three-dimensional sound reproduction system. in *JSST 2013 International Conference on Simulation Technology (JSST2013)* (2013), pp. 45
34. K. Tsuchida, K. Ueno, S. Shimada, Modulation of EEG mu and beta rhythm in the mirror neuron system to action-related sounds in a three-dimensional sound reproduction system, in *44th Annual Meeting of the Society for Neuroscience (Neuroscience2014)* (2014)
35. M. Kobayashi, K. Tsuichida, K. Ueno, S. Shimada, Measurement of mirror neuron system activation for the 3-dimentional reproduction sound fields (in Japanese). Trans. Virtual Real. Soc. Jpn. **21**(1), 73–79 (2016)
36. S. Kohno, Y. Watanabe, H. Yoshida, Y. Ikeda, S. Ise. Acoustic feedback cancellation for a sound-field simulation system based on boundary-surface control principle (in Japanese), in *Proc. of Mtg. of Acoust. Soc. Japan* (March 2015), pp. 653–654
37. M. Kobayashi, S. Tamura, K. Ueno, Auditory impression of flutes at a concert hall (in Japanese), in *Proc. of Mtg. of Acoust. Soc. Japan* (September 2013), pp. 889–890
38. A. Nagai, S. Numakami, Y. Ikeda, Y. Watanabe, S. Ise, K. Ueno, Development of virtual table tennis system between the two persons for sound cask (in Japanese), in *Proc. of Mtg. of Acoust. Soc. Japan* (March 2016)
39. W. Woszczyk, J. Cooperstock, J. Roston, W.L. Martens, Shake, rattle, and roll: getting immersed in multisensory, interactive music via broadband networks. J. Audio Eng. Soc. (AES) **53**(4), 336–344 (2005)
40. T. Nagao, T. Watanabe, Y. Ikeda, K. Ueno, S. Ise, Study on the effect of sound delay conditions on ensemble performance (in Japanese), In *Proc. of Mtg. of Acoust. Soc. Japan* (March 2012), pp. 997–998
41. H. Yoshida, Y. Kitagawa, Y. Watanabe, S. Ise, Implementation of low-latency convolver using FPGA and its application for sound-eld sharing system (in Japanese), in *Proc. of Mtg. of Acoust. Soc. Japan* (September 2015), pp. 515–518
42. Y. Watanabe, H. Yoshida, S. Kohno, Y. Ikeda, S. Ise, Development of a sound-field simulation system and its evaluation on room acoustics—Examination of acoustic feedback cancellation (in Japanese), in *Proc. of Mtg. of Acoust. Soc. Japan* (March 2015), pp. 1061–1062
43. H. Aso, K. Ueno, M. Takahashi, M. Kobayashi, Examination on performance of the sound filed sharing system based on boundary-surface control principle,–Subjective evaluation by performing musicians–(in Japanese), in *Proc. of Mtg. of Acoust. Soc* (September 2016). (Japan (in Press))
44. E.G. Williams, *Fourier Acoustics: Sound Radiation and Nearfield Acoustical Holography* (Academic Press, London, 1999)
45. B.P. Hildebrand, B.B. Brenden, *An Introduction to Acoustical Holography* (Plenum Press, New York, 1974)
46. A. Omoto, S. Ise, Y. Ikeda, K. Ueno, S. Enomoto, M. Kobayashi, Sound field reproduction and sharing system based on the boundary surface control principle. Acoust. Sci. Technol. **36**(1), 1–11 (2015)

Chapter 3
User Generated Dialogue Systems: uDialogue

Keiichi Tokuda, Akinobu Lee, Yoshihiko Nankaku, Keiichiro Oura,
Kei Hashimoto, Daisuke Yamamoto, Ichi Takumi, Takahiro Uchiya,
Shuhei Tsutsumi, Steve Renals and Junichi Yamagishi

Abstract This chapter introduces the idea of user-generated dialogue content and
describes our experimental exploration aimed at clarifying the mechanism and conditions that makes it workable in practice. One of the attractive points of a speech
interface is to provide a vivid sense of interactivity that cannot be achieved with a text
interface alone. This study proposes a framework that spoken dialogue systems are
separated into content that can be produced and modified by users, and the systems
that drive the content, and seek to clarify (1) the requirements of systems that enable

K. Tokuda (✉) · A. Lee · Y. Nankaku · K. Oura · K. Hashimoto · D. Yamamoto · I. Takumi
T. Uchiya · S. Tsutsumi
Nagoya Institute of Technology, Nagoya, Japan
e-mail: tokuda@nitech.ac.jp

A. Lee
e-mail: ri@nitech.ac.jp

Y. Nankaku
e-mail: nankaku@nitech.ac.jp

K. Oura
e-mail: uratec@nitech.ac.jp

K. Hashimoto
e-mail: hashimoto.kei@nitech.ac.jp

D. Yamamoto
e-mail: yamamoto.daisuke@nitech.ac.jp

I. Takumi
e-mail: takumi@nitech.ac.jp

T. Uchiya
e-mail: t-uchiya@nitech.ac.jp

S. Tsutsumi
e-mail: tsutsumi.shuhei@nitech.ac.jp

S. Renals
University of Edinburgh, Edinburgh, UK
e-mail: s.renals@ed.ac.uk

J. Yamagishi
National Institute of Informatics, Tokyo, Japan
e-mail: jyamagis@nii.ac.jp

© Springer Japan KK 2017
T. Nishida (ed.), *Human-Harmonized Information Technology, Volume 2*,
DOI 10.1007/978-4-431-56535-2_3

the creation of attractive spoken dialogue, and (2) the conditions for the active generation of attractive dialogue content by users, while attempting to establish a method for realizing them. Experiments for validating user dialogue content generation were performed by installing interactive digital signage with a speech interface in public spaces as a dialogue device, and implementing a content generation environment for users via the Internet. The proposed framework is expected to lead to a breakthrough in the spread of using speech technology.

Keywords User-generated content · Spoken dialogue system · Speech recognition · Speech synthesis

3.1 Introduction

A human-centered information environment is an environment where everyone is a source of information, and is able to enjoy information naturally. Since speech is the most basic form of communication for humans, it is one of the ideals of modern society to realize the widespread availability of speech communication environments where people can naturally and freely interact other people wherever they may be, using advanced ubiquitous network telecommunication equipment. Although the fundamental technologies of speech recognition, speech synthesis and dialogue processing are making progress towards the sort of level needed for practical applications, it cannot yet be said that this sort of speech communication environment is available in the real world. There are other issues can be addressed, such as improving the accuracy of speech recognition, but in general it will probably not be possible to solve every issue simply by accumulating more technology. One such issue concerns the "attractiveness" of spoken dialogue systems to users. The ability to take part in a realistic interactive conversation is one of the important "draws" of speech interfaces that cannot be achieved with text processing alone. However, this can only be achieved by entering into regions where high-level human speech processing capabilities are required, such as facial expressions, gestures, voice quality and timing. The hardware and software limitations of current dialogue systems tend to make them rather inflexible and lifeless.

The aim of this study is to separate spoken dialogue systems into content that can be produced and modified by users and the systems that drive the content. In this way, we hope to clarify what sort of requirements must be met to produce "attractive" content and systems so that speech technology can spread widely among people (Fig. 3.1). However, attractiveness is created through the combination of human feelings and knowledge, and is not something that can easily be evaluated mechanically. Therefore, we have to inductively clarify the essential qualities of attractiveness by establishing a framework that makes it easy for users to create and evaluate large quantities of dialogue content. The basic strategy of this study is to construct a "circulatory system" of content generation as shown in Fig. 3.1 and empirically analyze

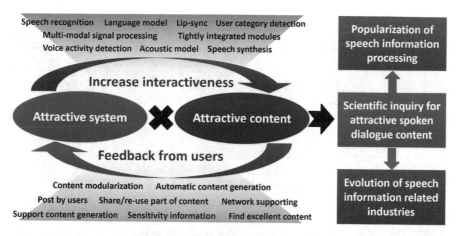

Speech recognition   Language model   Lip-sync   User category detection
Multi-modal signal processing   Tightly integrated modules
Voice activity detection   Acoustic model   Speech synthesis

Popularization of speech information processing

Increase interactiveness

Attractive system   Attractive content

Scientific inquiry for attractive spoken dialogue content

Feedback from users

Content modularization   Automatic content generation
Post by users   Share/re-use part of content   Network supporting
Support content generation   Sensitivity information   Find excellent content

Evolution of speech information related industries

Fig. 3.1 A circulatory system of content generation

the factors achieving a loop gain of more than 1 in order to establish techniques for constructing the framework of user-generated dialogue content. s

3.2 Background and Purpose of the Study

3.2.1 The Relationship with Industrial Structures

To establish a framework to facilitate the creation and evaluation of dialogue content, we need to separate the content from spoken dialogue system software, and make them widely available to creators and ordinary users without software engineering skills. This process resembles the evolution of industrial structures shown in Fig. 3.2. The telecommunications industry started out with the creation of electronic equipment, but as it grew larger, the software production parts and then the content creation parts were separated out, and ended up forming major industry fields. Mobile game production is a typical example, where content creation is progressively separated from development of game engine software. To bring about this sort of change with regard to speech technology, it will be necessary to accelerate the creation of attractive content by getting as many creators and users as possible involved in content creation.

3.2.2 Relationship with the UGC Approach

Today, attention is focused on content created by users as referred to by terms such as CGM (Consumer Generated Media) and UGC (User Generated Content). This is a

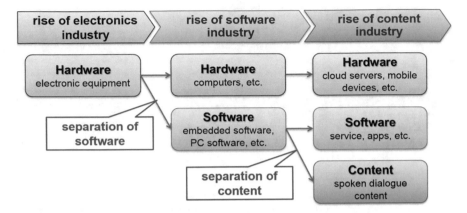

Fig. 3.2 The evolution of industry structure related to telecommunications

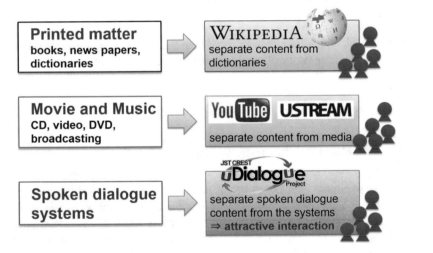

Fig. 3.3 Separation of content

system where users are mainly responsible for the creation of content—well-known examples include Wikipedia, YouTube, Facebook, Twitter and Instagram. The main features of these systems are that new content is continuously created by users, and that the users' assessments and wishes are directly reflected in the content. Our approach in this study can be regarded as a version of dialogue content, which aims to implement a users' information transmission environment based on a new type of media content (Fig. 3.3).

3.2.3   Devices for Implementing a Ubiquitous Speech-Based Information Environment

Devices for implementing a ubiquitous speech-based information environment can take many forms, such as ordinary PCs, information appliances or smartphones, and the created dialogue content will also vary according to the device characteristics and usage environments. In this study, we focused on digital signage placed in public spaces as one style of demonstration experiment. Digital signage is a medium for the delivery of information and advertising using digital communication technology and display technology such as large-sized liquid crystal displays. Its benefits include the ability to display rich media content such as audio and video, and change content at any time by using digital communication. In recent years, attempts have also been made to use technologies such as proximity sensors, touch panels and face recognition to control the display interactively. By further developing this idea to add voice interaction functions, it should become possible to produce a natural and impressive level of interactivity. In this study, digital signage devices equipped with speech processing functions were installed in various places such as a university campus, a tourist office and a city hall, and were used to perform demonstration experiments involving various cooperative mechanisms via the Internet.

3.3   MMDAgent: A Toolkit for Building Voice Interaction Systems

To comprehensively research the various elements of voice interfaces such as their level of engagement with users and their implicit attractiveness against other user interface, these systems need to develop into areas where human assessment and advanced processing are required, such as expressions, gestures, tone of voice and timing. To do this, we need a platform that is closely integrated with not just the voice processing system but also the image processing and virtual agent representation. Furthermore, since various data has to be collected for various tasks and situations, we require an advanced and flexible system where both users and system developers can work freely on every part of the system and dialogue content.

So far, we have continuously developed and released open-source research platform software tools that cooperate with speech technology including HTS (an HMM-based speech synthesis system) [1], Open JTalk (a Japanese text-to-speech system based on HTS) [2], and Julius (a speech recognition engine) [3]. Based on this group of software, we built "MMDAgent" toolkit for building voice interaction systems [4] by incorporating speech recognition, HMM-based flexible speech synthesis, embodied 3D agent rendering with simulated physics, and dialog management based on a finite state transducer (FST) and we released it as an open-source software toolkit (Fig. 3.4). The inter-module architecture is fairly simple: a single message queue is shared among all modules, and an output from a module will broadcast to all

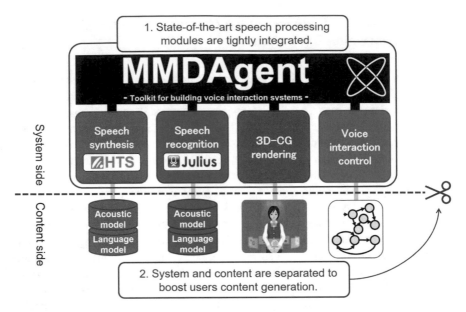

Fig. 3.4 A toolkit for building voice interaction systems (MMDAgent)

modules. The interaction control script is written in FST [5], a generic automaton representation converting the received messages (recognition result, sensor status, timer, etc.) into output messages (synthesis text, motion trigger etc.). This system uses open formats not only for the speech recognition and speech synthesis, but also for the virtual agent's 3D models and the motion data and FST definitions that drive these models. This makes it possible for users and developers to freely create, edit and replace any of the system's components using existing tools.

MMDAgent adopts a design policy that is geared strongly towards enabling not only speech technology experts but also ordinary people everywhere to enjoy creating systems using speech technology, and aims to support the continuous creation of attractive dialogue content. This is the main feature of MMDAgent. MMDAgent allows richly expressive dialogue and computer graphics to be produced with high performance, and is used as the technical platform of this study.

In this study, we use the MMDAgent toolkit for building voice interaction systems as a platform to separate spoken dialogue systems into the content provided to users and the systems that drive this content. Our aim is to clarify which factor is essential to create systems and content that are sufficiently engaging and attractive to utilize speech technology widely to many people. There are many issues that need to be addressed in order to achieve this goal. They can be summarized in the following three categories:

1. Enhancement of the baseline technology and software
2. Creating a framework for content creation
3. Public experiments of content creation

By addressing these issues, we established a framework that makes it easy for users to create and share dialogue content, and we clarified the mechanism whereby attractive dialogue content is created from the creation/sharing/evaluation of dialogue content by users. In the following three sections, the above three items will be described.

3.4   Enhancing the Baseline Technology

To create attractive dialogue content, it is essential to provide a technology infrastructure where spoken dialogue systems are able to engage users. This section describes our efforts to enhance the speech recognition, speech synthesis and other underlying technologies of the spoken dialogue system, and to optimize the underlying software for building the spoken dialogue system, and the design of the corpus/agents.

3.4.1   Underlying Technology

To optimize the underlying technology, we performed a lot of basic research for processing speech information, such as speech recognition and speech synthesis. Some typical examples are listed below.

- Integration of feature extraction and modeling for HMM based speech synthesis [6]
  In recent years, speech synthesis has been performed using statistical models called hidden Markov models (HMMs) to model the acoustic relationships between speech features and linguistic features. In this study, by integrating the extraction of features from speech into the HMM training process, we were able to directly model the speech waveforms with a unified framework. This improved the system's overall modeling capabilities, and greatly improved the quality of synthesized speech.
- Improvement of spectral modeling with an additive structure [7]
  We proposed an additive model for speech synthesis by assuming additive structures in the relationship between linguistic features and speech features. We also proposed a training algorithm for the efficient training of additive models. It was shown that the synthesized speech quality with an additive model was greatly improved.
- Conversational speech synthesis method [8]
  Dialogue between people often contains hesitations and filler pauses (like "ah" and "um"). We therefore examined the impact of hesitations and fillers on dialogue, and we studied how to automatically insert them into synthesized speech. This enabled us to make accurate predictions about where they will be inserted, and to perform speech synthesis in a more natural conversational style.
- Improving the precision of speech recognition using a language model based on a recurrent neural network [9]

For high-performance speech recognition, studies are being performed where recurrent neural networks are used for language models that model linguistic features. In this study, we proposed a learning method based on a neural network-based language model suitable for speech recognition, and we improved the speech recognition accuracy. We were also able to perform speech recognition with greater precision by making it possible to use acoustic features as additional information.

- Improvement of speech synthesis based on deep neural networks [10–12]
  It was recently reported that the performance of speech synthesis can also be greatly improved through the use of neural networks. In this study, we proposed methods for integrating multiple neural networks and methods for learning in neural networks that are suited to the problem of speech synthesis, demonstrated their effectiveness.
- Construction of text-to-speech systems for unknown-pronunciation languages [13]
  Ordinary speech synthesis consists of a text analysis part that predicts how text should be read, and a waveform generation part that creates the corresponding speech waveforms, but it is not possible to construct a text analysis part for languages whose pronunciation information is unknown. We therefore proposed a text-to-speech system construction method for unknown-pronunciation language, which involves the use of speech recognition systems for different languages. Using this construction method, we were able to construct text-to-speech systems for a wide variety of languages.
- Analysis of dialogue content using a topic model [14]
  The creation and management of dialogue content requires a framework where it is possible to perform operations such as searching for topics, detecting similar content, and recommending popular content. There are many different kinds of dialogue content, and it is difficult to perform procedures such as rule-based tagging. In this study, we proposed a method for automatic statistical classification of dialogue content by applying a topic model (a kind of language model).

3.4.2 Underlying Software

We summarized the results obtained in the advancement of underlying technology as research platform software, and we published the following open source software.[1]

- MMDAgent: Toolkit for building voice interaction systems
  (http://www.mmdagent.jp/)
  (61,000 downloads)
- Julius: Open-source large vocabulary continuous speech recognition engine
  (http://julius.sourceforge.jp/)
  (216,000 downloads)

---

[1] The number of downloads is the cumulative total from October 2011 to March 2016.

- HTS: HMM speech synthesis toolkit
  (http://hts.sp.nitech.ac.jp/)
  (371,000 downloads)
- hts_engine API: HMM speech synthesis engine
  (http://hts-engine.sourceforge.net/)
  (41,000 downloads)
- Open JTalk: Japanese text-to-speech system
  (http://open-jtalk.sourceforge.net/)
  (47,000 downloads)
- SPTK: Speech signal processing toolkit
  (http://sp-tk.sourceforge.net/)
  (42,000 downloads)
- Sinsy: HMM-based singing voice synthesis system
  (http://sinsy.sourceforge.net/)
  (1,400 downloads)

The development of this open-source software is ongoing, and new versions continue to be released. In particular, the MMDAgent toolkit for building voice interaction systems was developed as cross-platform software that can run on Windows, Mac OS, Linux, Android OS and iOS. It can run by itself on smartphones and tablet PCs, and makes it possible for a spoken dialogue system with small response delays to be used in smartphones and tablets (Figs. 3.5 and 3.6). It seems to be the first open-source implementation of a spoken dialogue system with a 3D agent capable of running on a stand-alone smartphone or tablet PC.

These software platforms include state-of-the-art technology, and as the number of downloads show, they have already achieved the status of de facto standards. In fact, as shown in Fig. 3.7, it is being widely used in many different situations, including academic papers, software development and events.

Fig. 3.5 Android-compatible MMDAgent

Fig. 3.6 iOS-compatible MMDAgent

Fig. 3.7 Examples of the usage of open-source software

3.4.3 Corpora and Agents

In order to obtain universal knowledge that is not language-dependent, it is necessary to perform validation experiments in parallel with various different languages. When doing so, it is necessary to give full consideration to cultural differences as well as linguistic differences. We therefore developed a spoken dialogue system targeting Japanese and English, and by performing experiments with the Japanese and English spoken dialogue systems, we verified which points are dependent on language and culture, and which are not.

First, we constructed a Japanese speech corpus and a British English speech corpus, which were needed to develop the spoken dialogue system.

- Japanese male voice actor corpus
  Recordings of 3,000 sentences in Japanese spoken by a male voice actor. The recorded utterances are selected from multiple domains including newspaper, etc. There are 5 speaking styles consists of 1800 normal utterances and 300 emotional utterances for angry, sad, happy and whisper, respectively.
- CSTR VCTK corpus [15]
  This corpus is a large-scale speech corpus containing about 60 hours of speech by 109 speakers with various British English accents. The recorded speech consists of about 400 sentences from each speaker, selected from multiple domains including newspaper articles. This corpus is 50% larger than the WSJCAM0 corpus (available from LDC for a fee), which is the current standard speech database for research on British English. It is expected that it will be used for diverse applications in many different fields in the future.
- Corpus of British English (Edinburgh) spoken by a female
  Recordings of 4,600 sentences in British English spoken by a female voice actor with an Edinburgh accent. Speech was recorded at two different speeds, with 800 sentences spoken at high speed, and 800 sentences spoken at low speed. 800 sentences spoken at low speed consist of 2 speaking styles: talking to a hearing impaired person and talking to a computer. There are also over 100 minutes of spontaneous conversation recordings.

Next, we created a conversation agent suited to dialogue (Fig. 3.8). To make the spoken dialogue system acceptable to users, it was necessary to make the system by taking cultural differences into consideration. In Japan, people are thought to have little resistance to animated 3D agents, so we created a female agent with a height of 2.5 heads, and a male agent. On the other hand, from the results of various discussions, it was considered that a realistic 3D agent would be more acceptable to a European audience, so we created a dialogue agent for the British English version of the spoken dialogue system.

Fig. 3.8 Animated dialogue agent and realistic dialogue agent

3.5 Building a Mechanism for the Creation and Sharing of Content

In this section, we discuss a mechanism for creating and sharing dialogue content by introducing the concept of user-generated dialogue content.

As shown in Fig. 3.9, it consists of a three-level hierarchy. The material layer contains specialized model data such as voice models and language models, and binary files such as images, music, 3D models and motion data. The action layer contains short action sequences, such as dialogue patterns for simple greetings, or for displaying weather forecast panels. The scenario layer combines the actions of the action layer to produce more complex dialogue scenarios. The scenario layer and action layer are scripted in FST format, while each material in the material layer is stored in its own format.

As shown in Fig. 3.10, we also assumed that the spoken dialogue system may cooperate with other systems instead of operating as a closed stand-alone system. In particular, the smartphone version of MMDAgent implements a mechanism that makes it easy to link up with networks and other smart phones [16].

3.5.1 Tools for Dialogue Content Creation

In the MMDAgent toolkit for building voice interaction systems, the dialogue scenarios are written in FST. However, it is difficult for most users to create FST scripts manually. We therefore implemented a mechanism that allows dialogue content to be edited easily.

Dialogue Script Editing Tool

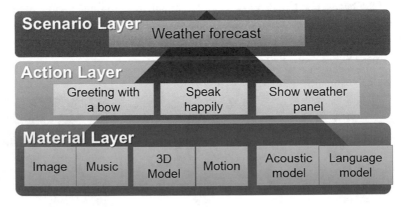

Fig. 3.9 Hierarchy of dialogue content

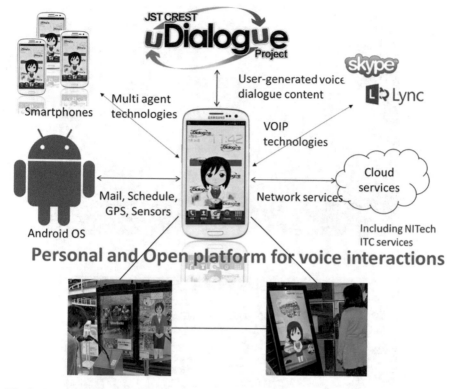

Fig. 3.10 Linking spoken dialogue systems with a network

To facilitate the creation of user-generated dialogue content, it is essential that users can easily create dialogue content. We therefore developed the EFDE dialogue content creation tool (Fig. 3.11) and the MMDAE dialogue content creation tool for advanced content creators using web browsers (Fig. 3.12).

- EFDE (Extended FST based Dialogue Editor) [17]
  A tool targeted at beginners using Android devices, where FST scripts displayed as state transition diagrams can be edited using a touch interface. The edited scripts can be run on demand so that users can easily edit scripts while checking the action of the dialogue content. Also, by providing typical parts of dialogue scripts as templates, we have made it possible to implement complex dialogues with a small number of steps. Furthermore, users can also input sentences and keywords in a dialogue content by speaking, thus a dialogue content can be created easily in a multi-modal manner.
- MMDAE (MMDAgent Editor) [18]
  A web-based FST editor for a detailed editing of FST scripts. Editing can be performed easily and reliably by active input suggestion for message formats and

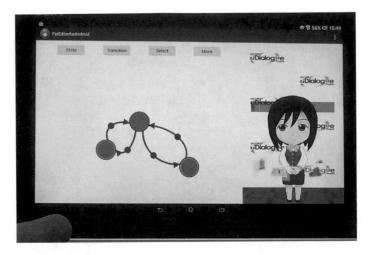

Fig. 3.11 Tablet interface for EFDE

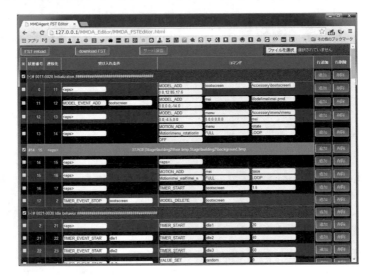

Fig. 3.12 Web browser interface for MMDAE

structured FST input view. Since this tool runs on a web browser, it can be used on a wide variety of platforms.

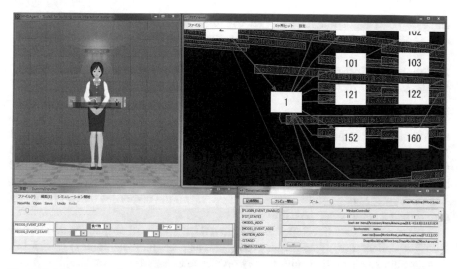

Fig. 3.13 Voice interaction builder

Voice Interaction Builder

To promote the creation of attractive high-quality content by users, a creator-oriented environment must be provided where users can exercise detailed control over the addition of dialogue content according. We therefore made a prototype voice interaction builder as a development environment where interactive dialogue content can be created with detailed control over the speech timing and other details, and where the action of this content can be verified (Fig. 3.13). This voice interaction builder consists of three components: (1) a function for grasping the structure of FST scripts by visualizing and browsing the state transition diagram in 3D space, (2) a function for tracing the operation of a script by means of an event input simulation, and (3) a function for verifying time-series interactions by storing and playing back a series of input/output events. In subjective tests, users reported that it was easier to create content than in the existing environment.

3.5.2 Construction of a Cloud Environment for Collaborative Content Editing

One of the characteristics of user-generated media is that it is frequently built as a collaborative effort with other users. In dialogue content, by constructing an environment where dialogue content can be created and edited over a network, it becomes easier to create complex content in collaboration with other users, and to incorporate and extend existing content. In this section, we discuss the construction of a collaborative editing environment for dialogue content based on a cloud environment.

Collaborative Editing System for Building Dialogue Content with Dialogue Context

One of the simplest way for the collaborative construction of dialogue content is to make system that gathers a set of questions and answers from users via Web. However, this system can only handle simple question-and-answer exchanges because it retains no context of previous utterances, and is thus clearly inadequate as a system intended to provide fun and attractive dialogue with continuity and situational awareness. Also, it is sometimes hard to build a system that covers all the responses that a user might give during a lengthy conversation.

We have therefore developed a user-generated spoken dialogue system makes it easy to collaboratively construct conversations with dialogue context (Fig. 3.14). Conversations are stored in units of keyword/response sets as same as simple QA systems, but can also include parent-child relationships, whereby users are able to collaboratively construct multiple consecutive question-and-answer type interactions. The whole dialogue content is stored in a tree structure consisting of keyword/response pairs as its building blocks. For instant registration of a dialogue content, we built an SNS (social networking service) chat-style Web interface where it is possible for anyone to intuitively grasp and edit the flow of a conversation (Fig. 3.15). This system can be used to create long continuous conversations, and allows dialogue registered by other users to be branched off into other conversations by another users. In subjective evaluation tests, it was found that this approach generates much more anticipation and interest among users than the conventional method, and enables the construction of user-generated systems with attractive conversations.

Construction of a Cloud-based Dialogue Content Editing Environment

To increase the variety of conversations in MMDAgent, it is generally necessary to describe a larger number of conversation scenarios. However, it is difficult for a person to create conversation scenarios on a large scale. We therefore developed a crowd sourcing system specialized for the creation of dialogue scenarios (Fig. 3.16). In this system, multiple users receive orders for dialogue scenario creation tasks based on a crowd sourcing scheme. This allows scenarios to be created by sharing the workload among multiple users. To make it easy for a user to create a scenario after receiving a dialogue scenario creation request, we also strengthened the functions for collaboration between MMDAE and a Skype version of the tool to debug the system easily. In an experimental evaluation, we confirmed its validity for the creation of dialogue scenarios based on crowd sourcing [19, 20].

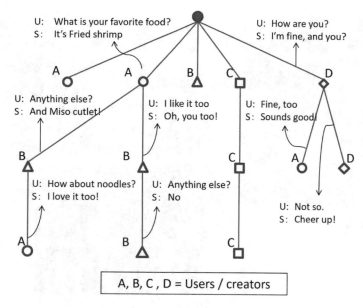

Fig. 3.14 Concept of interactive content with history

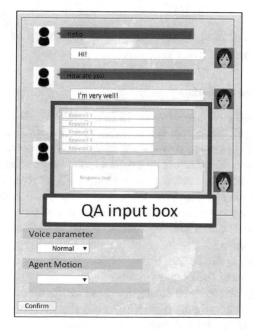

Fig. 3.15 Registration interface for interaction with history

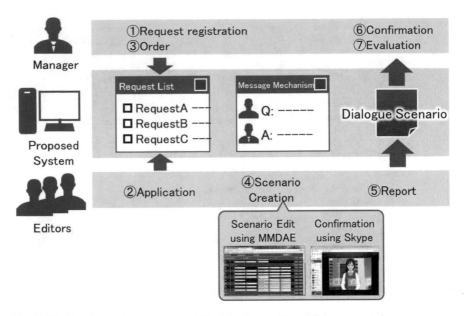

Fig. 3.16 Crowd sourcing system specialized for the creation of dialogue scenarios

3.5.3 Modularization, Networking and Inter-agent Collaboration

Packaging Dialogue Content

Most of the current dialogue systems are "Haute couture": they are built for a specialized task, tuning all the components especially for the task, and runs solely for the task. Their availability or portability toward various tasks or users as a media content is not well studied yet. We therefore proposed a framework for distributing and sharing user-generated dialogue content over a network via a server. First, we studied a packaging method by extending FST scripts for modularization and parallelization. This made it possible to update a part of FST script, or function-based script delivering, while at the same time making FST scripts easier to maintain. We also studied a framework for circulating content in package units by creating a prototype delivery framework as shown in Fig. 3.17.

We also proposed and built a user-generated spoken dialogue system architecture with the aim of implementing an environment where the user is free to reassemble, select and construct not only dialogue scripts but also each constituent element of dialogue content such as word dictionaries, voice data, 3D models or motion data (Figs. 3.18 and 3.19). By defining the part of dialogue content as general-purpose modules for the integrated handling of speech recognition/synthesis, dialogue management and all content including agent models, we made it possible to achieve consistency in the operation of packages and handle dependencies between modules. In practice, we proposed a mechanism for managing modules in packages for MMDAgent, and we implemented a framework for applying scopes to module name specifications (e.g., inside dialogue scripts), and for automatically detecting dependencies and conflicts between packages based on their external declarations.

A Platform for Cooperation Between Spoken Dialogue Systems Using Network Agent Technology

Spoken dialogue systems for existing smart phones either work as stand-alone applications or communicate with a remote server, and it has not been possible to build complex dialogue scenarios that efficiently link up with multiple terminal devices. We therefore introduced the system collaboration platform described below.

- We built an environment where MMDAgent can run cooperatively on multiple smartphone devices. Specifically, we developed a network connection mechanism for spoken dialogue systems based on agent/NFC/Bluetooth technology (Fig. 3.20)

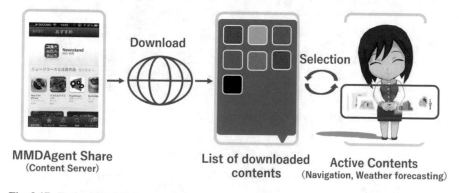

Fig. 3.17 Packaging of dialogue content

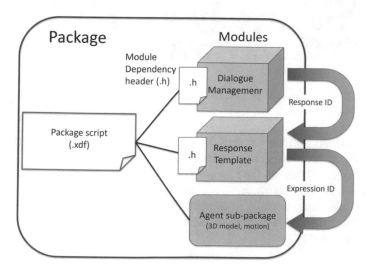

Fig. 3.18 Converting dialogue modules into packages

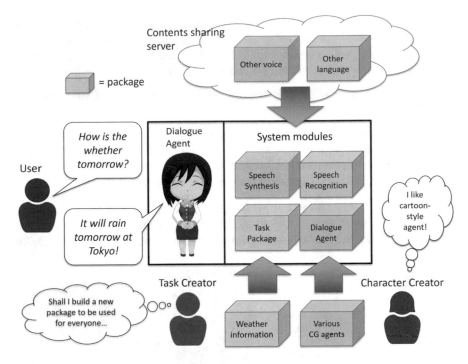

Fig. 3.19 Module-based sharing of dialogue content

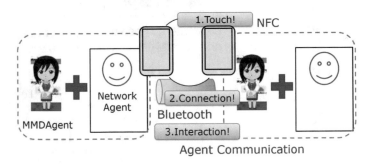

Fig. 3.20 P2P network connection mechanism

[21]. We made a prototype scheduling system to confirm the validity of services involving cooperation between multiple spoken dialogue systems.

• We built an environment for running MMDAgent cooperatively on multiple signage devices. This environment was designed to be highly scalable in order to accommodate large numbers of signage devices. We confirmed the validity of system collaboration between signage devices by making a prototype system to share the number of dialogues.

3.6 Public Experiments of Content Creation

The studies in the previous sections are essentially aimed for re-defining dialogue system as a player executing dialogue content, and we have worked on several aspect of both system and content creation/management, which are essential to make the dialog content applicable as a user generated media.

In this section, several public tests performed using the proposed system are summarized for discussion.

3.6.1 Building a Framework to Promote the Use of Content

In user-generated dialogue content, it can be expected that a large quantity of diverse dialogue content will be created by users. In such situation, it is important to maximize the usefulness of this content by organizing it into a suitable taxonomy. Here, we discuss the results of a study for the analysis, categorization and correlation of dialogue content groups in order to support the creation and use of spoken dialogue systems.

Related Word Recommendations Based on the Usage History of a Spoken Dialogue System

Fig. 3.21 Related word presentation method. (*red frame box* related words, *blue frame box* conversation history)

With the aim of promoting the use of spoken dialogue systems by beginners with no experience in the use of spoken dialogue systems, we studied a framework for presenting the user with a group of word candidates that can be said next. We then implemented a technique for acquiring relevant words from user's conversation data stored on the server using an information recommendation technique (Fig. 3.21). In user testing, we obtained results suggesting that the presentation of related keywords helps users make effective use of spoken dialogue systems. We also conducted a comparative study of four different related word recommendation methods (history-based recommendations, content-based recommendations, ranking recommendations and random recommendations), and a composite recommendation method that integrates all of these. In user testing, we confirmed that the composite recommendation method produces better overall results than individual content-based or random recommendation.

Strengthening of Mutual Incentives by Sharing Usage Histories Between Users

In user-generated media, sharing activity histories is essential in that it will cause mutual stimulation among users, leading to increased usage of the system and increased content creation. Thus, also in dialogue content, it is expected that sharing interactions with the spoken dialogue system and content usage histories between users can mutually increase the willingness of users to use the system, which is required to make the dialogue content as user-generated media. Therefore, in an open question-and-answer style spoken dialogue system in which any user can add any QA to the system, we examined several methods that provide user-oriented mutual incentives for interaction by (1) on-line sharing what other users are saying now, and (2) displaying information of "hot" content, which are extracted according

Fig. 3.22 Sharing conversation histories and displaying dialogue content rankings

to the frequency ranking and its registration time. As shown in Fig. 3.22, when this information was presented to the users and creators of dialogue content, users can share other user's activity and will be stimulated to use the system more. We also implemented a feedback from users to content creators by gathering user's out-of-domain utterances and give the statistics to the creators. In user testing, we confirmed that these frameworks can lead to an improvement in the motivation (incentivization) of both users and content creators.

3.6.2 Demonstration Experiments in Public Spaces

To demonstrate the proposed system's suitability for public installations, we installed and operated it at various locations including in front of the main gate at the Nagoya Institute of Technology, and at the tourist information office in Handa city. The dialogue content collected in these validation experiments will shed light on methods for making dialogue content more attractive. Some typical experiments are listed below.

Demonstration Experiment in a University Campus

To test the applicability of our system to public, an all-weather voice enabled digital signage system ("Mei-chan") was built by using MMDAgent and installed in an open public space at the main gate (Fig. 3.23). This system supports various functions including using multiple cameras and face recognition technology to control the line of sight of an animated character, and having the character actively address people detected using pyroelectric sensors. Content that integrates together not only the displayed text, images and dialogue text, but also the character's movements and speaking style when offering guidance can be updated dynamically from a server, and is used to display timely guidance ranging from information about events on campus that are recorded in a database at the information platform center to weather forecasts and other information optionally selected depending on the dialogue timing and content (Fig. 3.24).

The first version of the system went into operation on April 6, 2011, and on June 15, 2011, the content registration system was made open to be used by anyone in the university. By November 15, 2011, more than 100 items of content had been registered, and the number of user utterances captured per day was about 350 on average, even including holidays. There were 243 submissions of dialogue content from students and faculty staff (of which 4 were from students). Figure 3.25 shows examples of the submitted panel displays. Since September 2014, the system has also been installed in the open space ("Yume Room") at the university (Fig. 3.26). The guidance system installed in the student space allows dialogue content to be submitted easily not only from a PC but also from a smart phone with near field communication (NFC). During the six-month period following installation, a total of 437 dialogue content contributions were made by students and others, totally spontaneously.

Fig. 3.23 "Mei-chan": Digital signage in Nagoya Institute of Technology main gate

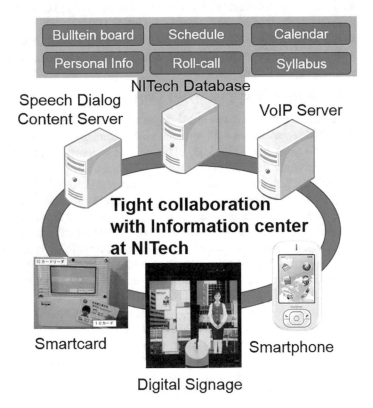

Fig. 3.24 Cooperation with the information infrastructure system

Fig. 3.25 Panel display

Fig. 3.26 Open space at the Nagoya Institute of Technology

Fig. 3.27 Handa city tourist information office (inside view)

Fig. 3.28 Handa city tourist information office (outside view)

A network questionnaire was held to conduct a survey of Mei-chan's popularity and frequency of use. Of the 262 valid responses, nearly everyone (99%) were aware of this system. A high percentage (77%) had also attempted conversations, showing that the spoken dialogue system using MMDAgent and its user-oriented way of making dialogue content attracts people inside the university. The free questionnaire drew a response rate of 33%, showing that one out of three users actively offered suggestions on how to improve the spoken dialogue system, etc.

Demonstration Experiment Outside the University

Next, the system was experimented on several places outside the campus for public test. An indoor digital signage prototype was installed at a tourist information office of a sightseeing spot in Handa city (Figs. 3.27 and 3.28). Since the room for this system was confined, the screen layout and expressions were optimized for close use.

Fig. 3.29 Handa city hall

We also implemented a localization whereby users (in this case, the tourist office staff) could add and update the dialogue content with ease. This enabled them to freely modify and adapt the content to the varying daily needs on the site by their own, which could made this system more applicable and attractive to tourists. In fact, a large amount of tourist information content was registered by the staff at the tourist office. This system was featured on television and in the newspapers, and appeared on the front page of Handa city's official newsletter, generating interest from other regions in connection with the use of this technology for tourism and PR.

Another spoken dialogue systems were also installed at other locations including the Handa city hall building, the National Institute of Informatics, and the NHK's Nagoya broadcasting station (Figs. 3.29, 3.30 and 3.31). For the National Institute of Informatics, we built a spoken dialogue system using a 3D model of their mascot (a cartoon dog called "Bit") (Fig. 3.30). At the NHK Nagoya broadcasting station, we performed a demonstration experiment where the equipment was used in TV broadcasts and events. This system was extended to include extra features such as being able to operate multiple characters by linking them together. We also constructed a speech database matched to our character, and a speech synthesis system that uses the character's voice.

Other Validation Experiments

More experiments has been conducted to explore the use of spoken dialogue systems and user generated dialogue content creation, namely on mobile environments.

- A video streaming version of our system has been developed (Fig. 3.32) [22]. This system was implemented by linking MMDAgent with Skype. A public trials and a questionnaire survey was conducted at the annual conference of IPSJ to serve as a conversation-based guidance for the sessions and venues. From the results

Fig. 3.30 National institute of informatics

Fig. 3.31 NHK Nagoya broadcasting station (from NHK news program "Hot Evening" on August 28, 2015)

of 120 questionnaires, it is found that it can provide information in a friendly conversational manner, whereas its network response delay might annoys users.

- A mobile campus tour support system based on dialogue was developed and used for junior high school students (Fig. 3.33) [23]. In this system, a dialogue agent on a smart phone provides each of them with information about the Nagoya Institute of Technology campus and its facilities. Subjective evaluation tests demonstrated the effectiveness of the system.
- It would be useful to link it up with systems such as the public telephone network for more availability. We therefore developed a framework that links MMDAgent with a VoIP client [24]. We created a middleware to connect the system to Skype for business. At the same time, to connect with the internal VoIP phone system of the internal unified communication system at Nagoya Institute of Technology,

Fig. 3.32 MMDAgent
skype version

Fig. 3.33 Campus tour
support system

we developed middleware for connecting a software phone, and we subjected it to
interconnection tests.

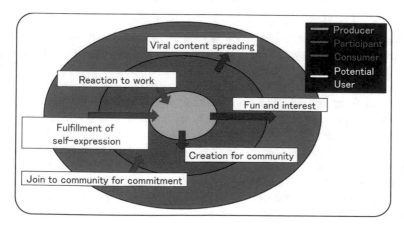

Fig. 3.34 User layer categories and incentives

3.6.3   Demonstration Experiment in a Network Environment

To obtain cues on the implementation of user-generated dialogue content in a broader social environment, we performed demonstration experiments involving a general network environment.

First, we analyzed the motivations and draw factors (incentives) that persuade users to engage with the system, which is an essential requirement for the growth of user-generated dialogue content in society.

We classified factors that motivate and attract users into the following four types according to the user's degree of involvement with the content, and we analyzed their respective interrelationships and movements (Fig. 3.34).

- Potential user—someone who has never used the system.
- Consumer—someone who is using or has used the system. Passive user.
- Participant—someone who actively engages with the system while commenting, favoriting and evaluating. Active user.
- Producer—someone who creates and posts content.

The requirements that should be met by a spoken dialogue system so that dialogue content can be created in a network environment as user-generated media for our system are as follows:

- From potential users to consumers: expanding the dialogue content playback environment to multiple devices including smart phones.
- From consumers to participants: stimulating interest in the overall system by providing periodic information by SNS or by designing user flow lines
- From participants to producers: using facilities reachable for users to promote them to create dialogue content on a particular theme (Fig. 3.35).

We built a multi-platform question-and-answer type dialogue content distribution/registration system incorporating the above improvements, and we used it to perform social experiments (Fig. 3.36). The content server on which the dialogue content was stored was placed, and a multiplatform (Windows/Linux/Android) system was provided to facilitate access. In this experiment, we prepared several flow line to draw users into the usage of the system and support system to attract ordinary users, and we performed public testing for one month. About 30,000 people found out about the system via tweets on Twitter, and we obtained 6,300 dialogues and 232 newly registered dialogue content registrations. 55% of the users participated from Android devices, and 15% performed light content registration by participating in the provision of "themes" using the Twitter library functions. In this way, we were able to confirm the effectiveness of the proposed method and accumulate valuable materials relating to user trends.

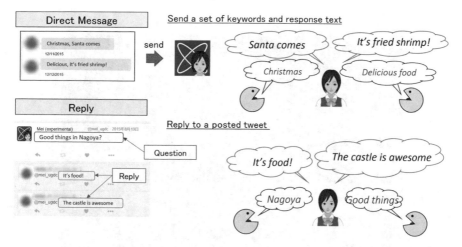

Fig. 3.35 Themed dialogue content creation

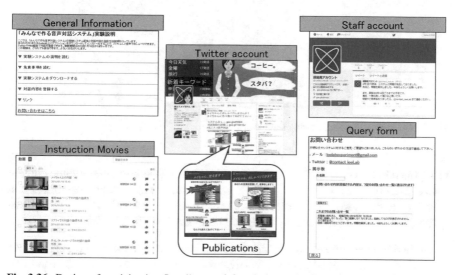

Fig. 3.36 Design of participation flow lines and description pages for ordinary users in the social experiment

3.6.4 Dialogue Content Sharing Service: MMDAgent SHARE

No framework was available for the sharing of dialogue content between the creators and users of this content, and the created dialogue content ended up being distributed to various different locations. We therefore considered that providing a place where dialogue content can be presented and shared would lead to more dialogue content being produced. Specifically, we launched a dialogue content sharing ser-

Fig. 3.37 Dialogue content sharing service

vice "MMDAgent SHARE" as a framework to facilitate sharing of dialogue content between users (Figs. 3.37 and 3.38). In general, there are various difficulties that may need to be addressed in order to share dialogue content easily, but the proposed system solves these problems by using the methods described below.

1. Since dialogue content often consists of a set of many files and is cumbersome to work with, we defined our own MMDA format that allows them to be used as a single file.
2. We created a function whereby MMDA format files can be produced easily on the server.
3. We developed a new MMDAgent installer for Windows to make it possible to run MMDA format content with a single click.
4. To make the service easy to use, we enabled cooperation with Open IDs services such as Google accounts.
5. We developed a framework that automatically detects script errors and warnings when content is posted.

Fig. 3.38 Shared dialogue content

6. We are carefully preparing a user agreement and privacy policy for this service.
7. We developed some features that are very useful for copyright holders, such as a framework whereby all the attached text included in the content (README files, etc.) can be automatically checked from this service.

We also built a prototype service that makes it easy to create Web pages containing dialogue content. This framework facilitates the creation of dialogue content by allowing the user to input data such as images, keywords and text via an ordinary Web browser (Fig. 3.39).

3.7   Encyclopedia MMDAgent

So far, in addition to developing the dialogue content production support tool and underlying software, including MMDAgent, we have also conducted numerous demonstration experiments both on and off campus, written review papers, held MMDAgent workshops, and published tips on an Internet blog, and we have completed a set of materials on the use of MMDAgent and the production of dialogue content including guide books/tutorials, lecture slides, reference manuals, and sample scripts. By integrating these achievements and carrying out further expansion and maintenance, we constructed an all-in-one "Encyclopedia MMDAgent" package that includes a set of software, manuals, basic dialogue libraries and dialogue content design guidelines. This package includes the following items:

Fig. 3.39 Dialogue content
creation service

1. The MMDAgent toolkit for building interaction systems (Windows, Mac OS, Linux, Android OS and iOS compatible)
2. MMDAgent Primer (Japanese and English)
3. MMDAgent creators reference manual (Japanese and English)
4. MMDAgent developers reference manual (Japanese and English)
5. MMDAgent lecture slides (Japanese and English)
6. MMDAgent lecture videos (MOOC, OCW)
7. Voice interaction content creation support tools (Web application for editing dialogue content, tablet application for editing dialogue content, voice interaction builder, etc.)
8. Dialogue content library (basic dialogue library, sample 3D models, speech synthesis models, etc.)
9. Dialogue content design guidelines

This package comprises a coordinated collection of multi-platform software, user-oriented content production support tools, dialogue content design guidelines based on the results of long-term demonstration experiments, reference manuals and lecture slides for content creators and developers, tutorial videos for MOOC/OCW courses, and a library of dialogue content, providing an environment where users can easily create their own content.

3.8   Future Prospects

The essential differences between the services offered by the leading IT companies and the user content creation concept discussed in this project are tabulated in Fig. 3.40. The services of leading IT companies have a top-down structure where users can only use content within a framework provided by the company. Recently leading IT companies often have teams responsible for the creation of spoken dialogue content, giving rise to a workflow whereby the construction of the spoken dialogue system is treated as a content production issue. However, commercial services are only able to progress within their own closed worlds, and it is not possible to share the generated content over as wide a range as user-generated content in the true sense. On the other hand, when taking the user content generation approach, it becomes possible to share content without having to rely on any particular service, and any type of content can be produced and shared without any constraints. The content and knowledge that is shared and integrated in this sort of way becomes a form of common property, and it is expected that this shared content will be divided into different content types, and that new types of content will be discovered. This sort of content and knowledge may of course be used to provide feedback to services offered by the leading IT industries, and in addition is also expected to fuel the growth of completely new modes of use and business applications (bottom-up approach).

To facilitate user creation in the abovementioned true sense over a broad range, including industrial applications, it is necessary to have a platform for this purpose, which could perhaps be fulfilled by the encyclopedia MMDAgent that brings together the MMDAgent of this project and the related achievements. Furthermore, if the user content creation shown in Fig. 3.40 can be deployed while expanding into industrial applications, then it should be possible to generate a diverse range of technical research topics as shown in Fig. 3.41. In other words, it is liable to open up the new academic field of spoken dialogue content studies, and the research achievements of this project are expected to provide a platform for this sort of expansion.

Fig. 3.40 Bottom-up approach—opening up voice interaction systems to the people

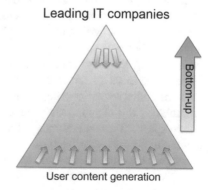

Leading IT companies

Bottom-up

User content generation

Fig. 3.41 What sort platform will emerge from the next stage of research based on the current research achievements?

3.9 Conclusion

In this study, by separating spoken dialogue systems into the content provided by users and the systems that drive this content, we have created a content creation framework based on enhanced technology where users and creators with abilities close to those of users can be expected to create a continuous supply of attractive dialogue content. We have also conducted demonstration experiments to show how this system can be used to create content. Based on the number of times the software tools have been downloaded and on the diverse uses of this software on the Internet, we have seen a lot of content being created. We have created and published an "Encyclopedia MMDAgent" that integrates all the results obtained so far. Furthermore, we have built a content sharing server in order to analyze this content. In the future, we hope that by operating this content sharing server, we will encourage the creation of more attractive content while gaining further insights into the system's use.

In this study, we set out to consider speech technology from the new perspective of building an environment for the creation of user-generated dialogue content. We are hopeful that it will not only yield useful insights into the creation of dialogue interfaces, but will also lead to future breakthroughs in the spread of voice interfaces. In fact, the latest spoken dialogue systems are increasing their attractiveness by engaging in witty exchanges with users, based on content produced by people who could be called scenario writers. This sort of situation is consistent with the outlook presented in this chapter. Also, the implementation and testing of digital signage in public spaces is an embodiment of a new kind of ubiquitous information environment, which could soon become more widespread and more commercialized. In the future, if it becomes possible to collect large numbers of actual dialogue samples and examples of dialogue content, then it could become possible to perform statistical modeling of dialogue based on these large data sets.

References

1. HTS: HMM speech synthesis toolkit, http://www.hts.nitech.ac.jp/
2. Open JTalk: Japanese text-to-speech system, http://open-jtalk.sourceforge.net/
3. Julius: Open-source large vocabulary continuous speech recognition engine, http://julius.sourceforge.jp/
4. MMDAgent: Toolkit for building voice interaction systems, http://www.mmdagent.jp/
5. T. Funayachi, K. Oura, Y. Nankaku, A. Lee, K. Tokuda, A simple dialogue description based on finite state transducers for user-generated spoken dialog content, in *Proceedings of ASJ 2013 Autumn Meeting, 2-P-28*, pp. 223–224, 25–27 Sept 2013. (in Japanese)
6. K. Nakamura, K. Hashimoto, Y. Nankaku, K. Tokuda, Integration of spectral feature extraction and modeling for HMM-based speech synthesis. IEICE Trans. Inf. Syst. **E97-D**(6), 1438–1448 (2014)
7. S. Takaki, Y. Nankaku, K. Tokuda, Contextual partial additive structure for HMM-based speech synthesis, in *2013 IEEE International Conference on Acoustics, Speech, and Signal Processing (ICASSP)*, Vancouver, Canada, pp. 7878–7882, 2013
8. R. Dall, M. Tomalin, M. Wester, W. Byrne, S. King, Investigating automatic & human filled pause insertion for speech synthesis, in *Proceedings of Interspeech*, 2014
9. S. R. Gangireddy, S. Renals, Y. Nankaku, A. Lee, Prosodically-enhanced recurrent neural network language models, in *Proceedings of Interspeech 2015*, Dresden, Sept 2015
10. K. Hashimoto, K. Oura, Y. Nankaku, K. Tokuda, The effect of neural networks in statistical parametric speech synthesis, in *Proceedings of 2015 IEEE International Conference on Acoustics, Speech, and Signal Processing (ICASSP 2015)*, Brisbane, Australia, pp. 4455–4459, 19–24 Apr 2015
11. S. Takaki, S. Kim, J. Yamagishi, J.J. Kim, Multiple feed-forward deep neural networks for statistical parametric speech synthesis, in *Proceedings of Interspeech*, vol. 2015, pp. 2242–2246, 2015
12. K. Hashimoto, K. Oura, Y. Nankaku, K. Tokuda, Trajectory training considering global variance for speech synthesis based on neural networks, in *Proceedings of 2016 IEEE International Conference on Acoustics, Speech, and Signal Processing (ICASSP 2016)*, Shanghai, China, pp. 5600–5604, 20–25 Mar 2016
13. K. Sawada, K. Hashimoto, K. Oura, Y. Nankaku, and K. Tokuda, "Evaluation of text-to-speech system construction for unknown-pronunciation languages," Technical Report of IEICE, vol. 115, no. 346, SP2015-80, pp. 93–98, 2–3 Dec 2015
14. S.R. Gangireddy, Q. Huang, S. Renals, F. McInnes, J. Yamagishi, in *Topic Model Features in Neural Network Language Models*, (UK Speech Meeting, 2013)
15. CSTR VCTK Corpus, http://www.udialogue.org/ja/download-ja.html
16. D. Yamamoto, K. Oura, R. Nishimura, T. Uchiya, A. Lee, I. Takumi, Keiichi Tokuda, Voice interaction system with 3D-CG human agent for Stand-alone smartphones, in *Proceedings of the 2nd International Conference on Human Agent Interaction* (ACM digital library, 2014), pp. 320–330
17. K. Wakabayashi, D. Yamamoto, N. Takahashi, A voice dialog editor based on finite state transducer using composite state for tablet devices, computer and information science 2015. Stud. Comput. Intell. **614**, 125–139 (2016)
18. R. Nishimura, D. Yamamoto, T. Uchiya, I. Takumi, Development of a dialogue scenario editor on a web browser for a spoken dialogue system, in *Proceedings of the Second International Conference on Human-agent Interaction*, pp. 129–132, 2014
19. Y. Matsushita, T. Uchiya, R. Nishimura, D. Yamamoto, I. Takumi, Crowdsourcing environment to create voice interaction scenario of spoken dialogue system, in *Proceedings of the 18th International Conference on Network-Based Information Systems (NBiS-2015)*, pp. 500–504, 2015
20. Y. Matsushita, T. Uchiya, R. Nishimura, D. Yamamoto, I. Takumi, Experiment and evaluation of crowd sourcing model for creation of voice interaction scenario. Proc. IEEE GCCE **2015**, 321–322 (2015)

21. T. Uchiya, R. Nakano, D. Yamamoto, R. Nishimura, I. Takumi, Extension with intelligent agents for the spoken dialogue system for smartphones. Proc. IEEE GCCE **2015**, 298–299 (2015)
22. T. Uchiya, D. Yamamoto, M. Shibakawa, M. Yoshida, R. Nishimura, I. Takumi, Development of spoken dialogue service based on video call named "Mobile Meichan". Proc. JAWS2012 (2012). (in Japanese)
23. T. Uchiya, M. Yoshida, D. Yamamoto, R. Nishimura, I. Takumi, Design and implementation of open-campus event system with voice interaction agent. Int. J. Mob. Multimed. **11**(3, 4), 237–250 (2015)
24. R. Nishimura, K. Sugioka, D. Yamamoto, T. Uchiya, I. Takumi, A VoIP-based voice interaction system for a virtual telephone operator using video calls. Proc. IEEE GCCE **2014**, 529–532 (2014)

Chapter 4
Enabling Harmonized Human-Robot Interaction in a Public Space

Takayuki Kanda

Abstract We aim to realize a future city environment in which social robots roam in public spaces and offer such useful services to visitors as information-providing and flyer-distributing, will make three types of research contributions from our project. First, we developed a sensor network that can cover a large area in a shopping mall. Second, based on the rich information from that sensor network, we developed models of pedestrian behavior to increase our understanding of their behavior. Third, these models of pedestrian behavior enable us to harmonize robots into public spaces. That is, without hindering the movement of people, robots will be able to offer useful services.

Keywords Human-Robot Interaction · Social robots · Service robots · Pedestrian modeling

4.1 Introduction

In the near future, robots are expected to navigate in daily human environments and provide services for various tasks (Fig. 4.1). For instance, for museums, robots have been developed that guide visitors and explain exhibits [1–4]. Similarly, another robot led people to items in a big shop [5]. Other robots provide carrying services, e.g., shopping-cart [6] and garbage-collecting robots [7]. Some involve more human-like dialogs. For instance, a receptionist robot in an office [8] receives input from keyboards, provides directions, and engages in small talk. A city explorer robot [9] collects information from people by asking questions. Humanoid robots are also used for daily greetings and direction-giving in shopping malls (e.g. [10]). We found that people prefer services from a robot rather than from a person for troublesome tasks [11], and they enjoy a robot's presence even if it does not offer a concrete service [12]. In the future, we expect such robots to provide various new services in daily human environments.

T. Kanda (✉)
ATR Intelligent Robotics Communication Laboratories, Kyoto, Japan
e-mail: kanda@atr.jp

© Springer Japan KK 2017
T. Nishida (ed.), *Human-Harmonized Information Technology, Volume 2*,
DOI 10.1007/978-4-431-56535-2_4

Fig. 4.1 Image of future shopping mall with robots

Fig. 4.2 Harmonization
problem: congestion around
robot

However, we observed some problems in harmonizing robots with human environments. Since they still lack common sense, they often fail to detect problematic situations. For instance, Fig. 4.2 shows an information-providing robot in a shopping mall. Because the robot is novel, too many visitors stopped to look at it and obstructed other pedestrians from passing through the environment. Since the robot itself was unable to recognize this situation, it continued to cause congestion until human personnel intervened [13]. We also observed a situation where a moving robot failed to naturally avoid other pedestrians [14]. We also encountered a problem where robots disturbed shop activities because it failed to recognize the importance of locations, e.g., around entrances and shelves in shops, although the robot was in a public corridor [15]. Such obstruction scenes were common during our field studies.

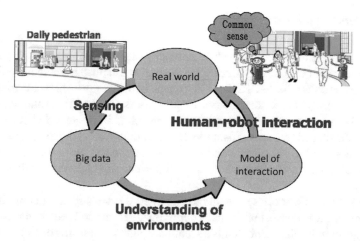

Fig. 4.3   Basic framework of project

The fundamental problem is that robots lack common sense. In human environments, people understand such unwritten knowledge and rules (e.g. [16, 17]) that they share and apply harmoniously without disturbing others. However, unless programmed or implemented in other ways, robots do not have such common sense that can be applied to avoid disturbing others. Thus, future robots must develop human-like common sense.

Our research project specifically focuses on such a common sense problem in the domain of an open public space, like a shopping mall corridor, where pedestrians are walking. We believe that such open public spaces will be one location where robots will be used even in their early deployment phase. If we can establish techniques that harmonize robots (even just in expensive robots with limited capability) in daily human environments, they might be able to offer many useful services in such contexts.

As illustrated in Fig. 4.3, our approach to this problem starts by sensing the daily activities of pedestrians. Such real-world sensing yields a large amount of data about daily behavior. Then from such real-world data, we retrieve an understanding of environments and establish models of interaction. Finally, we will incorporate the established models into robots and test them in the real world. If they serve harmoniously based on the models, we can confirm that our established models contain the critical essence of common sense. With this approach, we can simultaneously improve the capability of robots as well as confirm the meaningfulness of our established model.

In the next three sections, we briefly overview each element in the above basic framework and explain the state-of-art contributions: Sensor Network, Pedestrian Modeling, Enabling Harmonized and Human-Robot Interaction. The final section, Examples of Robot Services, describes some examples of enabled services from the robots.

4.2 Sensor Network

One key element in our framework is sensing pedestrians. Even though there are many studies with various approaches, we wanted to establish a stable infrastructure that can be used for further studies. Thus, our two main priorities are robustness and wide coverage. For instance, laser range sensors attached to a robot can detect people within a few meters, although that approach is inadequate for our purpose. Thus, we developed our own sensing infrastructure based on depth sensing, which is very robust, and used multiple depth cameras on the ceiling of the environments so that the sensing infrastructure does not interfere with people's daily activities (Fig. 4.4).

For a sensor network based on depth cameras, we developed a people-tracking algorithm. Its basic idea is that for each depth image from each sensor, it runs a clustering algorithm for the point clouds so that each individual forms one cluster. Then from the top, it creates layers to analyze the head and shoulder locations (Fig. 4.5). Finally, it combines the information from all of the sensors with a particle filter. This algorithm has an advantage in computation complexity; since it only performs simple and light computation, it can run in real time even with more than 20 depth cameras

Fig. 4.4 Tracking people by depth cameras on ceiling

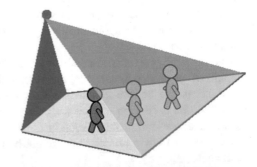

Fig. 4.5 Feature retrieval from depth images: *green* points represents shoulders and *top* of head

Fig. 4.6 Tracking people locations using depth cameras: *left* tracking result, *right* sensors on ceiling

(Fig. 4.6 shows a tracking scene). The locations of people are estimated and provided every 33 ms. Further, we can estimate the height of people to determine whether they are adults or children. The algorithm's details are available in our previous work [18]. To calibrate the location parameters of the sensors in the computation, we prepared supporting tools, e.g., 3-dimensional visualization support. A technique exists that automatically calibrates parameters [19]. The sensor network can also be used to help a robot localize itself [20].

We installed our developed sensor network in a shopping mall in Osaka, Japan. Its area includes an approx. 70, 3–6 m wide corridor with four shops alongside it that is connected to a big hall of approx. 300 m^2. The corridor connects the hall to a train station and is relatively more crowded with pedestrians. Both the corridor and the hall were covered with our people-tracking infrastructure using 49 3-D range sensors on the ceiling (Fig. 4.7) (combination of Panasonic D-Imager, ASUS Xtion, and Velodyne HDL-32E) to estimate the people's locations every 33 ms. Each sensor was

Fig. 4.7 Depth sensors attached to ceiling of shopping mall corridor

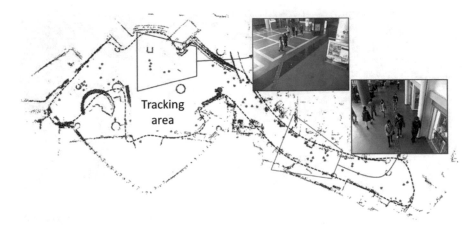

Fig. 4.8 Tracking infrastructure installed in shopping mall

connected to a computer, which only receives data from the sensor and transfers them to the central computer, which performs all the remaining tracking computations. In total, an area of approx. $900\,m^2$ was covered (Fig. 4.8).

Our system performs well in a real shopping mall [18]. We evaluated its performance using a clear MOT method [21], which yielded 94.47% of Multiple Object Tracking Accuracy (MOTA) value, indicating quite stable tracking. For instance, PETS09 SL.L2 datasets resemble our situation in terms of pedestrian density for which other algorithms using RGB cameras show performance of 50–67% of MOTA value. Unfortunately, PETS09 only contains data from adults; our shopping mall is populated by children, baby strollers, and shopping carts that complicate the situation. For those interested in depth sensing, our data are available at the following URL: http://www.irc.atr.jp/crest2010_HRI/ATC_dataset.

4.3 Pedestrian Modeling

People behave daily under certain norms based on common sense. For instance, people behave appropriately based on locations, though such behavior is often done unconsciously. When they stop to talk, common sense dictates that they do so in a large open square rather than in the middle of a busy corridor. Our approach retrieves such common sense about pedestrian behavior from the analysis of big data measured from the real world.

Figure 4.9 illustrates the series of models we have developed for our research approach. Our sensing infrastructure, reported in Sect. 4.2, enables us to observe pedestrian behavior even in large spaces or crowded situations. One method is to directly use such a model to replicate human behavior. For instance, with our collision avoidance model, we developed a robot that avoids pedestrians in a way that

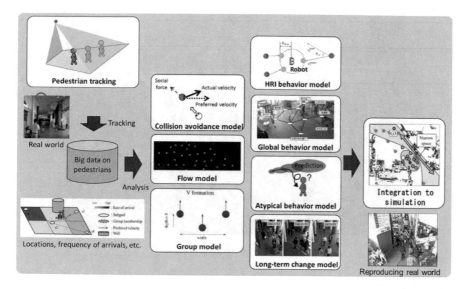

Fig. 4.9 Overview of developed pedestrian models

resembles how other pedestrians avoid collisions. Further, we integrated the models into a pedestrian simulation, which enables the robot to anticipate near future situations in its planning module.

In the following sections, we explain two of the models: collision avoidance and HRI behavior. We also developed a flow model that reproduces pedestrian flow (since people tend to walk on the left side of corridors in Japan, the flow of people in each direction is clearly separated) [22], group behavior [23–25], global behavior [26], and long-term change [27].

4.3.1   Collision Avoidance Model

Pedestrians avoid each other in natural ways. Researchers have developed such a model of collision avoidance. One most famous scheme is the "social force model," in which collision avoidance behavior is modeled as a simple repulsive force [28]. If the distance between two persons is small, a large repulsive force is assumed, as if an invisible "social" force is being applied among people in a way that mimics a physical force. While people's behavior can be well explained with such modeling if their density is high (like panic and escape situations), no relatively low-density situations (less than 0.25 person/m^2) have been modeled well in such previous approaches, which are the typical situations in open public spaces (Fig. 4.10).

In contrast, our model was specifically developed for such low-density situations where people avoid each other at the earliest possible moment and behave in such a

Fig. 4.10 Example of density in a public space: approx. 0.1 person/m^2

Fig. 4.11 Collision
avoidance model with a
prediction

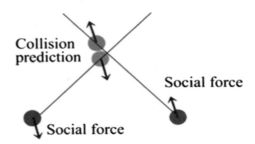

way to avoid blocking each other's paths. For this phenomenon, our model includes
the concept of prediction. For each agent, social force is computed based on a future
moment (Fig. 4.11). In other words, each agent anticipates the motion of each other
agent, anticipates potential future collisions, and navigates a course that avoids a
collision. The detailed specifications were previously reported [29]. In a laboratory
environment, we tested the model and collected trajectories where four and eight
people walked and avoided each other at the same time in a situation that imitates a
busy shopping mall. We compared the proposed model with other existing models
and demonstrated that our proposed model outperformed the others.

4.3.2   HRI Behavior Model

Even though a pedestrian model assumes people walk straight toward a goal, they
sometimes deviate from their own goals, particularly around a robot. Some change
their behavior when they see a robot. Figure 4.12 shows one such moment with a

Fig. 4.12 Woman stopped in front of a robot (*right*) and observed it [14]

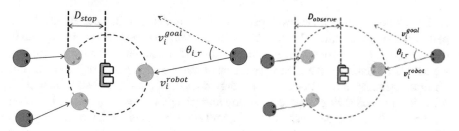

Fig. 4.13 HRI behavior model: adopted from [14]

group of walkers who noticed the robot, and one member darted toward it and stopped in front of it while her friend stopped and observed her interaction with it.

Although diverse types of human-robot interaction (HRI) exist, if we limit our scope to navigational behavior, we can classify people into four categories. Thus, to reproduce peoples behavior in a pedestrian simulation, we developed the following. Further details are available [14].

1. Stopping to interact: Some people approached the robot, stopped to interact at an acceptable social distance (Fig. 4.13, left), and stayed there for a short period. In a simulation, we reproduced this behavior as follows. When a robot is within D_{notice} distance in front of a person, he/she changes course and approaches the robot until it reaches $D_{interact}$ distance. After stopping for Tstop time, he/she walks away from the robot and continues moving toward his/her original goal.
2. Stopping to observe: Some pedestrians stopped to observe the robot outside of the social zone (Fig. 4.13, right). Similar to the stopping to interact behavior, people in this category approach the robot and stop; however, stopping distance $D_{observe}$ is large, suggesting that they are merely observing the robot from a distance without actually being involved in any social interaction.
3. Slowing down to look: Some slowed down to look at the robot without changing their course and passed without stopping.
4. Uninterested: A considerable number of persons showed almost no interest in the robot. They avoided the robot as if it were just another pedestrian. Except for such collision-avoiding behavior, their walking course and velocity were not affected.

The ratio of pedestrians for each cluster depends on various factors, such as the robot's appearance, its role, and the types of visitors (e.g., business or leisure contexts). For instance, pedestrian behaviors in a shopping mall were analyzed where a human-like robot moved around [14]. 26.3% were classified as stopped to interact, 25.9% as stopped to observe, 4.1% as slowed down to look, and 43.7% as uninterested.

4.3.3   Integration into a Simulation

As illustrated in Fig. 4.9, we developed a series of models and integrated them into a pedestrian simulation, which consisted of three elements: generation of new pedestrian agents, a trajectory manager, and human-robot interaction. For the generation, we computed statistics about the appearance of new pedestrians from the big data of observed pedestrian trajectories from a large dataset of one-year observations [27]. We also analyzed their groups, e.g., family and friends who walk together, based on our previously developed technique [30], and prepared statistical models of group differentiation. Once pedestrians appear in the simulated world, then the trajectory manager computes their behavior, based on the models we have developed. With our global behavior model [26], we established a probabilistic model about the final goals and the sub-goals (routes) of each pedestrian. Thus, each pedestrian agent has its own goal toward which it moves at each moment in the simulation. When pedestrians are near the simulated robot, their behavior follows the HRI behavior model. Some pedestrian agents were influenced by the robot and might stop and stay near it.

Figure 4.14 illustrates an example where we simulated congestion caused by a robot. The congestion itself was not directly modeled: only the microscopic behaviors of the pedestrians. All of the pedestrians individually behaved from which such a congestion phenomenon emerges. Because people stopped near the robot, it also stopped. When it started a conversation with people, they tended to stop near the robot more frequently [13]. The corridor in Fig. 4.14 only suffers from congestion when the robot is there; if it tries to pass, some people start to stop, rather quickly escalating

Fig. 4.14 Congestion where pedestrians pass through corridor's narrow part: *left* simulated scene, *right* actual scene

the tendency of others to stop, which increases the congestion. In our simulation, we reproduced a macroscopic phenomenon from such microscopic modeling and used this emergent way of modeling to plan the robot behavior and explain such mechanism in subsequent sections.

4.4 Enabling Harmonized Human-Robot Interaction

Our goal is to harmonize robots into daily human environments. For this purpose, we developed a series of models of the natural behaviors of pedestrians. We assume that such human models will enable a robot to behave in concordance with human common sense, to avoid disturbing human activity, and be well harmonized with its environment. In this section, we introduce three examples of human-robot interaction techniques that are typically enabled with such a model: collision avoidance, congestion prevention, and escaping from abuse. We also developed other techniques: friendly patrolling where a robot exhibits its availability by its navigational behavior [31]; a polite-approaching method where a robot selectively approaches pedestrians who seems interested [32]; a model of appropriate locations for waiting [33]; a model of 'territory' nearby shops [15]; and a model of human-like side-by-side walking [34]. In addition, as can be seen in our examples, harmonized interaction is often enabled with our developed sensing infrastructures. A robot often needs to observe human behavior at specific distances to behave proactively and must adjust its behavior quickly to avoid causing problems.

4.4.1 Harmonized Collision Avoidance

One harmonization problem we faced is collision avoidance. Figure 4.15 shows an unsafe situation caused by a robot, although no actual collision occurred. A man is approaching the robot, which is moving toward him. It was operated by a well-established collision avoidance method: the time varying dynamic window (TVDW) method [35]. It plans its future velocity by projecting other moving entities and avoids a velocity that might cause a collision. In this example, the robot turned right before it too closely approached this man who gazed at the robot and quickly moved to the side as if he suddenly found it unsafe. He looked back at the robot after a moment with an irritated expression. Like this example, we identified such "unsafe" situations in 3.6% of the crossing interactions when the robot was operated with the TVDW method at such shopping mall corridor.

Figure 4.16 shows examples of the robot and pedestrian trajectories during collision avoidance. In both examples, the robot moves from left to right when a pedestrian is approaching from right to left. The example on the left is with the TVDW method. The robot only starts to change its course when it determines that it might collide with the person. Even it does not collide, it passes too near the person and causes

Fig. 4.15 An unsafe situation (the robot closely approached the man who gazed at the robot and quickly moved to the side as if he suddenly found it unsafe)

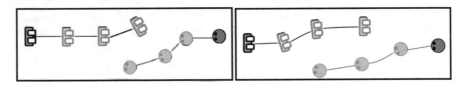

Fig. 4.16 Collision avoidance behavior of robot: *left* with TVDW method, *right* with a CP-SFM (proposed method)

an unsafe situation, as shown in the above example. This behavior might also confuse pedestrians. Since its course suggests that it will approach the person, some people might mistakenly believe that the robot has a particular goal or purpose and wonder what to do. In either case, such inadequately harmonized behavior fails to appropriately mimic human-like collision avoidance.

In contrast, the example on the right in Fig. 4.16 is with our pedestrian model: CP-SFM. It computes the social force based on future moments when a collision is anticipated. If a pedestrian is on the same course as the robot, the robot has already started to deviate to the side. Such collision avoidance resembles what we humans ourselves do in such low-density environments.

We experimentally validated this collision avoidance method. First, we investigated how people perceive the robot's behavior. When we compared the CP-SFM and TVDW methods, we found that people evaluated the former method higher since they can walk at their preferred speed without obstruction from the robot. We also investigated how often the robot caused unsafe situations in a natural setting. As mentioned above, in the TVDW method, the robot caused 3.6% unsafe situations; no such situations occurred in the proposed CP-SFM method [36] (Fig. 4.17). Thus, with a model of human-like natural collision avoidance, we can more effectively harmonize the robot in daily human environments in the context of collision avoidance.

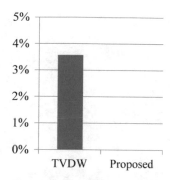

Fig. 4.17 Experiment result about ratio of unsafe situations: reported in previous work [36]

Fig. 4.18 Congestion problem. Robot interacted in a narrow part of a corridor, which inconvenienced passages of others

4.4.2 Preventing Congestion

Since robots are novel, they attract much attention. During their navigations, people typically stop walking, gather near them, and start interacting. However, such gatherings often cause congestion. When they happen in a narrow location, other pedestrians who wanted to pass are often inconvenienced (Fig. 4.18).

We pondered what to do in such situations. Humans have the capability to anticipate future situations and speculate about what happen if we go somewhere and attract visitors. We can foresee how we might aggravate the situation. We can anticipate an appropriate amount of visitors: not too few, not too many. We wanted to endow our robot with such an anticipation capability to consider future situations without causing congestion problems.

Fig. 4.19 Simulation of comfort-discomfort around robot. Robot agent (*green*) was surrounded by pedestrian agents who stopped to interact with it (*gray*). Other pedestrian agents are indicated with *yellow* to *red*, where *red* represents pedestrian agents who were more uncomfortable going through other pedestrians and *yellow* represents pedestrian agents who were less uncomfortable

To achieve this capability, we used a pedestrian simulation in the robot's planning module. As explained in above, our pedestrian simulation emergently reproduces congestion phenomena with a microscopic model of pedestrian behavior to reproduce macroscopic phenomena. We can also use a pedestrian simulation to predict whether a congestion problem might occur. With a different situation for a microscopic model, we can foresee the degree of gathering a robot might cause. Further, we modeled how people perceive and suffer from congestion. After modeling with human participants, we found that pedestrians describe situations as more uncomfortable if the nearest distance to others is short.

We incorporated this comfort-discomfort model into our simulation to compute the level of disturbance caused by a crowd around a robot. Figure 4.19 shows a simulated scene where the comfort of the agents around the congestion was reproduced. When the robot agent was roaming in the corridor's narrow part, other pedestrian agents stopped around it, reducing the corridor's remaining space. Other pedestrian agents felt less comfortable when they were around the congestion. The robot simulates various future situations in its planning module and estimates comfort levels as well as the amount of service it can offer. Figure 4.20 shows a robot operated with this planning module. Among many possible choices, it chooses to move in this space because it can meet many people without causing congestion. We experimentally tested this planning module in this shopping mall and found that it effectively reduced congestion [37]. We extended this basic idea to a more dynamic situation, where the robot must interaction with nearby pedestrians or move away from them

Fig. 4.20 Robot with proposed method. It chooses a location where it can meet many visitors without causing congestion

[13]. People tended to stop near the robot when it was interacting with others. While people stop less frequently near the robot when it is moving, once it stops to interact with them, they tend to stop more frequently. In other words, the congestion tends to grow rather quickly once it starts.

4.4.3   Escaping from Robot Abuse

Robots are sometimes treated roughly by people, especially children. The term "robot abuse," first used by Bartneck and his colleagues [38], succinctly describes the tendency of people to continue to interact inappropriately with a robot even if the robot itself asks them to stop. In an open public environment, Salvini et al. observed such aggressive behaviors to robots as kicking, punching, or slapping [39].

We also observed such robot abuse from children in our field, particularly after we developed a technique to moderate the congestion caused by robots. Figure 4.21 shows an example of such robot abuse. Here, a group of children interacted with the robot, which was designed to roam around the environment. When its course was blocked, it requested the people to move. However, they continued to block its path. In some cases, children continued such persistent obstruction for up to 19 minutes, ignoring 45 requests from the robot. Sometimes their behavior escalated and included hitting and kicking. This resembles human bullying. The children seemed to enjoy abusing the robot, even though they understood that the robot can suffer [40].

Such abuse is a genuine problem for social robots. First, it might reduce the efficiency of the services they can offer. Second, more importantly, such abuse creates

Fig. 4.21 Robot abuse. Children persistently blocked its course: relevant video clip available at: https://youtu.be/CuJT9EtdETY

uncomfortable feelings in people and might harm children's development. This is also a problem in harmonizing robots into daily human environments.

Thus, we decided to study this phenomenon by identifying how to prevent it. Here, we briefly report our analysis results. (See previous work [41] for details). We identified two main tendencies. First, the risk of abuse increases when the number of children around the robot also increases. For instance, with four children around the robot, the robot is approximately five times more likely to be abused than when there are only two children. Such abuse risks increase as they continued to interact with the robot. Second, children tend to quit interacting with the robot when their parents are near or when many pedestrians are present. This matches our previous experiences. Now, with the congestion prevention mechanism (explained in Sect. 4.4.2), the robot tends to operate where the pedestrian flow is relatively small. Thus, children tended to interact with the robot longer, creating more chances for other children to simultaneously stay around the robot, which results in a higher risk of abuse.

We implemented this model of abuse occurrence in our pedestrian simulation and extended our planning framework for the congestion problem to this abuse problem. The robot system anticipates future situations using the simulator and chooses a plan that will yield the lowest risk of being abused. The robot tended to approach a parent when it was approached by a child. As a result, since parents typically took their children away from the robot, the risk of abuse was largely reduced [41].

4.5 Examples of Robot Services

Based on the advance of techniques that harmonize robots with open public environments, we developed some examples of robot services to emphasize the feasibility of our developed techniques as well as the social acceptance of such robot services.

4.5.1 Distributing Flyers

In Japan, people often distribute flyers in open public spaces. We believe that a robot will also be able to perform such a flyer-distribution service. Initially, we started with the assumption that the behavior required of a robot would be rather simple; however, we found that it is rather complicated. In our implementation, when a robot just approached a person and extended its arm to distribute a flyer, it did not perform well because its actions weren't natural [42].

Thus, we developed a model for how people behave in a flyer-distributing service and found a rather big individual difference. Some people are good at this task, yielding a successful giving rate of 60–80%; some are poor and achieve a 10–20% success rate. We analyzed the behavior of successful givers and found that they approached and extended their arms near the pedestrians. Good givers also slightly approach their targets from the left/right side instead of directly in front. This is the essence of simple, non-obstructive behavior to distribute flyers to targets.

To reproduce such human successful behavior in robots, they must have the capability to observe pedestrians from a distance that exceeds 10 m. A robot is usually slower than pedestrians, because excessively fast robots are not safe and might scare people. A robot needs to adequately plan its motion course in advance; otherwise, it is not possible to approach pedestrians from the front. We used our sensor network infrastructure to stably detect people far from the robot and implemented a model of human successful behavior. Figure 4.22 shows a scene where the developed robot approached a pedestrian and gave him a flyer. Overall, our implemented system yielded a success rate of 73.3%, which closely resembles the performance of successful human givers [42].

We also conducted a field study with our system's extended version and integrated the model with other techniques to harmonize the robot with its environment. We noticed that pedestrians tended to accept flyers more frequently if the pedestrian before them also accepted one. Thus, we implemented a planner whose preference was to give a flyer to a flow of people so that the robot can continuously handout flyers to pedestrians. Finally, the successful ratio of giving flyers reached 87.9%, which exceeds the average of human givers (40.7%) as well as the best giver in our dataset (77.5%). Figure 4.23 shows a scene of the field study. The robot navigated around the square and approached pedestrians to give them flyers. Figure 4.24 shows another

Fig. 4.22 Robot approaches from front right side to give a flyer: adopted from previous work [42]

Fig. 4.23 Scene of our field study. Robot navigates and gives flyers to pedestrians

Fig. 4.24 Visitors approach robot and extend their arms for flyers

scene where a group of visitors noticed the robot distributing flyers, approached it, and extended their arm to request one. We interviewed those who accepted flyers and asked why they took them. 55.6% mentioned such a robot-unique reason as its novelty or its easy-to-access nature, but 44.4% mentioned the human-like naturalness of the giving. This result is interesting since the robot service has both human-like and robot-unique natures.

4.5.2 Direction-Giving

Information-providing is one service people expect from a robot, particularly a direction-giving service [43]. Thus, we developed a robot system that offers such information as direction-giving and shop recommendations in a shopping mall.

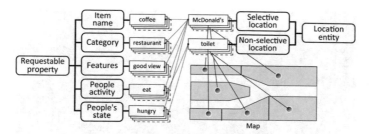

Fig. 4.25 Knowledge representation for information-providing services: adopted from previous work [43]

Fig. 4.26 Direction-giving service scene

We integrated the relevant techniques as well as techniques for harmonizing robots, as reported throughout this chapter. Regarding direction-giving interactions, previous work revealed how a robot should provide directions [44], and how environmental knowledge should be collected and stored [45]. Since automatic speech recognition remains difficult for a robot in noisy environments, we used a semi-autonomous approach where human operators take over simple processing of listening utterances; since one operator can control up to four robots [46, 47], it might even be feasible to use robots with such semi-autonomy. In addition, we prepared knowledge representation for information about shops and their items (Fig. 4.25) and designed behaviors to effectively offer direction information [43].

We conducted a field study with our developed robot. Figure 4.26 illustrates an interaction scene. The robot approached visitors and asked if they needed any help. When they asked for directions to an office, it pointed to explain the route. Figure 4.27 illustrates another scene where a child responded to a robot's pointing gesture. She mimicked the gesture and explained its meaning to her mother. People listened to the robot and seemed happy when it indicated a direction.

To investigate the social acceptance of its service, we interviewed 89 visitors who interacted with the robot. 96.6% reported that the service was good. They described

Fig. 4.27 Response to pointing gestures. A child mimicked the gesture and explained it to her mother

the direction-giving as comprehensive and also said that it was easier to ask the robot than the human staff. Children were happy during their interactions with it [48].

4.6 Future Directions

With the series of studies reported in this chapter, we developed fundamental capabilities with which robots can navigate in a future city environment and offer useful services to visitors. Built on these fundamental capabilities, one important future direction is to expand the types of services robots could offer. We have mainly worked with a human-like service robot so far. Nevertheless, the requirements for basic navigation capability are largely shared by other types of robots, such as autonomous wheelchairs and delivery robots. Within 5–10 years with an appropriate advance of research into the task-dependent nature of navigation for each service, we expect to see early deployment of such robot services that exploit autonomous navigation capabilities. Of course, for this future direction, we need to conduct applied research on various aspects to prepare the fundamental technologies.

Likewise, expansion of the roles of robots will occur in different types of environments. Our study so far focused on public spaces like shopping malls where people walk around and generally pass by. People remain in other environments, like shops, museums, hospitals, and hotels. In schools and homes, they stay much longer. Our realized principle might be expanded to such situations with an appropriate advance of techniques to deal with personalization and adaptation.

In the coming 5–10 years, we expect that rapid advancement of relevant robotics technologies will occur. For instance, manipulation capability is rapidly growing. Combining advanced navigation and manipulation capabilities will open up a future in which diverse labor is done by various robots in such future city environments.

4.7 Summary

Since our goal is to use robots in open public spaces, we developed a series of techniques to harmonize them into daily human contexts. Our sensor network infrastructure enables us to observe daily pedestrian behavior from which we established models that can be used to harmonize robots with their environments. With our sensor network as well as techniques based on the models, we demonstrated that robots can offer useful services. Our field studies revealed that they were harmonized in daily human contexts and encouraged people to acquire information from them. Through our project, we identified the potential possessed by one human-harmonized information technology.

Acknowledgements The authors of this chapter thank the following people who participated in this project: Satoru Satake, Drazen Brščić, Francesco Zanlungo, Masahiro Shiomi, Tetsushi Ikeda, Takahiro Miyashita, Kotaro Hayashi, Yoich Morales, Thomas Kaczmarek, Hiroyuki Kidokoro, Alessandra Maria Sabelli, Chao Shi, Yoshitaka Suehiro, Deneth Karunarathne, Yoshihiro Chigodo, Daniel Rea, Takuya Kitade, Hajime Iba, Ryo Murakami, Yusuke Kato, Keita Nakatani, and Kanako Tomita.

References

1. W. Burgard, et al., The interactive museum Tour-Guide robot, in *National Conference on Artificial Intelligence (AAAI1998)*, pp. 11–18, 1998
2. R. Siegwart et al., Robox at Expo. 02: a large scale installation of personal robots. Robot. Auton. Syst. **42**, 203–222 (2003)
3. M. Shiomi, T. Kanda, H. Ishiguro, N. Hagita, Interactive humanoid robots for a science museum. IEEE Intell. Syst. **22**, 25–32 (2007)
4. S. Thrun, et al., Minerva: a Second-Generation museum Tour-Guide robot, in *IEEE International Conference on Robotics and Automation (ICRA1999)*, pp. 1999–2005, 1999
5. H.-M. Gross, et al., Shopbot: progress in developing an interactive mobile shopping assistant for everyday use, in *IEEE International Conference on Systems, Man, and Cybernetics (SMC2008)*, pp. 3471–3478, 2008
6. V. Kulyukin, C. Gharpure, J. Nicholson, robocart: toward Robot-Assisted navigation of grocery stores by the visually impaired, in *IEEE/RSJ International Conference on Intelligent Robots and Systems (IROS2005)*, pp. 2845–2850, 2005
7. G. Ferri, et al., Dustcart, an autonomous robot for Door-to-Door garbage collection: from dustbot project to the experimentation in the small town of peccioli, in *IEEE International Conference on Robotics and Automation (ICRA2011)*, pp. 655–660, 2011
8. R. Kirby, J. Forlizzi, R. Simmons, Affective social robots. Robot. Auton. Syst. **58**, 322–332 (2010)
9. A. Weiss, et al., A methodological variation for acceptance evaluation of human-robot interaction in public places, in *IEEE International Symposium on Robot and Human Interactive Communication (RO-MAN2008)*, pp. 713–718, 2008
10. T. Kanda, M. Shiomi, Z. Miyashita, H. Ishiguro, N. Hagita, A communication robot in a shopping mall. IEEE Trans. Robot. **26**, 897–913 (2010)
11. K. Hayashi, M. Shiomi, T. Kanda, N. Hagita, Are robots appropriate for troublesome and communicative tasks in a city environment? IEEE Trans. Auton. Ment. Dev. **4**, 150–160 (2012)
12. A.M. Sabelli, T. Kanda, Robovie as a mascot: a qualitative study for Long-Term presence of robots in a shopping mall. Int. J. Soc. Robot. 1–11 (2015)

13. H. Kidokoro, T. Kanda, D. Brščić, M. Shiomi, Simulation-Based behavior planning to prevent congestion of pedestrians around a robot. IEEE Trans. Robot. **31**, 1419–1431 (2015)
14. M. Shiomi, F. Zanlungo, K. Hayashi, T. Kanda, A framework with a pedestrian simulator for deploying robots into a real environment, in *Simlation, modeling, and programming for autonomous robots (SIMPAR2012)*, 2012
15. S. Satake, H. Iba, T. Kanda, M. Imai, Y.M. Saiki, May I talk about other shops here?: modeling territory and invasion in front of shops, in *Proceedings of the 2014 ACM/IEEE International Conference on Human-Robot Interaction* (ed: ACM, 2014), pp. 487–494
16. J.B. Misyak, T. Melkonyan, H. Zeitoun, N. Chater, Unwritten Rules: Virtual Bargaining Underpins Social Interaction. Cult. Soc. Trends Cogn. Sci. **18**, 512–519 (2014)
17. M.J. Gelfand et al., Differences between tight and loose cultures: a 33-Nation study. Science **332**, 1100–1104 (2011)
18. D. Brščić, T. Kanda, T. Ikeda, T. Miyashita, Person tracking in large public spaces using 3D range sensors. IEEE Trans. Hum.-Mach. Syst. **43**, 522–534 (2013)
19. D.F. Glas, D. Brščić, T. Miyashita, N. Hagita, Snapcat-3d: calibrating networks of 3D range sensors for pedestrian tracking, in *2015 IEEE International Conference on Robotics and Automation (ICRA)* (ed: IEEE, 2015), pp. 712–719
20. D.F. Glas, Y. Morales, T. Kanda, H. Ishiguro, N. Hagita, Simultaneous people tracking and robot localization in dynamic social spaces. Auton. Robot. **39**, 43–63 (2015)
21. K. Bernardin, R. Stiefelhangen, Evaluating multiple object tracking performance: the clear mot metrics, in *Video Tracking in Complex Scenes for Surveillance Applications* (Eurasip Journal on Image and Video Processing), vol. 2008 (Hindawi Publishing Corporation, 2008)
22. F. Zanlungo, T. Ikeda, T. Kanda, A microscopic "Social Norm" model to obtain realistic macroscopic velocity and density pedestrian distributions. PLoS ONE **7** (2012)
23. F. Zanlungo, D. Brščić, T. Kanda, Spatial-Size scaling of pedestrian groups under growing density conditions. Phys. Rev. E **91**, 062810 (2015)
24. F. Zanlungo, T. Kanda, A. Mesoscopic, Model for the effect of density on pedestrian group dynamics. EPL (Europhysics Letters) **111**, 38007 (2015)
25. F. Zanlungo, T. Ikeda, T. Kanda, Potential for the dynamics of pedestrians in a socially interacting group. Phys. Rev. E **89** (2014)
26. T. Ikeda, et al., *Modeling and Prediction of Pedestrian Behavior Based on the Sub-Goal Concept Robotics: Science and Systems*, 2012
27. D. Brščić, T. Kanda, Changes in usage of an indoor public space: analysis of one year of person tracking. IEEE Trans. Hum.-Mach. Syst. **45**, 228–237 (2015)
28. D. Helbing, P. Molnar, Social force model for pedestrian dynamics. Phys. Rev. E **51**, 4282–4286 (1995)
29. F. Zanlungo, T. Ikeda, T. Kanda, Social force model with explicit collision prediction. Europhys. Lett. **93**, 68005 (2011)
30. T. Kanda, et al., Analysis of people trajectories with ubiquitous sensors in a science museum, in *IEEE International Conference on Robotics and Automation (ICRA2007)*, pp. 4846–4853, 2007
31. K. Hayashi, M. Shiomi, T. Kanda, N. Hagita, *Friendly Patrolling: A Model of Natural Encounters, Robotics: Science and Systems Conference (RSS2011)*, 2011
32. Y. Kato, T. Kanda and H. Ishiguro, May I Help You?: Design of Human-Like Polite Approaching Behavior, Proceedings of the Tenth Annual ACM/IEEE International Conference on Human-Robot Interaction (HRI2015), pp. 35–42, 2015
33. T. Kitade, S. Satake, T. Kanda, M. Imai, Understanding suitable locations for waiting, in *Proceedings of the 8th ACM/IEEE international conference on Human-robot interaction* (ed: IEEE Press, 2013), pp. 57–64
34. R. Murakami, L.Y. Morales Saiki, S. Satake, T. Kanda, H. Ishiguro, Destination unknown: walking Side-by-Side without knowing the goal, in *Proceedings of the 2014 ACM/IEEE international conference on Human-robot interaction* (ed: ACM, 2014), pp. 471–478
35. M. Seder, I. Petrovic, Dynamic window based approach to mobile robot motion control in the presence of moving obstacles, in *IEEE International Conference on Robotics and Automation (ICRA2007)*, pp. 1986–1991, 2007

36. M. Shiomi, F. Zanlungo, K. Hayashi, T. Kanda, Towards a socially acceptable collision avoidance for a mobile robot navigating among pedestrians using a pedestrian model. Int. J. Soc. Robot. **6**, 443–455 (2014)
37. H. Kidokoro, T. Kanda, D. Brščić, M. Shiomi, Will I Bother Here?-a robot anticipating its influence on pedestrian walking comfort, in *ACM/IEEE International Conference on Human-Robot Interaction (HRI2013)* (ed: IEEE, 2013), pp. 259–266
38. C. Bartneck, C. Rosalia, R. Menges, I. Deckers, Robot Abuse? a limitation of the media equation, in *Proceedings of the interact 2005 workshop on agent abuse, Rome*, ed, 2005
39. P. Salvini, et al., How Safe Are Service Robots in Urban Environments? bullying a robot, *IEEE International Symposium on Robot and Human Interactive Communication (RO-MAN2010)*, pp. 1–7, 2010
40. T. Nomura, et al., Why Do Children Abuse Robots?, in *Proceedings of the Tenth Annual ACM/IEEE International Conference on Human-Robot Interaction Extended Abstracts* (ed: ACM, 2015), pp. 63–64
41. D. Brščić, H. Kidokoro, Y. Suehiro, T. Kanda, Escaping from children's abuse of social robots, in *Proceedings of the Tenth Annual ACM/IEEE International Conference on Human-Robot Interaction* (ed: ACM, 2015), pp. 59–66
42. C. Shi, M. Shiomi, C. Smith, T. Kanda, H. Ishiguro, A Model of Distributional Handing Interaction for a Mobile Robot, Robotics: Science and Systems Conference (RSS2013), 2013
43. S. Satake, K. Nakatani, K. Hayashi, T. Kanda, M. Imai, What should we know to develop an information robot? Peerj Comput. Sci. **1**, e8 (2015)
44. Y. Okuno, T. Kanda, M. Imai, H. Ishiguro, N. Hagita, Providing route directions: design of robot's utterance, gesture, and timing, in *ACM/IEEE International Conference on Human-Robot Interaction (HRI2009)*, pp. 53–60, 2009
45. Y. Morales, S. Satake, T. Kanda, N. Hagita, Modeling environments from a route perspective, in *ACM/IEEE International Conference on Human Robot Interaction (HRI2011)*, pp. 441–448, 2011
46. D.F. Glas, T. Kanda, H. Ishiguro, N. Hagita, Teleoperation of multiple social robots. IEEE Trans. Syst. Man Cybern. Part A: Syst. Hum. **42**, 530–544 (2012)
47. K. Zheng, D. F. Glas, T. Kanda, H. Ishiguro, N. Hagita, How Many Social Robots Can One Operator Control?, in *ACM/IEEE Int. Conf. on Human-Robot Interaction (HRI2011)*, (ed. Lausanne, Switzerland, 2011), pp. 379–386
48. S. Satake, K. Hayashi, K. Nakatani, T. Kanda, Field trial of an information-providing robot in a shopping mall, in *2015 IEEE/RSJ International Conference on Intelligent Robots and Systems (IROS)* (ed: IEEE, 2015), pp. 1832–1839

Chapter 5
Behavior Understanding Based on Intention-Gait Model

Yasushi Yagi, Ikuhisa Mitsugami, Satoshi Shioiri and Hitoshi Habe

Abstract Gait is known as one of biometrics, and there have been many studies on gait authentication. In those studies, it is implicitly assumed that the gait of a certain person is always constant. It is, however, untrue in reality; a person usually walks differently according to their mood and physical/mental conditions, which we call "inertial states." Motivated by this fact, we organized the research project "Behavior Understanding based on Intention-Gait Model", which was supported by JST-CREST from 2010 to 2017. The goal of this project was to map "gait", in the broad sense of the term, to inertial states such as attention, social factors, and cognitive ability. In this chapter, we provide an overview of the three kinds of estimation technologies considered in this project: attention, social factors, and cognitive ability.

Keywords Gait analysis · Eye-head coordination · Visual perception · Gaze estimation · Group segmentation · Dual-task · Cognitive level estimation · Dementia diagnosis · Huge data collection

5.1 Introduction

Walking is a behavior that is fundamental to our daily lives. Because gait (i.e., way of walking) is unique to each person, it is regarded as a biometric property and can be applied to person authentication tasks. There have been many studies

Y. Yagi (✉) · I. Mitsugami
Osaka University, Osaka, Japan
e-mail: yagi@sanken.osaka-u.ac.jp

I. Mitsugami
e-mail: mitsugami@am.sanken.osaka-u.ac.jp

S. Shioiri
Tohoku University, Miyagi, Japan
e-mail: shioiri@riec.tohoku.ac.jp

H. Habe
Kindai University, Osaka, Japan
e-mail: habe@kindai.ac.jp

© Springer Japan KK 2017
T. Nishida (ed.), *Human-Harmonized Information Technology, Volume 2*,
DOI 10.1007/978-4-431-56535-2_5

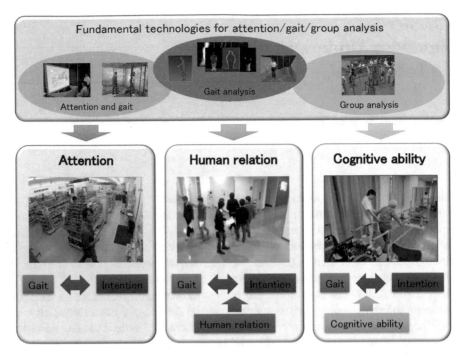

Fig. 5.1 Overview of JST-CREST "Behavior understanding based on Intention-Gait model"

on gait authentication [1–7], and they have revealed that gait is a very effective cue for identifying a person using public gait datasets, such as the CASIA Gait Database [8], the USF Human ID Gait Baseline Database [9], and the OU-ISIR Gait Database [10]. All of these studies, however, implicitly assume that the gait of a certain person is always constant, which is untrue in reality; a person usually walks differently according to their mood and physical/mental conditions, which we call "inertial states." Motivated by this fact, we organized the research project "Behavior Understanding based on Intention-Gait Model", which was supported by JST-CREST from 2010 to 2017. Note that in our previous research, "gait" simply denotes a way of walking, while in this study, we extend this definition to include eye and head motions and walking trajectory. The goal of this project was to map "gait", in the broad sense of the term, to inertial states such as attention, social factors, and cognitive ability. In this chapter, we provide an overview of the three kinds of estimation technologies considered in this project: attention, social factors, and cognitive ability, as shown in Fig. 5.1. Note that in the project we have also developed many fundamental methods for these estimation technologies; calibration of range sensors [11, 12], 3-D reconstruction of human body [13, 14], detection of injured people [15, 16], and gait analysis [12, 17, 18].

Attention is an inertial state that is known to be affected by the interests, feelings, and intention of an individual. For instance, security agencies report that shoplifters often show unique gazing behaviors. Thus, if one were to obtain and analyze gaze activity of people in shops, it may be possible to detect shoplifters. Similarly, customers usually gaze at products that they are interested in. If this type of gaze information were acquired, it might be possible to use it to effectively give customers salient information about promotions and sales. Considering these examples, gaze information has many potential applications. It is, however, usually impossible to obtain gaze information in real environments because such data collection requires the use of an eye tracker. Thus, it is necessary to consider other ways of collecting gaze information. For this purpose, in this project, we examined the relationship between gaze behavior and whole body behaviors, such as gait. We collected data from many participant to facilitate the development of appropriate models. Section 5.2 describes the details of our investigation.

Section 5.3 describes our approach to social interaction estimation. In the course of daily activities, humans often form social groups, such as families and groups of coworkers. When we are in such groups, our actions are strongly affected by and have a large effect on other group members. Investigating social relationships is thus an important way to understand and/or infer information about our daily activities. This section is focused on explaining our proposed method for identifying social groups by analyzing time-series range data.

Section 5.4 concerns cognitive ability estimation. According to a national investigation report, more than 4.4 million people in Japan present with dementia, which is associated with obstacles in brain function that affect understanding, judgment, and memory. An additional 37 thousand people nation-wide present with early-onset dementia due to cerebral vascular disease. It is important to detect dementia in its early stage and conduct treatments accordingly. To examine methods of detecting early onset dementia, we adopted a "dual-task" procedure, in which participants simultaneously complete a physical task (e.g., walking, stepping, and dancing) and a cognitive task (e.g., counting down numbers, telling words of a certain category). This section describes a measurement systems that we have developed for this purpose, and introduces some recent results.

5.2 Gaze Prediction from Body Movements

Gaze location is one of the most useful ways to glean information about people's interests and can be used to estimate intentions, because gaze location is usually assumed to be at the location of the attention focus, although these are not always consistent with each other. To predict gaze location, a number of models using saliency maps, which topographically represent the visual saliency of a given scene, have been proposed [19, 20]. Saliency maps are based on the bottom-up architecture of visual attention, which involves the hypothesis that the most salient locations in a visual scene tend to attract attention. Visual saliency is calculated by integrating the visual features of a scene, such as color, luminance, and orientation, often with a considerable variety of visual functions, like retinal inhomogeneity [21] and the canceling out of self-motion [22]. However, the accuracy of gaze prediction using visual saliency alone is limited because it is based on bottom-up factors such as visual features, and does not account for the influence of top-down factors such as the intention of the participant [23–25]. Models that account for top-down factors undoubtedly provide better gaze prediction. Machine learning techniques are one of the best ways to add information about possible gaze locations from empirical data, and are effective when the task and scenes are known, making learning possible beforehand. However, to improve the accuracy of gaze and attention prediction in generalized conditions, other techniques may be required. Previously, a method was proposed to predict gaze locations using head direction [26], following the purpose of the project to link body movements and intention as described hereafter.

Coordinative movements of the eye and head have been shown experimentally, by measuring eye and head movements during simple gaze shifts to targets present in the periphery from the central fixation [27, 28]. These previous studies revealed that eye-head movements are coordinated when gaze shifts are sufficiently large. Although these results suggest the potential use of head direction in gaze estimation, the conditions of these studies are far from natural conditions, where gaze predictions are desired. Therefore, as a first step, we investigated the relationship between eye and head movements when people are continuously shifting their gaze.

5.2.1 Eye-Head Coordination

We conducted three experiments to explore the relationship between the eye and head movements under more natural conditions than single gaze shifts. The first experiment used 360° surrounding display system and a visual search task [29], the second experiment used natural scene pictures on a large display with more than two hundred participants [26], and the third experiment used a movie in a wide field of view display, which was 7,680 pixels wide by 4,320 pixels tall (8 K) [30]. In all of the experiments, eye and head movements were measured while the participants performed the required tasks (Figs. 5.2 and 5.3).

In the first experiment [29], participants searched for a target across six displays, moving their eyes, head and body inside the space surrounded by the displays (Fig. 5.2). The search display consisted of one target, T, and seven distractors, Ls, on one of the six displays, and eight Ls on the other displays. To search for the target, the participant moved their body and head as well as their eyes to look at all the displays. The eye and head movements were recorded during the period of visual search. Figure 5.4 shows an example of the eye and head movements during visual search. There is one head movement in the figure, and coordination between the eyes and head can be seen. The eyes tend to shift in the direction of the head movement, and therefore the gaze location is farther away from the front than the head direction.

The distribution of the eye orientations was analyzed for different head directions to determine the relationship between the eye and head orientations. Figure 5.5 shows the results of the analysis. Horizontal head orientation is binned and noted at the top of each panel in Fig. 5.5a. The vertical axis shows the percentage of fixations, and the

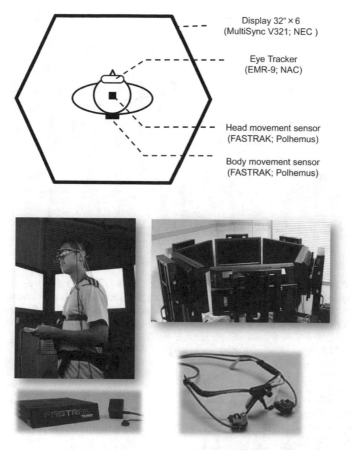

Fig. 5.2 The experiment was performed in a dark room using six 32-inch liquid crystal displays, arranged in the shape of a regular hexagon. Eye-in-head movements were recorded by an eye tracker, and head and body movements were recorded by an electromagnetic motion tracking system

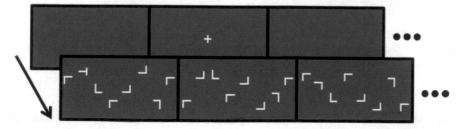

Fig. 5.3 Target letter, T, and distractor letters, Ls, were presented randomly on a *gray* background on one display, and only Ls were presented on the other five displays. Search frames were presented after fixation display

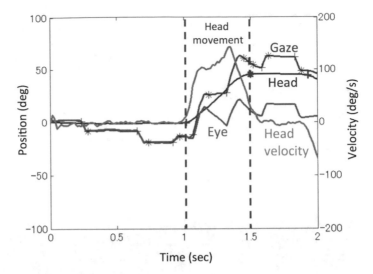

Fig. 5.4 An example of the eye and head movements. The blue line represents eye position, the *black line* represents head position, the *red line* represents gaze location, and the *green line* represents head velocity. The region between the two *red dashed lines* indicates the period of head movement, which was identified based on the head velocity (see the *green line*)

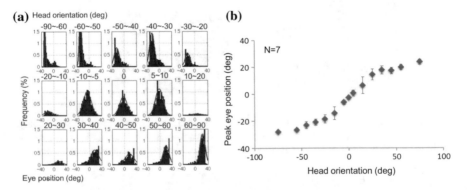

Fig. 5.5 **a** Distribution of eye direction during fixation plotted separately for different head orientations. The *red line* is the Gaussian function fitted to each set of data. **b** Peak eye directions estimated from the Gaussian functions fitted to each participant and averaged over the seven participants. Error bars indicate the standard error of the mean

horizontal axis shows the horizontal eye position relative to the head. To approximate the distribution, we fitted a Gaussian function to each set of data. The red line in each panel shows the function fitted to the average of all participants. Figure 5.5b shows the peak estimated from the Gaussian functions for different head orientations. There is a clear tendency for the eye to be directed in the same orientation as the head relative to the body. That is, when the head was oriented left (or right), the eyes also tended to orient to the left (or right) relative to the head.

Fig. 5.6 Natural scenes used in the second experiment. Outside scenes (*left*) and inside scenes (*right*) are used

In the second experiment [26], we investigated whether there was similar eye and head coordination as that found in the first experiment while viewing natural scenes presented on a 100-inch screen. A total of 30 natural scenes (six indoor and 24 outdoor) containing numerous objects (see Fig. 5.6) were prepared as stimuli and projected onto a large screen. The size of each image was designed to be $57° \times 44°$ from a viewing distance of 125 cm. The eye and head movements were recorded during a 5 s observation period. This experiment was conducted during an outreach activity at the National Museum of Emerging Science and Innovation in Tokyo, Japan, known as "Miraikan." Study participants comprised 228 museum visitors. All the participants had normal or corrected-to-normal vision.

Figure 5.7 shows the peak eye directions estimated from the Gaussian functions fitted to pooled data. There is a similar tendency to that of the results of the first experiment. The eyes tended to be directed in the same orientation as that of the head relative to the body. The eyes also tended to be directed to the left (or right) relative to the head when the head was orientated left (or right) when the participant was looking at natural scenes as well. The experiment also showed that this tendency was maintained for data pooled over more than 200 people.

It was also confirmed that there was similar eye and head coordination when the participants were watching a movie on an 85-inch 8 K ultrahigh-definition television

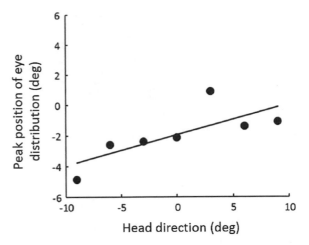

Fig. 5.7 Peak eye directions estimated from the Gaussian functions fitted to each participant and averaged over the seven participants

(UHDTV) in the third experiment [30], where two viewing distances were used to determine the effect of stimulus size on visual angle. The eye and head movements were recorded during the movie, which was 15 min. The movie included scenes of people performing activities such as walking in the streets, surfing, paragliding, and playing football, and nature scenes such as the sun rising, a sea of clouds, flowers, animals. The distribution of eye orientation was biased in the direction of head orientation. When the head was oriented to the left/right, the eyes also tended to orient to the left/right relative to the head. An important finding of the third experiment was that the eye-head coordination in the vertical direction was similar to that in the horizontal direction. In the first and second experiments, the vertical eye direction was distributed around the orientation of the head without showing a bias toward the direction of the head. Figure 5.8 shows the peak eye directions estimated from the Gaussian functions fitted to pooled data as in the previous experiments. In addition to the eye-head coordination in the horizontal direction, there was a similar tendency for the vertical direction. The distribution of eye orientation was biased in the direction of head orientation. When the head was oriented to the top/bottom, the eyes also tended to orient to the top/bottom relative to the head. The reason why we found that the eye orientation was biased toward the head orientation, even for the vertical direction in this experiment, may be because of the image size. The vertical dimensions of the stimuli were was 34, 44 and 53/90° (farther/closer viewing distance) for the first, second and third experiments, respectively. It is not surprising that the head moves more when there is a larger field of view. A question still remains as to why there is no eye-head coordination for field sizes smaller than 44°. Although we have no answer to this question, this is consistent with the finding from a single gaze shift that there is little head movement for a small gaze shift. Thus, this eye-head coordination may be unique to large gaze shifts.

Fig. 5.8 Peak eye directions estimated from the Gaussian functions fitted to each participant and averaged over all participants. The *top* panel shows horizontal movements and the *bottom* panel shows vertical movements. The *red* symbols and line represent the viewing distance of 110 cm and a smaller size of visual angle, and the *blue* symbols and line represent the viewing distance of 55 cm and the larger size of the visual angle

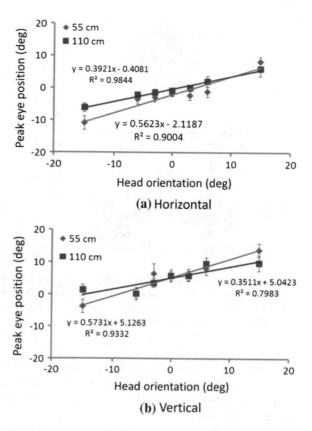

(a) Horizontal

(b) Vertical

5.2.2 Eye-Head Coordination and Visual Perception

The finding that there is similar eye-head coordination in different conditions suggests that head orientation is directly related to visual perception. Although the eyes do not orient in the same direction as the head, the difference between the eye and head orientation is smaller when the head moves, compared with the condition without head movements; that is, head movement reduces the difference. Studies of single gaze shifts have shown that the head tends to be immobile when the gaze shift is small: an estimation of the range for the immobile head is less than about 30° on average. To investigate the influence of head orientation on visual perception, Nakashima and Shioiri conducted visual search experiments in the present project [31, 32]. They controlled the head orientation: the head was oriented 30° in one condition (lateral viewing condition) and it was oriented straight ahead in the other (front viewing condition). The eye location relative to the stimulus display was virtually the same, and the visual system received identical retinal stimulation between the two conditions. Even with the same retinal stimulation, there was a difference in the reaction time to detect the target (the task was to respond to the orientation of

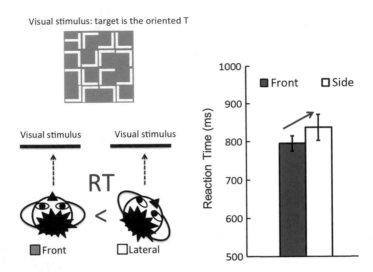

Fig. 5.9 Experimental condition (*left*) and reaction time results. There are two conditions: the head oriented to the visual stimulus in the front viewing condition, and the head oriented 30° from the visual stimulus in the lateral viewing condition. The reaction time is the time to detect and respond to the direction of the target T (*left* or *right*)

the target (left/right) as quickly as possible). A shorter reaction time was found in the front viewing condition, compared with the lateral viewing condition. That is, better performance was found when looking straight ahead (front viewing) than when looking to the side (lateral viewing).

The coordination of the eye and head movements supports the possible facilitation effect of visual processing via head orientation. It was found in the visual search experiment with the 360° surrounding display that there were frequent multiple gaze shifts during a single head movement [29], as shown in Fig. 5.4: the eye jumps twice (two sequential saccadic eye movements) during a single head movement to shift the gaze twice. If there were only one gaze shift in this case, the difference between the eye and head orientations would be larger, which could impair the visual perception (see Fig. 5.9). The analysis of the eye-head coordination revealed that single head movements with multiple saccades constituted as much as 57% of the total head movements with saccades in the visual search experiment in a 360° field of view. These results are different from those of studies using simple tasks, where eye-head coordination was derived from a single head movement with one saccade [27, 28]. No multiple saccades are found in such conditions in general, except for corrective saccades that are much smaller than a primary saccade. Multiple saccades may be critical to the performance of relatively difficult tasks, such as a visual search with sequential gaze shifts. Multiple saccades are one type of eye-head coordination that makes the difference between the eye and head orientations smaller. This smaller difference between the eye and head orientations possibly facilitates visual processing if front viewing is better than lateral viewing [31, 32].

The effect of eye-head coordination on visual perception is important for estimating intention based on gait as in the present project, or on action in general. To focus on an object, the head tends to orient to the object as well as the eye and attention. It is not only the eye, but the head and perhaps the body as well, that is the window to the mind.

5.2.3 Gaze Prediction with Head Orientation

The eye-head coordination results suggest that head orientation can be used to predict gaze location. The distribution of eye position varies systematically dependently on head orientation (Figs. 5.6, 5.7 and 5.8), and the reason that the head orients to the object of interest is to facilitate visual processing (Fig. 5.9). If head orientation can be used to predict gaze location, it has an advantage in terms of the effect on field of application. Usually gaze prediction systems work best for tasks, image types and other conditions specific to the situation of interest. Machine learning techniques are used to build an attention model with a certain bias toward a given task and image type [24], but the model cannot be applied to other tasks and image types easily. The eye-head coordination is general, and can be used without much restriction in terms of tasks and images, although head orientation needs to be measured using a device such as a monitoring camera.

Nakashima et al. proposed a method of gaze prediction using head orientation [26]. The basic idea of the model is to combine the head orientation effect and an attention model of the saliency map, which describes how much an area of the image attracts attention based on low-level visual features (bottom-up attention). The proposed model uses the eye position distribution for a given head orientation to the weighted value of saliency, using the knowledge of eye-head coordination experimentally obtained. The distribution of eye position is estimated based on head orientation, and used as the weighting function. In this study, we apply this model to an experiment using natural scenes presented on a 100-inch screen with 228 museum visitors (the second eye-head-coordination experiment).

Our model uses a saliency map [20], and modulates the map with head direction using weighting functions (Fig. 5.10b). To calculate the saliency map, visual input is decomposed into a set of topographic feature maps, such as those for color and orientation. The feature maps represent the spatial distribution of saliency of the individual features. The information from the individual feature maps is integrated into one map after normalization, and this is the saliency map. The saliency map estimates the activity of the visual cortex, and it is assumed that an area with higher cortical activity attracts attention and, thus, fixation. For each image, a saliency map was calculated following Itti et al. [19].

Assuming that head orientation is given, our model estimates the eye position distribution approximated by a Gaussian function for the head orientation. For this purpose, the relationship between the head orientation and the peak of the eye position distribution was modeled by a linear function as shown by the line in Fig. 5.6. Using

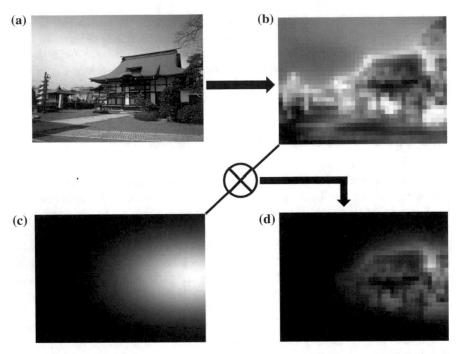

Fig. 5.10 The concept of gaze prediction using head orientation. **b** shows the saliency map of the input image **a**. **c** shows weights of fixation probability estimated from head orientation. **d** shows the gaze prediction map realized by multiplying the saliency map (b) and the weighting function **c**. Reproduced, with permission, from [26]

the linear function, the peak of the eye distribution function was derived for the head orientation. For the spatial spread of the weighting function, the model uses the average of the space constant of Gaussian functions fitted to the experimental results for different head directions. The weighting function was also a Gaussian function, so the peak and the space constant determined the shape. The weighting function was calculated from the head orientation measured experimentally (Fig. 5.10c), at each fixation location during the 5 s of picture viewing. The saliency map was modulated by the weighting function with multiplication for each fixation period to provide the model output of gaze prediction, the prediction map (Fig. 5.10d). The prediction map, therefore, changed with time alongside the head movements. The study used three additional models for gaze prediction for comparison. The first was the original saliency map; the second was our model but without eye-head coordination, which used the head orientation as the peak of the weighting function; and the third was weighted higher at the center of the stimulus scene, which models the tendency to look at the center of the images (the center bias). The last two models used the same spatial spread of the weighting function as the proposed model.

To evaluate model prediction, the study counted the number of fixations within the area defined by the model as the most probable one to attend to, which was the area with a weighted saliency value (or gaze prediction values) larger than a given threshold. If the prediction of the model is perfect, all the fixations should be within the area, and the percentage of fixations inside the area to all fixations should be 100%, with a lower percentage indicating a less accurate prediction. For the evaluation, the study divided the data into two halves. The eye-head-coordination data were obtained from one of the halves, which was then used for prediction of the other half. The head orientation was used from each participant, and was independent of the model. There was no overlap of participants and stimulus images between the two data sets: one for prediction and the other for testing.

To obtain the general characteristics of the model prediction, we drew receiver operating characteristics (ROC) curves for each model. For this purpose, the percentage of fixations inside the prediction area (hit rate) was calculated for different levels for the prediction values (threshold level): from 10% to 90% with steps of 10%. The top 10% area was determined so that the area size was 10% of the whole field and the gaze prediction values inside the area was larger than the levels outside. The ROC curve is the hit rate as a function of the threshold level (Fig. 5.11a). The study obtained the area under the ROC curve (AUC) to compare accuracy levels

Fig. 5.11 Evaluation results for each gaze prediction model: **a** ROC curves of the models. All of our proposed models are saliency maps with Gaussian distributions whose centers are head direction (head-direction model), the peak of the eye position distribution based on head direction (eye-head-coordination model), and the center of the images (image-center bias model). **b** AUCs of the models. Error bars indicate standard errors across the different scenes. Reproduced, with permission, from [26]

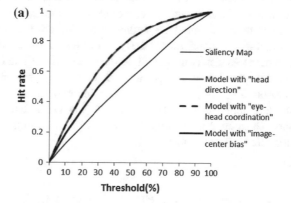

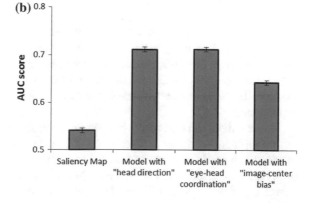

for different models. A larger AUC indicates a better prediction, because the AUC increases with more gaze fixations within higher saliency scores.

Figure 5.11b compares the prediction accuracy among four different models. Accuracy for the models with head direction information (either with or without eye-head coordination) was higher than that of the other two, and the accuracy of the center bias model was higher than that of the saliency map model. There was no significant difference between the two methods that used head direction information. This result indicates that the gaze bias from the head center based on head direction has little effect on gaze prediction accuracy. This is not surprising, because the variance of the Gaussian function is much larger than the peak shift in relation to head direction. Note that this does not imply that the eye-head coordination is completely useless. Recent analysis using the data from watching a movie from an 85-inch 8K UHDTV (the third experiment) [30] shows that the prediction accuracy is higher with eye-head coordination than without it. Although the result is still preliminary, there may be larger effects of eye-head coordination for movies than for static scenes (i.e., a higher slope in Fig. 5.8 than in Fig. 5.7).

The proposed model clearly shows the importance of head orientation for estimating gaze locations. It is interesting to consider the relationship of fixation to center bias. The center bias of gaze is usually consistent with the head orientation bias, because the head directs the center of the stimulus in typical experiments to record gaze shifts on stimuli. The studies of the present project showed the effect of head orientation independently of the center of the stimulus, which suggests that the center bias of the gaze may be a result of the head bias [29], at least partially. A central bias to the display has been reported with success in a model of attention to predict gaze location [33]. The prediction accuracy in our study showed that the model with head orientation (and eye-head coordination) was better than the model with image-center bias. Thus, head orientation likely plays a more important role in gaze estimation compared with the center bias.

5.2.4 Towards Gaze Prediction with Gait Information

We have described so far that gaze can be predicted accurately using head orientation. The goal of the present project is to build a system to predict gaze from gait information. Following studies of eye-head coordination and its application to gaze prediction, we investigated the relationship between gait information and gaze location. To measure gaze information during walking, we conducted the following experiments.

We constructed an immersive environment consisting of a treadmill and surrounding multiple screens and projectors as shown in Fig. 5.12. Figure 5.13 shows its metric. Each participant walked on the treadmill while gazing at the target object projected on the screens. The screens showed a corridor-like virtual space, which flowed based on the treadmill speed to make the participant feel as if they were actually walking in that space. There was also a gaze target (50 cm diameter, green sphere,

Fig. 5.12 Immersive
walking environment

Fig. 5.13 Dimension of the
immersive environment

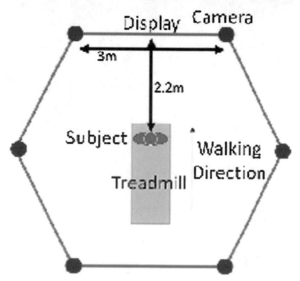

7.6° × 7.6° of visual angle from the participant). The target randomly appeared at
five positions as shown in Fig. 5.14. Six cameras connected to a motion capture
system (Bonita 10, Vicon Motion Systems Ltd., UK) were located around the environment. Using the motion capture system, we could obtain all body positions and
poses, including those of the head and chest.

Figure 5.15 shows the relationship between the gaze and head directions and
between the gaze and chest directions during walking. The horizontal axes denote
the gaze directions and the vertical axes denote the head or chest directions. In these
graphs, the obtained data and the averages and standard deviations of all participants
are shown. The dotted lines denote robust regression results. From these graphs, we
find that the angles of the gaze, head and chest have linear relationships similar to
those under the non-walking condition discussed in Sect. 2.1, even under the walking
condition.

Fig. 5.14 Target positions

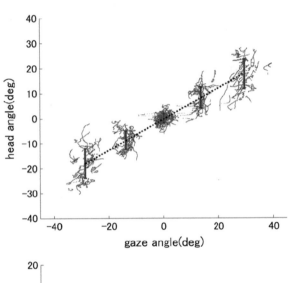

Fig. 5.15 Gaze-head and
gaze-chest relationships
while walking

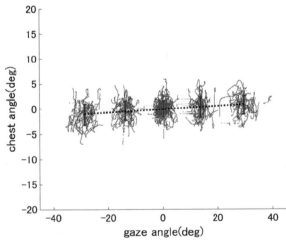

Moreover, it was found that not only the head but also the arm and leg movements are related to the gaze location. When the head was oriented to the left relative to the body, the right arm appeared to move more, as did the left leg [34, 35]. These results suggest that the arm and leg movements can be used to predict head orientation, which in turn predicts gaze location.

5.3 Attention-Oriented Pedestrian Group Segmentation

In the course of daily life, we are often with others in social groups such as family and coworkers. When we are in such groups, our actions are strongly affected by and have a strong effect on other members. Therefore, investigating social relationships is an important way to understand and/or infer our daily activities. In this section, we propose a method for determining social groups by analyzing time-series range data.

Many studies have been conducted on segmenting individuals into social groups. Most of them use human trajectories for segmentation. Typically, some features are computed from the trajectories and predetermined criteria or machine learning techniques are applied to the feature values for segmenting groups. Needless to say, additional features should be used if available.

Our idea is to extract a change of attention as a feature for group segmentation. As an example of this idea, consider the situation of walking with friends. We often talk with each other and make gestures for communication. During such interactions, our attention is directed, through speech and/or body language, toward a target, that is, the people with whom we are interacting. In contrast, two people who do not have a social relationship usually do not interact in this way while walking, even if they are in close proximity. This observation implies that we can discern whether two people are interacting with each other by observing their attentional shifts as signaled with speech and/or body language.

Our proposed method uses three types of information to determine whether two people are in the same group. The first is the motion trajectory, which has been commonly used in previous work. We also use chest orientation as a cue for human attention. To obtain these data, we use range sensors placed at chest height. Finally, we use video recording to detect gestures indicating that an interaction is occurring between people. We believe that the combination of this information enables us to detect social groups more accurately.

From the extracted features of motion trajectory, chest orientation, and video, we build a classifier to determine social groups. The classifier is based on multiple instance learning (MIL). When we are walking with a friend or colleague, we do not interact with them all the time. This means that meaningful information for group detection is embedded within only certain parts of the time-series data. To segment social groups accurately, we must detect the meaningful information and ignore the rest. MIL is used for efficiently detecting and focusing on the meaningful features.

To examine the proposed method, we conducted experiments using a practical data set, which was collected on a university campus. The experimental results show that the proposed method outperforms the existing method.

In the following sections, we first introduce related work in Sect. 5.3.1. We outline the proposed method in Sect. 5.3.2. Finally, we present experimental results in Sect. 5.3.3.

5.3.1 Related Work

As previously discussed, the most straightforward and essential information for group detection is a shared motion trajectory [36, 37]. However, additional information has been investigated for more effective group detection. Human attention is one of the most promising clues that reflects interaction among group members [38–40]. Our work is inspired by Chamveha [39], who also used attentional cues; however, we also use range sensors as input devices, videos for detecting interactions, and MIL to add efficiency in group detection.

Laser range sensors are widely used for obtaining reliable data, even outdoors. Scenarios for applying this work include pedestrian tracking [41]. It is relevant to note here that, to the best of our knowledge, existing studies have employed range sensors placed at leg height. This is because these studies have only considered the "footprint" of pedestrians. As mentioned earlier, consideration of human attention will enhance our understanding of human behavior. Our work aims to extend the possibilities of range sensor-based human analysis.

5.3.2 Proposed Method

The main features of our proposed method are twofold: (1) using the MIL framework for accurate and efficient group discovery, and (2) using video processing to detect gestural actions that indicate interactions. We describe each feature in the following section.

5.3.2.1 MIL Framework for Group Segmentation

In the latter part of the process, we pick two participants and classify whether or not they are in the same group. This is a common approach used in various studies [39].

Even when we are walking with another individual or a group, we do not interact with the other group member(s) all of the time. For example, each member of a group is sometimes looking at different objects, and at that moment, no interaction is observed among them. Many conventional approaches such as that used by Chamveha [39] employ a histogram of feature values. Histogram-based feature

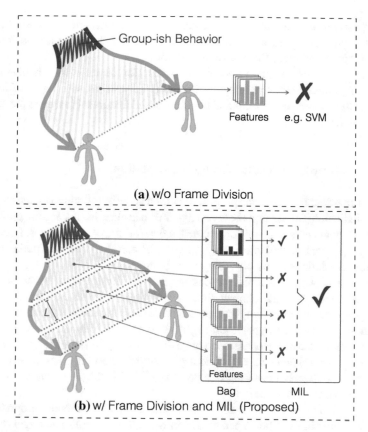

Fig. 5.16 Temporal Frame Division **a** conventional approach (w/o temporal division), **b** proposed approach

representation is commonly used because of its robustness. However, in our application scenarios, the irrelevant behavior contained in histograms conceals the relevant features.

MIL [42] can treat this type of ambiguity efficiently. A set of training data (instances) is treated as a bag, and each bag has a label. If a bag contains at least one positive instance, the bag becomes positive. If all of the contents of a bag are negative, the bag becomes negative.

In our case, as shown in Fig. 5.16, we divide time-series data $D = \{D_i\}$ into several subsets of data with shorter time lengths $D^{(k)}$, $D = \bigcup D^{(k)}$. Each subset is an instance in a bag for MIL. The bag consists of instances extracted from a single pair of walking participants. As mentioned earlier, even when two people are in the same group, not all of the instances will be clues to their social connection. Hence, all instances cannot be treated as positive examples, but at least one instance is positive.

We should note that the benefit of the MIL framework is in the training process. It is quite difficult to manually detect relevant actions for group discovery from long time-series data that include irrelevant behaviors. MIL automatically finds the relevant instance, i.e., actions, from a set of instances when the set is a positive bag. This significantly reduces the cost of annotation.

We use the same feature values for classification as used by Chamveha [39] because they have yielded reasonable results. Briefly stated, two types of features are used: attention-based features and position-based features. Please see the original paper for details.

5.3.2.2   Gesture Detection for Group Segmentation

Another important feature of the proposed method is the use of video images to detect gestures indicating interactions between a pair of participants. As argued previously, interactions between two people are a clue for determining social groups. Even when the two people are not walking closely together, we can still observe whether the two have a social relationship by observing their interactions.

In this paper, we use a simple processing method for detecting gestures such as pointing and hand-waving. Human action recognition is an active research area in the computer vision community and remains a challenging topic, especially in actual application scenarios. Our goal is not to classify a video into multiple action classes. If we can simply detect the occurrence of gestures, even without understanding what the gestures are, this can be a sufficient cue to understanding how a certain kind of interaction occurs between the two people. With this rationale, we use a simple method for gesture detection.

Figure 5.17 depicts a feature for gesture detection. We compute an optical flow for an observed video. When a person makes a gesture, its motion is larger than that of a normal walking action. Both Fig. 5.17a, b correspond to the optical flow for gestures. We can see large flows for both cases. To measure the likelihood that this

Fig. 5.17 Gesture Detection based on Optical Flow. Hue and saturation correspond to the orientation and strength of flows

(a) **(b)**

flow contains a gesture, we compute the feature $G = V_{max}/V_{min}$, where V_{max} and V_{min} denote the maximum and minimum of the strength of the optical flow. When G is large, the person is more likely to be making a gesture.

After computing the feature G, we simply concatenate it with information from other features introduced in the previous section. Each obtained feature is classified using the MIL framework.

5.3.3   Experiments

To confirm the basic effectiveness of the proposed method, we have carried out experiments using real data captured in a university building and a shopping mall.

5.3.3.1   Data Acquisition in a University Building

As mentioned in the previous section, we used a set of laser range sensors placed at chest height. A 2D range map captured by the range sensors can be integrated into a single map in a unified coordinate system. In the integrated range map, we subtract a background map from the obtained map and apply a conventional segmentation method to the subtracted map. Each segment can be assumed to be a person. Next, we fit an ellipse to the segmented map. The two axes of the ellipse are chosen so that they correspond to the body size. The ellipse has some "thickness" to allow for variations in body size. Finally, we connect the positions of the fitted ellipses to those detected in the previous frame, and obtain the time-series positions of walking people. We can assume that the shorter axis of the fitted ellipse indicates the chest direction. Because we found that the axis direction was not stable in a single frame, we applied temporal filtering to the direction for stabilization.

During data collection, various groups appear in the scene. One or more groups are instructed to move from a start point to a goal point. In some cases, each person in a group has a different start or goal point. Various kinds of instructions enable us to obtain a variety of group actions; however, instructions are only relevant to the start and goal positions. While walking between these two points, the people act naturally, without any instructions.

5.3.3.2   ATC Dataset

To evaluate the proposed method in more realistic scenarios, we used a public data set collected in a shopping mall. The dataset [43–45] hereafter ATC dataset, includes the positions and chest directions of walking pedestrians in a shopping mall. These data are collected using range sensors that are mounted so that walking people in a wide area can be monitored. The ATC dataset also includes manually annotated information about the group membership of the people. The dataset cannot be used for evaluating group detection using gesture because the data do not include visual information taken by cameras. However, the data can be used for the MIL-based group detection, which only requires trajectories and chest directions. Note that this dataset was collected by the CREST project led by Dr. Takayuki Kanda. Further details of the ATC dataset are described in Drazen [43].

5.3.3.3   Experiment 1—MIL Framework

First, we conducted an evaluation of the effect of the MIL framework described in Sect. 5.3.2.1. Table 5.1 summarizes the quantitative evaluation of the group segmentation results when the whole data set is divided into subsets of time length $L = 210$, where "w/o MIL" means that we did not divide the whole time-series data set. This can be regarded as the result of [39]. The MIL framework yields better results in terms of precision, recall, and F-measure.

To see the effect of the parameter L, we changed the parameter and evaluated performance. The graph in Fig. 5.18 shows the performance changes. The horizontal axis is the time length L. The dotted line shows the results when the whole data set is not divided. According to the graph, the choice of L has a strong effect on performance, so it should be determined for each individual scene.

Figure 5.19 shows typical examples of correctly and incorrectly classified samples. (a), (b), and (c) are successfully detected group pairs. (d) and (e) are false-positive samples, because the two participants are walking or standing close together but are

Table 5.1 Quantitative classification results for the MIL framework

	Proposed ($L = 210$) (%)	w/o MIL [39] (%)
Precision	**87.2**	85.7
Recall	**95.6**	90.3
F-measure	**91.2**	87.9

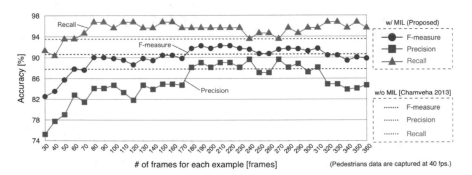

Fig. 5.18 Group Classification Results (Relationship between frame length and classification accuracy)

Fig. 5.19 Typical Classification Results Using Frame Division. **a**, **b**, and **c** are successfully detected group pairs even when they are not walking together all the time; **d** is an incorrectly detected pair that is coincidentally walking closely; **e** also shows incorrectly detected pairs who are not in a group but are standing closely; and **f** is an example of misdetection

not in the same group. (f) is a false-negative sample because the two participants are in the same group but have no interaction.

Next, the MIL framework was tested using the ATC dataset. We choose 1090 pedestrians, including 68 group pairs. The data were collected between 10 am and 11 am on January 9th, 2013. Table 5.2 summarizes the quantitative evaluation as in Table 5.1. These results also demonstrate that the MIL framework yields better results even under more realistic scenarios.

Figure 5.20 shows the relationship between time length L and accuracy, as in Fig. 5.18. Although performance varies as the time length changes, it is almost always better than the results without the MIL framework. Figure 5.21 shows the trajectories of a group pair. The pair was not classified as "in the same group" without the MIL

Table 5.2 Quantitative classification results for the MIL framework (ATC dataset)

	Proposed ($L = 240$) (%)	w/o MIL [39] (%)
Precision	**92.6**	87.1
Recall	**92.6**	89.7
F-measure	**92.6**	88.4

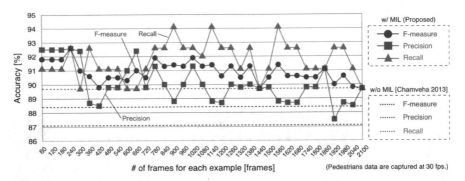

Fig. 5.20 Group classification results of ATC dataset (Relationship between frame length and classification accuracy)

Fig. 5.21 Typical Classification results using frame division (ATC dataset: these two persons are correctly classified as group members)

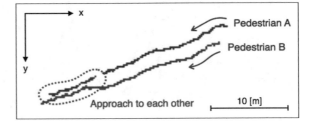

framework because the pair did not walk closely together. By applying the MIL framework, the pair was classified correctly as a group. This is a typical benefit of the proposed framework.

5.3.3.4 Experiment 2—Group Discovery Using Gesture Detection

When we take into account gesture detection described in Sect. 5.3.2.2, we add a scale factor C to the gesture likelihood G. We evaluated the performance at various values of C. Table 5.3 shows the results. Compared with no gesture detection, the parameter $C = 0.09$ produces the best result. Although we have to choose the parameter carefully, incorporating gesture detection has a positive effect on overall performance.

Table 5.3 Group classification results using gesture detection (Frame Length $L = 100$)

	w/o gesture features	w/ gesture features			
		$C = 0.07$	$C = 0.08$	$C = 0.09$	$C = 0.1$
True-Positive	96.7	94.6	94.6	95.6	92.4
False-Positive	6.5	5.4	4.4	4.4	4.4
F-measure	0.952	0.946	0.951	0.957	0.940

Fig. 5.22 Successful detection of group pair using gesture detection

Fig. 5.23 Successfully suppressed false detection using gesture detection

Fig. 5.24 Misdetected group pair using gesture detection

Figures 5.22, 5.23, and 5.24 show typical examples. Figure 5.22 is an example of a case in which gesture detection works well. This pair can only be classified successfully using gesture detection. Figure 5.23 is also an example of a successful result. In this case, the original method incorrectly detects a non-group pair as a group. This is because the two participants walk very closely together. By incorporating gesture detection, we can set an appropriate decision boundary for distance-related features. Finally, Fig. 5.24 is an example of the negative effects of the proposed method. Originally, the two participants are not detected as a group pair. However, one of the two participants incidentally makes a gesture that does not correspond to an interaction with the other participant. Gesture detection incorrectly detects the gesture, and the two are classified as a group pair.

5.4 Dual-Task Analysis for Cognitive Level Estimation

As mentioned, more than 4.4 million people in Japan present with dementia, while 37 thousand present with early-onset dementia due to cerebral vascular disease. Thus, dementia affects a large percentage of the population, and can threaten any individual as they age. Moreover, as the symptoms of dementia worsen, they can cause secondary damage, such as difficulties with interpersonal communication, co-morbid mental disorders such as depression, and loss of confidence and motivation. It is thus important to detect dementia in its early stage and treat individuals accordingly. However, dementia can be difficult to diagnose because there are often no clear symptoms in the early stages. In other words, by the time that symptoms are visible, dementia has generally progressed to a certain degree. It is therefore important to assess recognition function in our everyday lives.

Although cognitive ability can be assessed using interviews or questionnaires, these are often quite time-consuming and can thus be challenging methods for examining large numbers of people. Thus, assessments that involve simply observing activities in daily life are preferable. Among these, the "dual-task" method (Fig. 5.25) has received attention because it has been useful in identifying the early stages of dementia. Indeed, it has already been introduced in several elderly facilities and hospitals. However, that the assessment is subjective, i.e. it is performed by a doctor or a clinical psychologist, is problematic.

Considering the above situation, our goal was to develop a system that can be used to objectively assess cognitive ability by observing dual-task performance via sensors, such as cameras, range sensors, and microphones. We began by collecting observations from a diverse group of people, ranging from young healthy individuals to older adults with dementia. We extracted features that could be used to assess cognitive abilities. This section describes the measurement systems that we developed for this purpose and introduces some recent results obtained using our systems.

Fig. 5.25 Dual-task method for assessment of cognitive ability

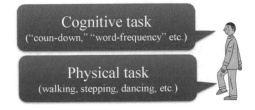

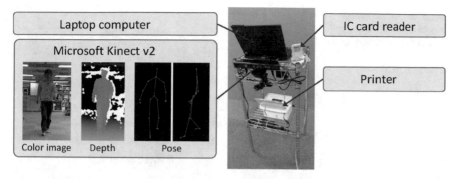

Fig. 5.26 Mobile measurement system

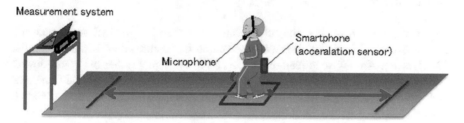

Fig. 5.27 Environmental setting for dual-task observation

5.4.1 Data Collection in an Elderly Care Facility

5.4.1.1 System Overview

We sought to collect data from elderly people with dementia. To this end, we designed a mobile measurement system that could be easily transported to elderly care facilities. Figure 5.26 shows the mobile system we constructed, which comprised a Microsoft Kinect and a laptop computer. An IC card reader was connected to the system for management of participant data.

As shown in Fig. 5.27, for the data collection, we prepared a pathway and located the measurement systems at its end points. Each participant was asked to perform stepping and walking back and forth along the pathway, and to perform the stepping/walking while engaged in cognitive tasks (dual-task). There were two kinds of cognitive tasks: a "count-down" task (reciting numbers from one hundred in descending order in a certain amount of time) and a "word-frequency" task (saying words which begin with a certain letter), which are standard tasks in clinical settings. For data analysis, we needed ground-truth score information about participant cognitive abilities in addition to our observations. We adopted the Mini-Mental State Examination (MMSE), which is a standard metric often used in elderly facilities. It ranges from 0 to 30; 30 means that a person has normal cognitive ability, and less than 23 signifies possible dementia.

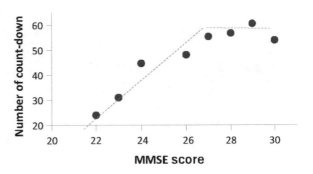

Fig. 5.28 Relationship between MMSE score and the number of "count-down"

5.4.1.2 Results

We thoroughly investigated the relationships between the MMSE score and any features extracted from the observation to search for features that would predict the MMSE score. Among such features, we used the average number of "count-down" numbers given in Fig. 5.28 The figure shows a curve, indicated by a dotted line. For MMSE scores ranging from 20 to 27, the number and the score are well correlated, and this converges with a "count-down" score of about 60, where the MMSE score is more than 27. Thus, the better the cognitive ability of a participant, the more numbers he/she can tell in a certain period. However the number cannot be larger than about 60.

5.4.2 Huge Data Collection in Miraikan

Throughout the process of data collection in elderly care facilities, as described in Sect. 5.4.1, we found several features that predict MMSE score. Thus, it should be possible to assess cognitive ability from the dual-task observation. On the other hand, we also found that we needed an increasingly large number of participants to ensure the reliability of the results. As we performed the data collection using identical procedures, doubling or tripling the number of participants doubled or tripled the length of the data collection period. Thus, the experiment was very time-consuming and a large effort was required to obtain a large dataset.

To address this problem, we adopted a new experimental method: We designed a fully automatic demonstration system (Figs. 5.29 and 5.30) that could administer the dual-task procedure and collect data and positioned the system in the National Museum of Emerging Science and Innovation, known as "Miraikan". Miraikan is located in the Tokyo bay area and receives several thousands of visitors per day. The demonstration period was approximately one year; from 15 July 2015 to 27 June 2016. With the help of Miraikan, the demonstration was optimized so that participants could enjoy it as if it were a game. Figure 5.31 shows the statistics of

Fig. 5.29 Demonstration system in Miraikan

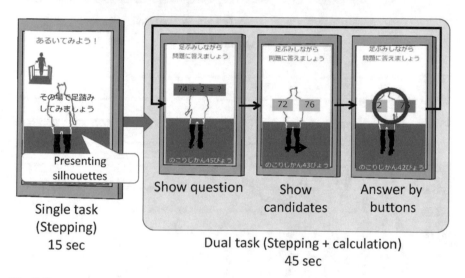

Fig. 5.30 Flow of demonstration

the participants. As a result, we collected data from more than 95,000 participants, making it one of the largest datasets in the world.[1]

---

[1] We also placed another system in Miraikan. It captures videos of a person walking from multiple viewpoints. The video dataset obtained by the system is not for assessment of cognitive ability but for gait authentication purpose, which is an most important research topic for us. This dataset is also among the largest in the world.

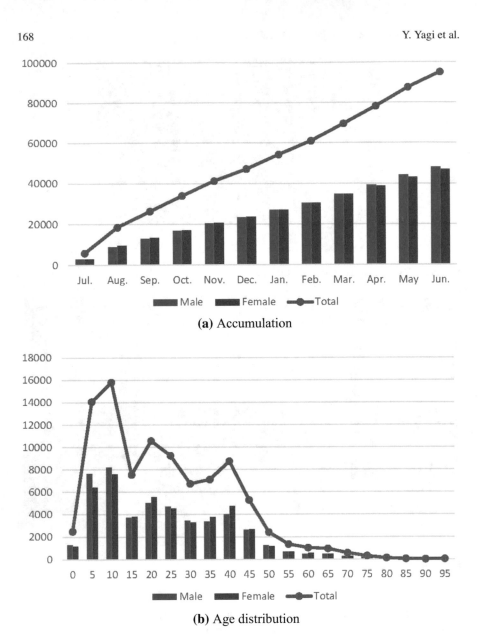

(a) Accumulation

(b) Age distribution

Fig. 5.31 Statistics of demonstration in Miraikan

5.5 Discussion and Future Work

The achievements in Sects. 5.2 and 5.3 have great potential to be applied in our daily lives, especially in commercial facilities. By applying the models and knowledge in Sect. 5.2 and extending them to more natural cases, it should be possible to estimate attention of each customer from his/her behaviors captured by security cameras, which are located anywhere in such facilities nowadays. When it is realized, it might be possible to detect shoplifters from his/her suspicious gaze behavior. It should be also possible to find customers who are interested in a certain product and effectively give them salient information about promotions and sales. Indeed, there have already been several works that analyzed the relation between person's intention or interest and his/her gaze behavior motivated by the similar consideration to ours. They are, however, still quite far from real applications, because in all those studies they need eye-trackers, which is in fact an unsatisfied condition; customers and shoplifters will never wear wearable eye-trackers, and a stationary eye-tracker usually has very limited view area so that it is impossible to measure gaze of a person walking freely around the space. We can conclude, therefore, our techniques for gaze estimation without eye-tracker have a really great impact for reaching the expected future. In addition, the achievements in Sect. 5.3 also take on an important role in the commercial facility scenario. In the course of daily activities, humans often form social groups, such as families and groups of coworkers. When we are in such groups, our actions are strongly affected by and have a large effect on other group members. If we can know how many groups there are in the space, which group each person belongs to, what kind of group each of them is, which person in a group is taking initiative, for example, it is helpful for a facility manager to analyze purchasing behaviors of customers and offer commercial advertisement effectively.

The systems for cognitive level assessment and experiences in the elderly facilities are also important achievements in this project. The design/process/stability of the systems have been evaluated from several viewpoints; system developers (the members in the project including the authors) who chose sensors and implemented software, staffs in the elderly facilities who observe the elderly/dementia people every day, and the elderly people who are in fact the participants of the systems. Especially the long-term exhibition in Miraikan, whose details are mentioned in Sect. 5.4.2, was a meaningful opportunity for establishing a good system. Through the one-year exhibition, the system was well brushed up and became stable, safe, and interesting for the participants. Fortunately, the improved system was decided to be installed in the elderly facilities for long-term (more than three years) data collection. By the data collection, we will obtain another kind of data; long-term history of the dual-task performance of a certain person combined with cognitive level assessed by clinical psychotherapists. It is really interesting data because it would be possible to model degradation of cognitive level, which is meaningful to realize "prediction" of dementia.

5.6 Conclusion

Gait has been regarded as one of biometrics and thus mainly studies for authentication task. In that scenario it is implicitly assumed that the gait of a certain person is always constant. It is, however, untrue in reality; a person usually walks differently according to their mood and physical/mental conditions. In our project "Behavior Understanding based on Intention-Gait Model" supported by JST-CREST, therefore, we focused on the variation of gait within a person, and have studied the relation between the gait variation to the inertial states. This chapter introduced some of our achievements related to three kinds of the inertial states; attention (gaze direction), human relation (group segmentation), and cognitive level (assessment of dementia). Though those about attention and human relation estimation are on still developing stage, they indicate possibility of realizing skill of "reading minds." Those about cognitive level assessment are also important contribution for the coming "super-aging society." We would be happy if our achievements would contribute to make our daily lives safer, more convenient, and more agreeable.

Acknowledgements We appreciate Honorary Professor Masatsugu Kidode in Nara Institute of Science and Technology for his great contribution as an editorial supervisor of this chapter.
Section 5.2 describes achievements by Mr. Yu Fang, Dr. Ryoichi Nakashima, Dr. Yasuhiro Hatori, and Associate Professor Kazumichi Matsumiya in Tohoku University. Section 5.3 is about the collaborative research with Professor Kazuhiko Sumi in Aoyama Gakuin University and Mr. Ryota Sato in Kindai University. The dual-task system in Sect. 5.4 was constructed in collaboration with Dr. Mitsuru Nakazawa, Dr. Masataka Niwa, Dr. Kota Aoki and Assistant Professor Fumio Okura in Osaka University, and Lecturer Hirotake Yamazoe in Ritsumeikan University. We appreciate these members for their efforts in the project.
This project was also supported by some institutes. Dr. Takayuki Kanda in ATR, who is a leader of another CREST project, and his colleagues Dr. Drazen Brscic and Dr. Satoshi Satake had discussion with our projects members to share ideas several times during our project period. Moreover, They kindly shared their datasets captured in a commercial facility. The ideas and datasets helped us to get better achievements. Mr. Masuhiro Okuda, who is the president of Social Welfare Corporation "Misasagikai," kindly believed the future we designed about elderly care systems, and gave us many opportunity to capture data of elderly people in his facilities, and accepted us to locate our dual-task system in each building. Staffs in his facilities were also kind and contributed professionally for our project. This project would never achieve the success without his understanding and help. We sincerely appreciate him for the contribution.
We also acknowledge the discussion to initiate the study in the meeting of the Cooperative Research Project of the Research Institute of Electrical Communication in Tohoku University and the Institute of Scientific and Industrial Research in Osaka University.

References

1. N. Lynnerup, J. Vedel, Person identification by gait analysis and photogrammetry. J. Forensic Sci. **50**(1), 112–118 (2005)
2. J. Han, B. Bhanu, Individual recognition using gait energy image. IEEE Trans. Pattern Anal. Mach. Intell. **28**, 316–322 (2006)
3. Y. Makihara, R. Sagawa, Y. Mukaigawa, T. Echigo, Y. Yagi, Gait recognition using a view transformation model in the frequency domain, in *Proceedings of the 9th European Conference on Computer Vision*, pp. 151–163, 2006
4. Y. Makihara, R. Sagawa, Y. Mukaigawa, T. Echigo, Y. Yagi, Adaptation to walking direction changes for gait identification. IEEE Int. Conf. Pattern Recognit. **2**, 96–99 (2006)
5. P.K. Larsen, E.B. Simonsen, N. Lynnerup, Gait analysis in forensic medicine. J. Forensic Sci. **53**(5), 1149–1153 (2008)

6. T.H.W. Lam, K.H. Cheung, J.N.K. Liu, Gait flow image: A silhouette-based gait representation for human identification. Pattern Recognit. **44**, 973–987 (2011)
7. I. Bouchrika, M. Goffredo, J. Carter, M. Nixon, On using gait in forensic biometrics. J. Forensic Sci. **56**(4), 882–889 (2011)
8. S. Zheng, J. Zhang, K. Huang, R. He, T. Tan, Robust View transformation model for gait recognition, in *Proceedings of the IEEE International Conference on Image Processing*, 2011
9. S. Sarkar, P. Jonathon Phillips, Z. Liu, I. Robledo, P. Grother, K.W. Bowyer, The human ID gait challenge problem: data sets, performance, and analysis. IEEE Trans. Pattern Anal. Mach. Intell. **27**(2), 162–177 (2005)
10. H. Iwama, M. Okumura, Y. Makihara, Y. Yagi, The OU-ISIR gait database comprising the large population dataset and performance evaluation of gait recognition. IEEE Trans. Inf. Forensics Secur. **7**(5), 1511–1521 (2012)
11. H. Yamazoe, H. Habe, I. Mitsugami, Y. Yagi, Easy depth sensor calibration. Int. Conf. Pattern Recognit. (2012)
12. M. Nakazawa, I. Mitsugami, H. Habe, H. Yamazoe, Y. Yagi, Calibration of multiple kinects with little overlap regions. IEEJ Trans. Electr. Electron. Eng. **10**(S1) (2015)
13. H. Nakajima, Y. Makihara, H. Hsu, I. Mitsugami, M. Nakazawa, H. Yamazoe, H. Habe, Y. Yagi, Point cloud transport. Inte. Conf. Pattern Recognit. (2012)
14. M. Nakazawa, I. Mitsugami, Y. Makihara, H. Nakajima, H. Yamazoe, H. Habe, Y. Yagi, Dynamic scene reconstruction using asynchronous multiple kinects. Int. Conf. Pattern Recognit. (2012)
15. C. Zhou, I. Mitsugami, Y. Yagi, Detection of elderly gait impairment by Patch-GEI. IEEJ Trans. Electr. Electron. Eng. **10**(S1) (2015)
16. H. Yamazoe, T. Ogawa, I. Mitsugami, Y. Yagi, Gait analysis of simulated left knee disorder, in *9th International Conference on Bio-inspired Information and Communications Technologies* (2015)
17. H. Nakajima, I. Mitsugami, Y. Yagi, Depth-based gait feature representation. IPSJ Trans. Comput. Vis. Appl. **5**, 94–98 (2013)
18. T. Ikeda, I. Mitsugami, Y. Yagi, Depth-based gait authentication for practical sensor settings. IPSJ Trans. Comput. Vis. Appl. **7**, 94–98 (2015)
19. L. Itti, C. Koch, E. Niebur, A model of saliency-based visual attention for rapid scene analysis. IEEE Trans. Pattern Anal. Mach. Intell. **20**, 1254–1259 (1998)
20. L. Itti, C. Koch, Computational modelling of visual attention. Nat. Rev. Neurosci. **2**, 194–203 (2001)
21. H. Kubota, Y. Sugano, T. Okabe, Y. Sato, A. Sugimoto, K. Hiraki, Incorporating visual field characteristics into a saliency map, in *Symposium on Eye Tracking Research and Applications*, pp. 333–336, 2012
22. A. Hiratani, R. Nakashima, K. Matsumiya, K. Kuriki, S. Shioiri, Considerations of self-motion in motion saliency. International Joint Workshop on Advanced Sensing/Visual Attention and Interaction. presented at the International Joint Workshop on Advanced Sensing/Visual Attention and Interaction-Toward Creation of Human-Harmonized Information Technology-, Okinawa, Japan
23. J. Henderson, J.R. Brockmole, M.S. Castelhano, M. Mack, Visual saliency does not account for eye movements during visual search in real-world scenes, in *Eye movements: a window on mind and brain*, ed. by R. van Gompel, M. Fischer, W. Murray, R. Hill (Elsevier, 2007), pp. 537–562
24. A. Torralba, A. Oliva, M.S. Castelhano, J.M. Henderson, Contextual guidance of eye movements in real-world scenes: the role of global features in object search. Psychol. Rev. **113**, 766–86 (2006)
25. A. Kimura, R. Yonetani, T. Hirayama, Computational models of human visual attention and their implementations: a survey. IEICE Trans. Inf. Syst. **96-D**, 562–578 (2013)
26. R. Nakashima, Y. Fang, Y. Hatori, A. Hiratani, K. Matsumiya, I. Kuriki et al., Saliency-based gaze prediction based on head direction. Vis. Res. **117**, 59–66 (2015)

27. J.S. Stahl, Amplitude of human head movements associated with horizontal saccades. Exp. Brain Res. **126**, 41–54 (1999)
28. A.L. Cecala, E.G. Freedman, Amplitude changes in response to target displacements during human eye-head movements. Vis. Res. **48**, 149–66 (2008)
29. Y. Fang, R. Nakashima, K. Matsumiya, I. Kuriki, S. Shioiri, Eye-head coordination for visual cognitive processing. PLoS One **10**, e0121035 (2015)
30. Y. Fang, M. Emoto, R. Nakashima, K. Matsumiya, I. Kuriki, S. Shioiri, Eye-position distribution depending on head orientation when observing movies on ultrahigh-definition television. ITE Trans. Media Technol. Appl. **3**, 149–154 (2015)
31. R. Nakashima, S. Shioiri, Facilitation of visual perception in head direction: visual attention modulation based on head direction. PLoS One **10**, e0124367 (2015)
32. R. Nakashima, S. Shioiri, Why do we move our head to look at an object in our peripheral region? Lateral viewing interferes with attentive search. PLoS One **9**, e92284 (2014)
33. C.H. Tseng, Z. Vidnyanszky, T. Papathomas, G. Sperling, Attention-based long-lasting sensitization and suppression of colors. Vis. Res. **50**, 23–416 (2010)
34. T. Okada, H. Yamazoe, I. Mitsugami, Y. Yagi, Preliminary analysis of gait changes that correspond to gaze directions, in *International Joint Workshop on Advanced Sensing/Visual Attention and Interaction*, pp. 788–792, 2013
35. I. Mitsugami, Y. Nagase, Y. Yagi, Primary analysis of human's gait and gaze direction using motion sensors, in *Asian Conference on Pattern Recognition*, 2011
36. M. Manfredi, R. Vezzani, S. Calderara, R. Cucchiara, Detection of static groups and crowds gathered in open spaces by texture classification. Pattern Recognit. Lett. **44**, 39–48 (2014)
37. M. Zanotto, L. Bazzani, M. Cristani, V. Murino, Online bayesian non-parametrics for social group detection, in *Proceedings of the British Machine Vision Conference* (BMVA Press, 2012), pp. 111.1–111.12
38. S. Calderara, R. Cucchiara, A. Prati, Group detection at camera handoff for collecting people appearance in multi-camera systems, in *Proceedings—IEEE International Conference on Video and Signal Based Surveillance 2006, AVSS 2006*, 2006
39. I. Chamveha, Y. Sugano, Y. Sato, A. Sugimoto, Social group discovery from surveillance videos: a data-driven approach with attention-based cues, in *BMVC 2013*, 2013
40. F. Setti, H. Hung, M. Cristani, Group detection in still images by F-formation modeling: a comparative study, in *2013 14th International Workshop on Image Analysis for Multimedia Interactive Services (WIAMIS)* (IEEE, 2013), pp. 1–4
41. H. Zhao, R. Shibasaki, A novel system for tracking pedestrians using multiple single-row laser-range scanners. IEEE Trans. Syst. Man Cybern. Part A: Syst. Hum. **35**(2), 283–291 (2005)
42. G. Doran, S. Ray, A theoretical and empirical analysis of support vector machine methods for multiple-instance classification. Mach. Learn. **97**(1–2), 1–24 (2013)
43. D. Brscic, T. Kanda, T. Ikeda, T. Miyashita, Person tracking in large public spaces using 3D range sensors. IEEE Trans. Hum.-Mach. Syst. (2013)
44. F. Zanlungo, D. Brscic, T. Kanda, Spatial-size scaling of pedestrian groups under growing density conditions. Phys. Rev. E **91**(6), 062810 (2015)
45. Pedestrian Group Dataset: http://www.irc.atr.jp/sets/groups/

Chapter 6
Inter-Personal Displays: Augmenting the Physical World Where People Get Together

**Takeshi Naemura, Yasuaki Kakehi, Shunsuke Yoshida,
Tomoko Hashida, Naoya Koizumi and Shogo Fukushima**

Abstract The aim of this project is to design and demonstrate the future of information environment where people get together. Personal computers and smart devices have succeeded in augmenting the ability of each person. At now, even when people meet at a place, they tend to gaze at their own displays. As a result, they cannot concentrate on face-to-face communication among them. This means that current information technology well designed for personal activities is insufficient for group ones. The authors believe that this problem is mainly caused by the limitation of current display technology. For exceeding this limitation, this article introduces three approaches: (1) privacy control of display content for promoting discussion in groups, (2) projection-based control of physical objects for suppressing the incompatibility between the physical and digital worlds and (3) spatial imaging for augmented reality among people without wearable displays. These contributions can transform existing personal display technology to novel inter-personal one which is useful for people getting together.

T. Naemura (✉) · S. Fukushima
The University of Tokyo, Tokyo, Japan
e-mail: naemura@nae-lab.org

S. Fukushima
e-mail: shogo@nae-lab.org

Y. Kakehi
Keio University, Kanagawa, Japan
e-mail: ykakehi@sfc.keio.ac.jp

S. Yoshida
National Institute of Information and Communications Technology, Tokyo, Japan
e-mail: shun@nict.go.jp

T. Hashida
Waseda University, Tokyo, Japan
e-mail: hashida@waseda.jp

N. Koizumi
The University of Electro-Communications, Tokyo, Japan
e-mail: koizumi.naoya@uec.ac.jp

© Springer Japan KK 2017
T. Nishida (ed.), *Human-Harmonized Information Technology, Volume 2*,
DOI 10.1007/978-4-431-56535-2_6

Keywords Augmented reality · Computer supported cooperative work · Group work · Visible light communication · Paper computing · Spatial imaging

6.1 Introduction

Information technology has matured in the sense that you can access the internet anywhere you want, and computers can act for much of human activities. This was brought about by virtue of the research fields on Ubiquitous Computing, Internet of Things (IoT), Big Data and Artificial Intelligence (AI). Indeed, personal computers and smart devices have succeeded in augmenting the ability of each person. However, people are still forced to utilize digital equipment with 2D flat displays, and wander the boundaries between the physical and digital worlds.

Augmented Reality (AR) is one of the promising ways for solve this problem. It tries to merge both worlds to provide intuitive spatial interaction. Most of the AR product can be categorized into two types: 2D flat display and head mounted display (HMD). Both capture an image of the physical world in front of you, and superimpose a digital image onto the captured one. You can see this synthetic image on your 2D flat display in the first type, or on your HMD in the second type. This means that your gaze is restricted to the 2D flat display or covered by the HMD.

The authors consider that this situation is useful for personal use, but has some difficulties in group use. The aim of this project is to design and demonstrate the future of information environment where people get together. In other words, existing "personal" display technology should be transformed to some kinds of "inter-personal" one. For this purpose, it is important to exceed the limitation of current display technology for group use. Section 6.2 explains the concept of this project. Sections 6.3, 6.4 and 6.5 illustrate three categories of technical contributions of the project:

- Section 6.3: privacy control of display content for promoting discussion in groups,
- Section 6.4: projection-based control of physical objects for suppressing the incompatibility between the physical and digital worlds and
- Section 6.5: spatial imaging for augmented reality among people without wearable displays.

Section 6.6 concludes and indicates the future direction.

6.2 Concept

Personal computers and smart devices have succeeded in augmenting the ability of each person. At now, even when people meet at a place, they tend to gaze at their own displays. As a result, they cannot concentrate on face-to-face communication among them as shown in Fig. 6.1a.

(a) Current display technology has some difficulties in group activities.

(b) The future of information environment that can promote people's active communication.

Fig. 6.1 Concept of this project

The authors believe that this problem is mainly caused by the limitation of current display technology. The future of information environment should not restrict the people's gaze onto their personal displays. In this project, the authors have pointed out the following three aspects as the limitations of current display technology:

1. Personal displays are powerful for private use, but sometimes inconvenient for public use. You don't want to show your private content to the others, and the others will try to avoid to look at it.
2. The digital world is imprisoned within the personal displays. Displayed content is positioned apart from physical objects. Image projector can display images next to the physical objects, but its effect is limited to visual augmentation.
3. The physical world is inherently three dimensional (3D), and several 3D displays certainly exist. Most of existing approaches to fuse both 3D worlds, however, require wearing special glasses which cover people's gaze.

As for the first limitation, you will see both public and private content in your display. Public content is something you are going to show group members: shared documents, recommended web pages, presentations and so on. By contrast, private one is just for you; you don't want to show it to the group members and they bear in mind so as not to look at it. Recent progress in information technology enables very powerful support for personalizing your computer. At now, your display is full of your private content: several messaging services, pop-up alerts from some applications, lists of files, web search histories and so on. For promoting discussion in groups, however, it is important to lead the group members to look at the other members' display. The first contribution of this project is the privacy control of display content and its application to group work facilitation. Section 6.3 describes the detail.

As for the second limitation, the physical and digital worlds are separated by display devices which can be regarded as small windows to access the digital world. As a result, people are gazing at their own display while interfering with face-to-face communication. Image projector is one of the simple ways to avoid this situation: we can display digital data next to the corresponding physical objects. In other words, image projector can visually merge the physical and digital worlds. However, the effect of current image projector is limited to visual augmentation of the physical world. The second contribution of this project is to extend the function of image projector for more advanced augmentation of the physical world: changing colors of ink on a paper chemically and sending pixel-by-pixel data for controlling physical objects. Section 6.4 describes the detail.

As for the third limitation, HMDs and 3D special glasses are effective for single user, but not for group use. This is because such devices interfere with face-to-face communication while obscuring people's gaze. Spatial imaging is a promising way to provide 3D visual sensation without forcing users to wear something. In order to utilize this technology to augment the physical world, however, 3D combination of physical objects and spatial imaging is essential. In addition, the ideal viewing angle of spatial imaging is 360° for the people surrounding a table. The third contribution of this project is some optical designs of spatial imaging for tabletop augmented reality among people. Section 6.5 describes the detail.

6.3　Group Work of the Future

This section proposes a privacy control method "SHelective" for sharing display, and a group work facilitation system "Inter-Personal Browsing" for collaborative web searching. These proposals illustrate the future of group work with PCs.

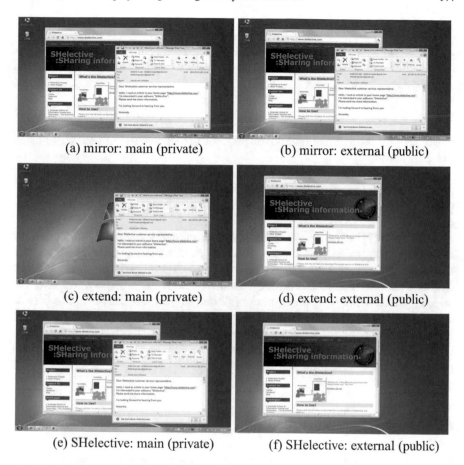

(a) mirror: main (private)   (b) mirror: external (public)

(c) extend: main (private)   (d) extend: external (public)

(e) SHelective: main (private)   (f) SHelective: external (public)

Fig. 6.2 Comparison among existing methods and SHelective for sharing display

6.3.1 SHelective

There are two major methods for sharing display content using an external display: mirror and extend. Consider that your main display is just for your private use, and the external display is for showing something to the audience. In other words, the external display is for public use.

"Mirror" shows the identical content on your main and external displays as shown in Fig. 6.2a, b. This means that all the private content including web search histories, lists of files and some pop-up alerts will appear even on the external (public) display. "Extend" shows different content on the two displays as shown in Fig. 6.2c, d. In this case, you have to watch both displays; If you want to control the application on the external display, you cannot handle it on your main display. When you try to search

Table 6.1 The ideal condition for sharing display

	Main display just for you	External display for the audience
Private content	✓	
Public content	✓	✓

a web page on the external (public) display, the audience will see your private web search histories.

To solve these problems, the authors consider that the ideal condition for sharing display should be as summarized in Table 6.1. You may want to see both private and public content on your main display, and limit the public content on the external display.

SHelective [1] is the method for satisfying this condition. At first, all the content appears on your main display. Then, you can select a window for mirroring to the external display by clicking SHelective icon on the right-upper area of the window. You can see both public and private window on your main display, and only the selected public window appears on the external display. As shown in Fig. 6.2e, f, even the hidden area of the public window on your main display (right-lower area of a web browser) appears on the external one. When you try to search a web page on the selected browser, the pop-up window showing your search histories just appears on your main display, but not on the external one.

6.3.2 Inter-Personal Browsing

In the fields of education and business, there has been renewed recognition of the importance on group work, where people work on multifaceted problem-solving or emergent tasks by cooperating and sharing the workload. Recently, there have also been greater opportunities for people to bring laptops into group work situations, but in this case the attention of users is drawn towards their individual displays, thus depriving them of the communication opportunities that group work is supposed to provide.

To solve this problem, the authors have introduced the concept of SHelective to the group work facilitation with laptops. Figure 6.3 illustrates the setup of the proposed system named Inter-Personal Browsing [3]. Each user has a set of a laptop and a small external display. The external display shows a web browser mirrored from each user's laptop, and is placed beside each user so that other users can see it. This means that only the browser window is made public to the others. Users can check each other's work status without having to exercise restraint, resulting in group work with smoother communication.

After making it possible for users to keep track of each other in this way, the next important requirement is to make it possible for users to interact with the system

Fig. 6.3 Inter-Personal Browsing: Each user's external display shows a mirrored public window

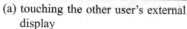

(a) touching the other user's external   (b) the same page is transferred to own
    display   display

Fig. 6.4 Transferring information from another user's public display to own display

in order to transfer information from another user's public display to their own
laptops. To allow group work to proceed smoothly while sharing information, it is
important to make it easy for users to transfer pages to their own laptops where they
can view them in more detail without interrupting the work of other users. For this
purpose, the authors implemented a mechanism whereby a user can use the touch
input functions to receive pages without anyone else's involvement. Specifically,
as shown in Fig. 6.4, this is done by touching the other user's public screen while
holding down a control key. To implement this function, a framework for specifying
the laptop of a specific user out of multiple other users is required. We may think
of some automatic specification method using a camera for image recognition. The
authors, however, adopted a non-automatic method which requires users to hold down
a control key to declare who is requesting the data transfer. This is because when
user A touches user B's external display, even the other users C and D can receive

(a) Paper-based group work   (b) PC-based group work

(c) Proposed system

Fig. 6.5 Appearance of group work in the lecture course

the same data by just pushing a control key. Non-automatic approach sometimes provides a room for utilizing the tool in different ways, and this feature can give an opportunity for discussion among people.

To examine how the quality of group work is changed by using Inter-Personal Browsing, the authors performed group work tests in a lecture course (Fig. 6.5). The specific aim of practical research through this course is to use Inter-Personal Browsing in a comparative study to see if it changes the quality of group work with regard to communication. For comparison, the authors also provided group work based on notes written on paper (paper-based group work) and group work using existing digital tools like Google Documents and Dropbox running on PCs (PC-based group work).

Table 6.2 shows the result of questionnaires in the lecture course. There were eight students in 2012 and twenty-four in 2013. Each group work was composed of three weeks: 1st week for brainstorming, 2nd for summarizing and 3rd for presentation. The authors asked the question "Did your group actively discuss in your group work?" twice (1st and 2nd week). The last week of 2013, one student was absent. Concerning activity of communication in the group work, over 90% of the students responded that they could actively discuss in paper-based group work and proposed

Table 6.2   Positive answers for the question "Did your group actively discuss in your group work?"

	2012	2013
Number of students	8	24
Paper-based	100% (16/16)	92% (44/48)
PC-based	44% (7/16)	52% (25/48)
Proposed system	100% (16/16)	91% (43/47)

one, suggesting that active communication had taken place. On the other hand, in PC-based group work, mostly half of the students responded that they could not play an active role in discussions.

6.4   Projection-Based Augmentation

This section introduces a chemical augmentation system "Hand-rewriting" for paper computing and a bit-data projection system "Pixel-level Visible Light Communication (PVLC) projector." Both are functional extension of existing image projectors to realize more advanced augmentation of the physical world.

6.4.1   Hand-Rewriting

More and more researchers are looking into paper computing, in which papers and printed materials are connected to the digital world, enriched with additional content, and even transformed into interactive interfaces. In this field, the authors are particularly interested in approaches for combining computing with handwriting using pen and regular paper, something with which all generations are familiar.

We can project computer-generated content onto paper by using a normal image projector. In this case, however, the image projection is emissive displaying, while the handwriting by pen is non-emissive. So, we will feel that the emissive digital world is separated from the non-emissive paper work.

To solve this problem, the authors have proposed a novel system named Hand-rewriting [2] that enables both human users and computer systems to write and erase freely on the same piece of paper. When the user writes on a piece of paper with a pen, the system can erase a part of the written content as shown in Fig. 6.6a, and write and print additional content on the paper in natural print-like colors as shown in Fig. 6.6b. To achieve these features, the authors focused our attention on chromic material, in which external stimuli can control the appearance and disappearance

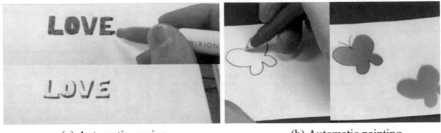

(a) Automatic erasing   (b) Automatic painting

Fig. 6.6 Hand-rewriting

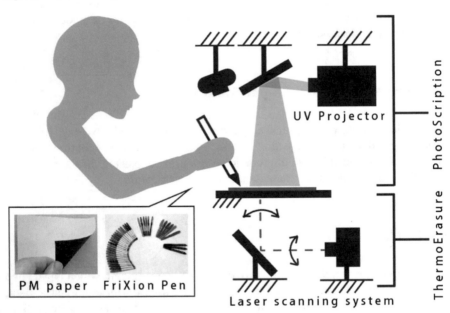

Fig. 6.7 System configuration of Hand-rewriting

of color. Specifically, thermochromic material and photochromic material are introduced, since both can be controlled without contact by heating or by exposing light.

Figure 6.7 shows the system configuration. The Hand-rewriting system combines two technical innovations: ThermoErasure and PhotoScription. The ThermoErasure system is comprised of a thermochromic FriXion pen and a 405 nm laser controlled by a galvanometer scanner. When the laser light hits the underside of the paper, it is converted into heat, and when the temperature reaches about 64 °C, the colors of local areas are erased. The PhotoScription system is comprised of photochromic (spiropyran-coated) paper, a UV mirror, and a UV projector. A single color appears locally on the paper when UV light pattern is projected. To project any type of invisible UV pattern locally, the authors have developed a UV projector with 365

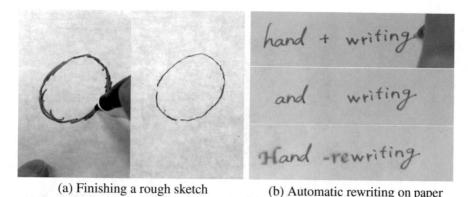

(a) Finishing a rough sketch   (b) Automatic rewriting on paper

Fig. 6.8   Applications of Hand-rewriting

nm wavelength light source and a digital micromirror device (DMD) of 1024 × 768 resolution.

We can develop several applications. When a user draws a rough sketch, the Hand-rewriting system can automatically erase unnecessary parts of the sketch and transforms it into a finished drawing as shown in Fig. 6.8a. When the user makes a mistake while writing something, it can automatically erase the incorrect part and displays a guide giving the correct entry in color as shown in Fig. 6.8b.

6.4.2   Pixel-Level Visible Light Communication Projector

A large display can support group work as an effective workspace, since users can put physical objects on it. The physical objects are not limited to just papers, but include smart devices, digital tools, robotic machines and so on. In this case, the dynamic combination of displayed image and the placed objects enables more intuitive interaction with each other. For this purpose, such objects should be controlled in such a way that is strongly related to the image content. In addition, users want to use a lot of such objects at once, and to put and remove them freely. Thus, the control method should satisfy the following features:

- Position-dependent control: the placed object should receive such data that is strongly related to the position in the displayed image,
- Parallel control: all the objects should be controlled in parallel, since the sequential control limits the number of controlled objects, and
- Calibration-free control: any calibration process before putting an object degrades the interactivity of the system.

If each pixel of the displayed image itself has the function of transmitting bit data to the placed object, all the requirements are satisfied. What is important here is that

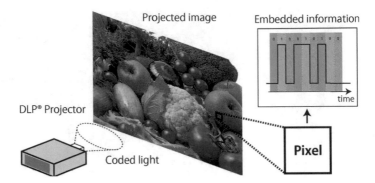

Fig. 6.9 Principle of PVLC: PVLC projector can embed bit data at each pixel by human-imperceptible high speed flicker

this data transmission should be imperceptible for users while the displayed image is visible.

Figure 6.9 illustrates the proposed principle of the Pixel-level Visible Light Communication (PVLC) projector which displays a visual image whose pixels contain imperceptible metadata which can be decoded by dedicated receivers [10]. The method is basically based on pixel-by-pixel ON-OFF Keying, and can be implemented with a DMD. When two inverted patterns are displayed alternatively at high-frequency, we would see just a flat gray image. Though we cannot perceive and distinguish each image, the receiver with a photo sensor can detect them as different signals. The luminance of a pixel is expressed by the ratio of time between on-and-off period, so the luminance does not depend on the order of on-and-off. Consequently, we can embed some bit patterns by replacing the order of on-and-off. As for the hardware design of dynamically updating the embedded data is presented in [15].

Several applications using the PVLC projector have been developed. EmiTable [9] is a tabletop system as shown in Fig. 6.10. The receiver has a photo diode and a dot-matrix display. When users put the receivers onto the tabletop, the receivers read out the position-dependent metadata and display the embedded data. With this example, users can see the embedded forecast data of the areas where users put the receivers as shown in Fig. 6.10b. Moving the receiver to another area on the map, users can obtain the forecast of that area.

Not only read out the position-dependent metadata, iPVLC [6] can recognize the relative position and inclination of the receiver as shown in Fig. 6.11. Two photo detectors are placed apart on the backside of personal Smart Mobile Device (SMD). By embedding two-dimensional coordinates in each pixel, the relative position and inclinations of the SMD placed on the screen can be calculated. With this application, colorful aerial photographs appear in SMDs placed on a blank map image. Users can see that the photographs and the map image are precisely aligned. The SMD can interactively superimpose the detailed information on the projected large image.

PVLC projector is also applicable for controlling a swarm of robots. Phygital Field [4, 5] utilizes two-dimensional coordinates and velocity vector for navigation

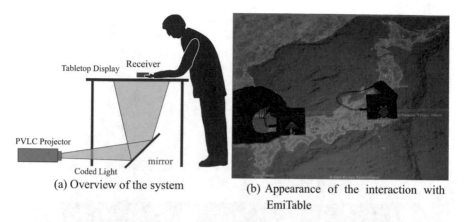

(a) Overview of the system

(b) Appearance of the interaction with EmiTable

Fig. 6.10 EmiTable: A tabletop surface pervaded with imperceptible Metadata

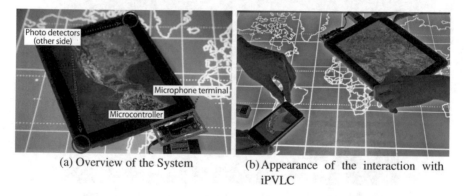

(a) Overview of the System

(b) Appearance of the interaction with iPVLC

Fig. 6.11 iPvlc: Pixel-level visible light communication for smart mobile devices

of robots as shown in Fig. 6.12. Since the entire pixel of the projected image contains both information, Phygital Field enables the robots to always recognize their inclinations and to follow a visual target using the coded velocity vector field. Further, the spatial deviation between the images and robots does not occur in principle. Therefore, the robots can recover its direction immediately if users push or move them.

6.5 Spatial Imaging

This section illustrates a tabletop spatial augmented reality system "EnchanTable," an application of spatial imaging to digital fabrication "MiragePrinter," and 360° viewable 3D display "fVisiOn." These proposals illustrate the future of tabletop augmented reality among people without wearable displays.

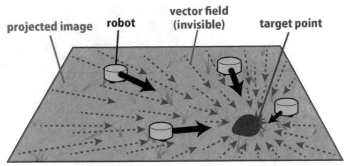

(a) System concept of Phygital Field

(b) Appearance of the interaction between moving robots
and users' hands

Fig. 6.12 Phygital Field: An integrated field with a swarm of physical robots and digital images

6.5.1 *EnchanTable*

Most of the augmented reality system require users to wear special glasses. Spatial imaging optics is one of the promising way to overcome this limitation. As for the tabletop system, Fig. 6.13 illustrates two types of system configurations.

When we set up an optical system behind a table, users can see spatial images above the tabletop as shown in Fig. 6.13a. One of the examples of this approach is the MARIO system [7] shown in Fig. 6.14a. Users can handle physical blocks to interact with a virtual character jumping on the blocks. In order to display spatial images directly onto the tabletop, we need to set up an optical system under the table as shown in Fig. 6.13b. HoVerTable [8] is one of the examples of this approach as

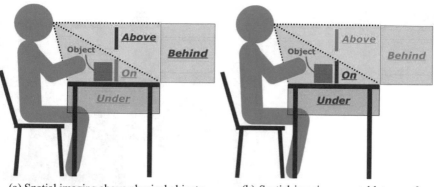

(a) Spatial imaging above physical objects by an optical system behind a table.

(b) Spatial imaging on a tabletop surface by an optical system under the table.

Fig. 6.13 Two types of tabletop spatial imaging

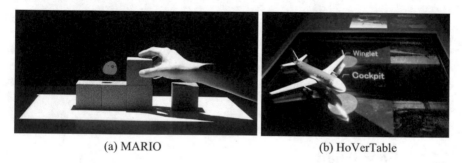

(a) MARIO

(b) HoVerTable

Fig. 6.14 Examples of tabletop spatial imaging

shown in Fig. 6.14b. Annotations "Cockpit" and "Winglet" to a 3D physical object (airplane) are displayed in mid-air.

Both enable spatial interaction with physical objects and computer-generated images. The second type can display spatial images closer to the physical objects than the first type. In contrast, the merit of the first type is that we can utilize a normal table since the optical system is attachable.

EnchanTable [11] is the combination of both types: displaying spatial images on the tabletop by an attachable optical system behind the table. Figure 6.15 illustrates its optical design consisting of a display (D), an actuator, an aerial-imaging plate (AIP), a louver-film (LF), and a reflective table surface (HM: Half Mirror). Light, emitted from D, forms a temporary image D' through the AIP. Reflected by the table surface, it forms a mid-air image (I) which we can move around by the actuator. The LF can block the light to the users directly passing through the AIP (upward), while the light for D' (downward) passes through the LF. We can display a 75 mm image, which can move in space at a depth of 50–150 mm.

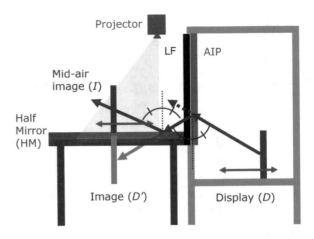

Fig. 6.15 Optical design of EnchanTable

The requirement of the proposed system is limited to the reflectiveness of the tabletop surface. Owing to its compactness, this method can be applied to other tabletop-interaction systems. Figure 6.16 shows the result of EnchanTable. Users can play with an up-standing virtual character by using an RFID card which can be detected by an RFID reader under the table. The virtual character can walk around on a wooden tabletop surface.

6.5.2 MiragePrinter

The rapid proliferation of digital fabrication machines has resulted in enabling more people to make various creations. It is, however, often pointed out that interfaces bridging between the physical and digital environment are necessary. Focusing on the 3D printing, the authors propose a new type of fabrication machine named MiragePrinter [12] that connects users' digital works and physical works seamlessly. More concretely, three contributions are the followings:

- Firstly, the authors have developed a novel printer hardware which can show mid-air images on a 3D printer stage. Users can simultaneously view optical images of their models and physical manifestations in identical positions.
- Secondly, the authors have implemented software and interfaces, so that users can control the displayed images and the printer actuations simultaneously. The user can design models using existing CAD software overlapped on the 3D printer's stage in real scale. Moreover, the user can manipulate the mid-air images through embodied interactions using head movements or rotating the stage.
- Thirdly, the authors have realized several interactive functions for connecting modeling process and materializing process seamlessly. Users can design digital models by referring to the parameters of existing physical objects placed on the stage. They can make additional parts of the objects themselves.

(a) Playing with an RFID card and a virtual character.

(b) The virtual character can walk around on a wooden tabletop surface.

Fig. 6.16 EnchanTable

MiragePrinter consists of a 3D printer (Solidoodle 2nd Generation), a mid-air display with an aerial imaging plate (AIP). It can show mid-air images without interfering the printing mechanism and users' activities such as removing parts of the stage, since all the optical equipments can be installed backside of the stage. The distance from the printed object on the stage to the plate was 300 mm, and the distance from the plate to the display was also 300 mm as shown in Fig. 6.17.

Users can create and modify mesh models using a standard Rhinoceros toolbox. The displayed mid-air image consists of a black background and white wireframe models. Since this mid-air display can show only 2D images, the authors installed a rotation stage on the 3D printer. According to the orientation of the stage, users can manipulate the rotation of the mid-air model (Fig. 6.18). The printing software converts model data to G-code, and prints the models. Even during the printing process, the user can stop the printing temporarily and modify the models. In this case, the system erases parts of G-code that has been already printed, and resume the print using the modified G-code to keep printing on the already printed object.

The followings are the scenarios to support the users' design process using MiragePrinter shown in Fig. 6.19:

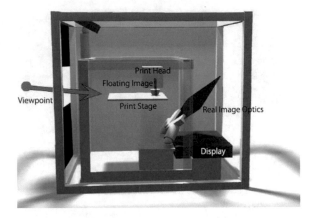

Fig. 6.17 System Design of MiragePrinter

(a)   **(b)**

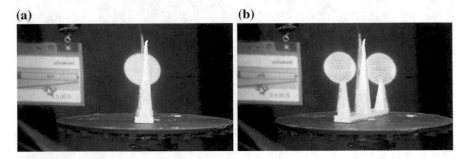

Fig. 6.18 A rotation stage on MiragePrinter

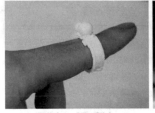  

   (a) Editing 3D Objects   (b) Quick Shape Scanning   (c) Direct Printing onto
      While Printing   of Existing Objects   Existing Physical Objects

Fig. 6.19 Application scenarios of MiragePrinter

Editing 3D Objects While Printing   Consider a case where a user creates a ring.
Firstly, the user makes a model of a base part by comparison with the actual
size of a finger. Then, after printing the base part, the user can design the upper
ornament models, while wearing the base on her finger.

Quick Shape Scanning of Existing Objects   The user can scan and modify physical
  objects easily without using a high spec 3D scanner, and design an additional part
  for an existing toy according to the tracing shape data.

Direct Printing onto Existing Objects   This system enables the user to directly add
  new parts to an existing physical object. Consider a situation where the user
  wants to add a new handle at the top of an existing cup. There have been still
  some limitations with regard to this function: the printed surface should be flat
  and the adhesiveness depends on the material of the existing object. However, this
  function could open up a new method for fixing or customizing existing physical
  objects.

6.5.3 fVisiOn

The proposed glasses-free tabletop 3D display, named *fVisiOn*, floats virtual 3D
objects on an empty tabletop surface and enables multiple viewers to observe raised
3D images from any angle at 360° as shown in Fig. 6.20. The entire principle is
installed beneath the table, so the tabletop area remains clear. No ordinary tabletop
activities are disturbed. Many people can naturally share the 3D images displayed
together with physical objects on the table.

To realize natural tabletop communication, the authors consider that the following
requirements must be satisfied: (1) 3D images of 360° should be observed by each
viewer from a correct angle; (2) ordinary tabletop activities should not be inhibited;
(3) the number of viewers should not be limited; and (4) no special 3D glasses or
wearable tracking system should be required.

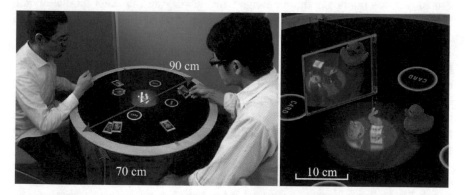

Fig. 6.20 Glasses-free tabletop 3D display, *fVisiOn*. Exterior of the latest prototype looks like an
ordinary round table of 90 cm diameter and 70 cm height (*left*). Virtual 3D objects are produced in
the center of the table. The 3D image can be seen from any direction and it can be reflected by a
real mirror as if they are actually there (*right*)

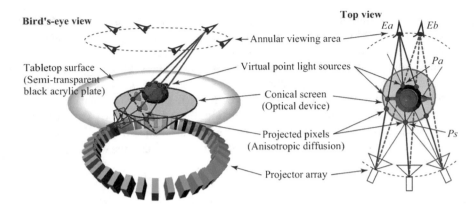

Fig. 6.21 Proposed principle for generating 360°-viewable tabletop 3D images [13, 14]. Our method employs a conical optical device (screen) and circularly arranged projectors. The combination of those static components produces a light-field of virtual 3D objects' surface and provides horizontal parallax in a circular direction

Recent VR systems using a head-mounted display would be utilized for collaborative works and satisfy conditions (1). However, its experience is closed in a totally immersive virtual world and people depart from a real-life communication. It does not satisfy conditions (2) and (4), and condition (3) is depending on the prepared device number. Several glasses-free tabletop 3D displays have been proposed which fully satisfy the conditions. These methods generally employ a horizontal high-speed rotation disk on the table and one or a few high-refresh-rate projectors. However, the high-speed component requires tradeoffs among the color depth range, refresh rate, and the number of directions to be displayed in a second. Therefore, these systems generally entail important shortcomings when displaying full-color animation and interactive contents. Moreover, the moving component is usually bulky, involving difficulty of momentum control when the display is enlarged.

The proposed system *fVisiOn* consists of only static components as illustrated in Fig. 6.21. The complete mechanism is installed underneath a round table to satisfy condition (2). The display forms a 360° annular viewing area around the table and provides horizontal parallax without 3D glasses or head tracking in the horizontal plane to satisfy conditions (3) and (4). Therefore, any number of viewers seated around the table, as in condition (1), can observe the 3D images with a correct perspective from any direction.

Figure 6.22 shows components of the system. There is a conical rear-projection screen underneath the table. Its curved surface is as an anisotropic radiation characteristic for the incoming rays; it diffuses in the direction of the shape's edge line and passes directly in the direction of the circumference. As sources to generate numerous directional light rays, 288 tiny projectors are arranged in a circle. Each pixel cast by the projectors corresponds to a particular ray. On a vertical plane, each ray enters the screen and extends at an angle. Part of the fan-like diffused light from the ray is

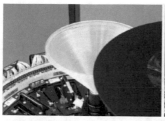

Fig. 6.22 Circularly arranged projectors and conical screen (*left*). The screen is covered by a semi-transparent *black plate*, and then a 3D image has appeared (*middle*). One projection module covers 30° of viewing area. All together, 12 modules accomplish production of the 360°-view 3D images (*right*)

caught by the viewer's eyes (Fig. 6.21, left). In contrast, on a horizontal plane, the orientation of the rays produced from a series of projection centers is preserved after they pass through the screen (Fig. 6.21, right). Our viewing area forms a circle. At any eye position on the annular viewing area, the eye observes the slit-like parts in each projector's rays. Therefore, the retina collects fractional slit-like images from different projectors to form an appropriate image for the perspective at each viewing point. For ease-of-use and portability, we fabricated modular projector arrays. Each module has 24 projectors and a video splitter. It inputs a video signal of 2400 × 1600 pixels in 60 Hz. Thereby, the video is split into 24 projection images of 400 × 400 pixels.

The principle of our tabletop 3D display is optimized for seating conditions. We set the radius of the annular viewing area as 50 cm and the height of the area as 35 cm from the level of the tabletop. These parameters of the annular viewing area were inferred from the general seating condition. This configuration enables users to reach their hands to the center of the tabletop and touch the floating virtual 3D characters. This seating situation gently leads viewers' eyes to the designated annular viewing area. However, their viewpoints occasionally deviate from the area because of their body movement. The vertical diffusion of our principle guarantees that the viewers see 3D images even though the eyes might deviate slightly from the sweet spots.

Figure 6.23 presents results obtained for a generated virtual 3D scene. From the photographs, one can confirm that the reproduced 3D images provide parallax without special glasses. Note that the reflection and the shadow cast on the imaginary blue floor on the tabletop surface are also reproduced appropriately.

Figure 6.20 left also presents an example of usage in which two persons are individually watching generated 3D images from each side. This photograph was taken at the third person's viewpoint. However, the 3D images can be photographed in the right perspective because the display provides every horizontal parallax in 360°. This photograph demonstrates interactive live content of playing 3D card game; creatures printed on physical cards are summoned on the table as virtual 3D characters by putting the cards on sensors embedded in the table. Figure 6.20 right portrays another symbolic result achieved by *fVisiOn*. In this photograph, a real mirror and a

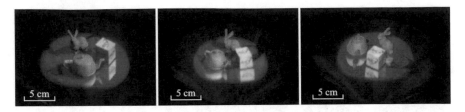

Fig. 6.23 Generated virtual 3D scene. These are photographed from different angles at three separate viewpoints on the annular viewing area. The reproduced 3D images provide parallax without use of special 3D glasses and multiple people can share the experience of watching same virtual 3D media on the table

toy duck are added around the generated 3D objects. It is readily apparent that the glasses-free 3D objects and the duck coexist on the table, naturally. Additionally, both the virtual and physical objects can be reflected by the mirror because of the existence of horizontal parallax around the table.

6.6 Conclusion

Personal computers and smart devices are extremely powerful for personal use, but sometimes interferes with face-to-face communication among people. For the purpose of group use, it is important to exceed the limitation of current display technology. From this point of view, this article introduced the following three approaches to investigate the future of display technology:

- privacy control of shared display content,
- projection-based augmentation of the physical world, and
- spatial imaging optics for merging the 3D physical and digital worlds.

The authors believe that these contributions will open up the next stage of information environment which can be called as "inter-personal digital media." Advanced collaboration between information technology and physical control creates a place to encourage people's activities. Rapid progress of Artificial Intelligence (AI) can support much of computer-substitutable activity. This leads to that the remained human-responsible activity becomes more important. For the human-responsible activity, Virtual Reality (VR) systems with HMDs are powerful for extending the ability of each person. Figure 6.24 illustrates the covered area of AI, VR, and the inter-personal digital media. The next stage of information environment should encourage the human-responsible group activity.

The achievements described in this article are already drawing attention from various fields including digital signage, education, group work, creative office, entertainment, gaming interface, and personal fabrication. Future directions of this project include the following research themes:

Fig. 6.24 The next stage of information environment should encourage the human-responsible group activity

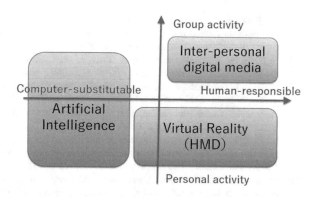

- interaction design for driving motivation and promoting action,
- minimal design of information device,
- much more augmentation of the physical world, and
- advanced utilization of physical objects.

As for the interaction design, non-automatic approach sometimes provides a room for utilizing the tool in different ways, and this feature can give an opportunity for discussion among people as mentioned in Sect. 6.3.2. Paper computing described in Sect. 6.4.1 is one of the examples of the minimal design which has almost no barrier to utilize digital technology. Projection-based augmentation in Sect. 6.4.2 has application possibilities for wireless power projection, intelligent lighting control and 3D spatial augmentation in collaboration with the systems in Sects. 6.5.1 and 6.5.3. Spatial imaging in Sect. 6.5.2 has illustrated the essential collaboration of physical objects and digital imaging. It shows the potential applicability for more advanced utilization of physical objects including shape-changing interfaces.

References

1. H. Fushiki, T. Naemura, SHelective: sharing information by selectively mirroring windows onto external displays, in *Proceedings of Human Interface Symposium (HIS2012), Human Interface Society* (2012), pp. 731–736
2. T. Hashida, K. Nishimura, T. Naemura, Hand-rewriting: automatic rewriting similar to natural handwriting, in *Proceedings of International Conference on Interactive Tabletop and Surfaces (ITS2012)* (ACM, 2012), pp. 153–162
3. T. Hashida, K. Nomura, M. Iida, T. Naemura, Inter-personal browsing: supporting cooperative web searching by face-to-face sharing of browser pages, in *Proceedings of International Conference on Computer Supported Collaborative Learning (CSCL2013)*, vol. 1, (International Society of the Learning Sciences, 2013), pp. 224–231
4. T. Hiraki, S. Fukushima, T. Naemura, Phygital field: an integrated field with a swarm of physical robots and digital images, in *Proceedings of SIGGRAPH ASIA 2016 Emerging Technologies* (ACM, 2016), pp. 2:1–2:2

5. T. Hiraki, S. Fukushima, T. Naemura, Projection-based localization and navigation method for multiple mobile robots with pixel-level visible light communication, in *Proceedings of International Symposium on System Integration (SII 2016)* (IEEE/SICE, 2016)
6. Y. Kato, N. Fukasawa, T. Naemura, iPvlc: Pixel-level visible light communication for smart mobile devices, in *Proceedings of SIGGRAPH 2011 Posters* (ACM, 2011), pp. 45:1–45:1
7. H. Kim, I. Takahashi, H. Yamamoto, S. Maekawa, T. Naemura, MARIO: mid-air augmented reality interaction with objects. Entertain. Comput. **5**(4), 233–241 (2014)
8. H. Kim, H. Yamamoto, N. Koizumi, S. Maekawa, T. Naemura, HoVerTable: combining dual-sided vertical mid-air images. Trans. Hum. Interface Soc. **17**(3), 275–286 (2015)
9. S. Kimura, M. Kitamura, T. Naemura, EmiTable: a tabletop surface pervaded with imperceptible metadata, in *Proceedings of International Workshop on Horizontal Interactive Human-Computer Systems (Tabletop2007)* (IEEE, 2007), pp. 189–192
10. M. Kitamura, T. Naemura, A basic study on positon-dependent visible light communication using DMD, in *Proceedings of Forum on Information Technology (FIT2006)*, vol. 5, (Information Processing Society of Japan, 2006), pp. 293–295
11. H. Yamamoto, H. Kajita, N. Koizumi, T. Naemura, EnchanTable: displaying a vertically standing mid-air image on a table surface using reflection, in *Proceedings of International Conference on Interactive Tabletops & Surfaces (ITS2015)* (ACM, 2015), pp. 397–400
12. J. Yamaoka, Y, Kakehi, MiragePrinter: interactive fabrication on a 3D printer with a mid-air display, in *Proceedings of SIGGRAPH 2016 Talks* (ACM, 2016), pp. 82:1–82:2
13. S. Yoshida, fVisiOn: 360-degree viewable glasses-free tabletop 3d display composed of conical screen and modular projector arrays. Opt. Express **24**(12), 13194–13203 (2016)
14. S. Yoshida, S. Yano, H. Ando, 16.1: prototyping of glassesfree tablestyle 3d display for tabletop tasks, in *SID Symposium Digest of Technical Papers*, vol. 41(1), (2010) pp. 211–214
15. L. Zhou, S. Fukushima, T. Naemura, Dynamically reconfigurable framework for pixel-level visible light communication projector, in *Proceedings of Emerging Digital Micromirror Device Based Systems and Applications VI*, vol. 8979, (SPIE, 2014), pp. 89790J:1–89790J:14

Chapter 7
Reading-Life Log as a New Paradigm of Utilizing Character and Document Media

Koichi Kise, Shinichiro Omachi, Seiichi Uchida, Masakazu Iwamura, Masahiko Inami and Kai Kunze

Abstract "You are what you read." As this sentence implies, reading is important for building our minds. We are investing a huge amount of time for reading to input information. However the activity of "reading" is done only by each individual in an analog way and nothing is digitally recorded and reused. In order to solve this problem, we record reading activities as digital data and analyze them for various goals. We call this research "reading-life log." In this chapter, we describe our achievements of the reading-life log. A target of the reading-life log is to analyze reading activities quantitatively and qualitatively: when, how much, what you read, and how you read in terms of your interests and understanding. Body-worn sensors including intelligent eyewear are employed for this purpose. Another target is to analyze the contents of documents based on the users' reading activities: for example, which are the parts most people feel difficult/interesting. Materials to be read are not limited to books and documents. Scene texts are also important materials which guide human activities.

K. Kise (✉) · M. Iwamura
Osaka Prefecture University, 1-1 Gakuencho, Naka, Sakai, Osaka 599-8531, Japan
e-mail: kise@cs.osakafu-u.ac.jp

M. Iwamura
e-mail: masa@cs.osakafu-u.ac.jp

S. Omachi
Tohoku University, 6-6-05, Aramaki Aza Aoba Aoba-ku, Sendai, Miyagi 980-8579, Japan
e-mail: machi@ecei.tohoku.ac.jp

S. Uchida
Kyushu University, 744, Motooka, Nishi, Fukuoka 819-0395, Japan
e-mail: uchida@ait.kyushu-u.ac.jp

M. Inami
The University of Tokyo, 7-3-1 Hongo, Bunkyo, Tokyo 113-8654, Japan
e-mail: inami@inami.info

K. Kunze
Keio University, 4-1-1 Hiyoshi, Kohoku, Yokohama, Kanagawa 223-8526, Japan
e-mail: kai.kunze@gmail.com

© Springer Japan KK 2017
T. Nishida (ed.), *Human-Harmonized Information Technology, Volume 2*,
DOI 10.1007/978-4-431-56535-2_7

Keywords Reading-life log · Document image retrieval · Scene character recognition · Scene character dataset · Font generation · Eye-tracking · Wordometer · Smart eyewear · Document annotation · AffectiveWear · Augmented narrative

7.1 Introduction

"Reading[1] is to the mind what food is to the body." This sentence emphasizes the importance of reading for building our minds. By knowing what you have been read, we are able to know more about you. Reading-Life Log (RLL) is a project that focuses on a human's reading activity and to know and enhance human ability.

For the majority of people, reading is a primary means of acquiring information. Few can spend a whole day without reading anything in their modern life. In other words, people's life is to input information by reading and to process it. However, the activity of "reading" is done only by each individual in an analog way. Although people spend a great deal of time reading, the activity of reading itself cannot be used later, because of its analog nature. In order to solve this problem, we record reading activities as digital data and analyze them for various goals. We call this research "reading-life log."

There is a wide variety of research items in the "reading-life log": what, when, and how much you read, and how you read in terms of your interests and understanding. In the research of the reading-life log, we obtain the above information by observing both readers and objects to be read. To observe readers, we employ various sensors most of which are body-worn: for example, an eye-tracker for the analysis of eye gaze, and an EEG device for the analysis of brain activity. To observe objects to be read, we employ a camera mounted on the reader. It enables us to extract character information read by people.

By acquiring the above information from a single person, we are able to estimate the quality and the quantity of knowledge he/she has acquired through reading. This information can be used for many purposes. For example, if the reader wishes to improve his/her ability in a language, we can help him/her by visualizing the amount of learning, as well as by showing the weak points. This process can be viewed as knowing people through materials to be read. On the other hand, by accumulating reading activities and reactions regarding a material, we are able to grasp information about who reads it, who likes it, which parts interest whom, and so on. This type of information is valuable for revising the contents of the material. A step forward would be to use it to establish the relationship among its readers, as well as the relationship among materials through their readers.

[1]Table 7.1 and Figs. 7.1, 7.3, 7.4, 7.5, 7.6, 7.7, 7.8, 7.9, 7.10, 7.11, 7.12, 7.13, 7.17, 7.18, 7.19, 7.20 are originally published in [1] and copyrighted by IEICE. They are granted to use in this article with the permission number 16KB0074. The research described in this chapter has been approved by the research ethics committee in Osaka Prefecture University.

Materials to be read are not limited to books and documents, but include posters, sheets of paper on bulletin boards, and signboards. When these materials are considered, information processing by readers is not limited to acquiring knowledge but to guiding their activities by the information. An easy example is a sign: we can guide ourselves by reading directions to the goal. From the opposite viewpoint, reading text on such materials allows us to estimate the reader's goal.

In order to realize the abovementioned information processing, what are the necessary functions we need to implement? It is at least necessary to read the characters in documents and other materials. Detection of reading activities and analysis of them are also important functions. In this chapter, we describe our latest results towards realizing the reading-life log.

Section 7.2 overviews the whole research of the reading-life log. Section 7.3 first describes fundamental technologies and tools for implementing the reading-life log. Section 7.4 is the main part of this chapter and describes several different reading-life logs and their technologies. Section 7.5 concludes this chapter with some future work to be undertaken.

7.2 Overview of the Research Field

7.2.1 Functions

An overview of all our research topics is shown in Fig. 7.1. The purpose of the research is to establish mutual analysis of materials (characters/documents) and their reading activities to establish a human-harmonized information environment for reading. The left-hand part of the applications indicates the analysis of reading activities based on characters and documents. On the other hand, an analysis of characters and documents based on reading activities is shown on the right.

The goal of the applications in the left-hand part is to build a reading-life log about what, when, and how much the reader reads. Depending on the materials to be read, this application is subdivided into two areas: reading-life log for documents and reading-life log for scene text.

The reading-life log for documents requires the computer to read documents simultaneously like the reader does. This function can be supported by two fundamental technologies: real-time character recognition and real-time document image retrieval. By using either of them, we can access the contents that the reader reads.

For the reading-life log for scene text, we employ real-time character recognition and omnidirectional character recognition as its fundamental technologies. The former recognizes characters pointed out by a camera. The latter on the other hand requires no pointing action; all characters around the reader are recognized to characterize the scene.

Both real-time and omnidirectional character recognition are based upon the technologies of basic character detectors and recognizers as well as a large-scale char-

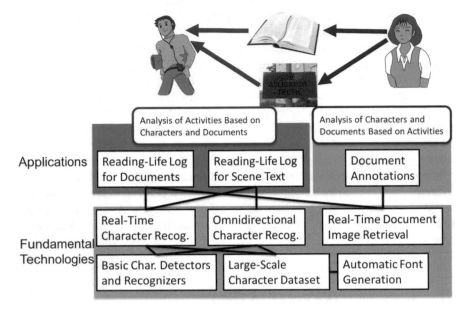

Fig. 7.1 Overview of research on the reading-life log

acter dataset, which is used as learning samples of recognizers. Although most of the samples in the dataset are labeled manually, this can be automatically done by using other technologies. For example, a technology called automatic font generation allows us to produce any font automatically, which can be used as a learning sample. Another way is to employ real-time document image retrieval for automatic labeling of camera-captured characters.

The right-hand part of the figure represents the processing of the opposite direction. Documents and characters are analyzed based on their reading activities. For example, difficult words for a reader are automatically recognized by analyzing eye gaze while reading. Although this is an example of automatic annotation of documents in terms of difficult words, we also provide the functionality of annotating documents manually. Annotated documents can be used in many different ways. In the case of difficult words, a direct application is to give the list of difficult words at the end of the day to encourage the reader to review them. Another, more sophisticated, way is to create an entertainment by playing annotations of a document.

7.2.2 Devices

For the case of the reading-life log for scene text, the main and only device we use is a camera. In the case of omnidirectional recognition, an omnidirectional camera that

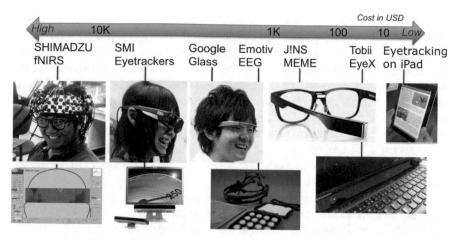

Fig. 7.2   Various devices for the reading-life log

enables us to capture 360-degree images is used. For other cases, a normal camera is employed.

To implement the reading-life log for documents, on the other hand, we employ various devices as shown in Fig. 7.2. The most expensive device we use is functional near-infrared spectroscopy (fNIRS), which measures brain activity from localized blood flow. We also employ EEG for a similar purpose. Eye-trackers ranging from expensive ones (SMI) to free ones (software implementation on iPad) are used to know where the reader is looking. Google Glass allows us to detect blinks, which can be used for recognizing activities. In addition to the same function, J!NS MEME enables us to sense eye movement based on electrooculography (EOG). The details of how to use and what kind of information we can obtain are explained at each application.

7.3   Fundamental Technologies

Before explaining the application technologies of the reading-life log, let us show some basic technologies and building blocks of the reading-life log.

7.3.1   Basic Character Detectors and Recognizers

Recent character recognition methods for scanned business documents can provide satisfactory recognition performance, by huge research efforts in a long history from the Tauschek patent (1829). In fact, commercial OCR software is now very common and bundled with scanning machines and document viewers, such as Adobe Acrobat.

In contrast, character recognition for text captured in photographs is still a difficult task. This task is so-called scene text recognition and many researchers are still tackling it. Possible reasons that make scene text recognition difficult are as follows: various font designs, especially decorated fonts, complex backgrounds, various illumination conditions, and non-frontal camera angles. In addition to these difficulties in "recognizing individual characters," another, more serious, difficulty lies in "detecting scene texts." Although scene text detection is no difficulty for human beings, it is still very difficult for computers; even state-of-the-art techniques cannot achieve an f-ratio of more than 90 [2, 3].

We have tried to develop breakthrough techniques for these tasks, i.e., scene text detection and scene text recognition. In later subsections, the techniques will be detailed. It is worth noting that development of techniques and their results are valuable for detection and recognition tasks for more general visual objects. Characters should be the easiest subject of detection and recognition tasks because they have been designed artificially and revised for error-less communication for thousands of years. Accordingly, characters are one of the best subjects for observing the fundamental performance of individual detection and recognition methodologies.

7.3.1.1 Trials of Scene Text Detection

As noted above, scene text detection is still an open problem and an unavoidable problem for scene text recognition systems. Various detection methods have been proposed so far [4, 5]. The most typical approach to scene text detection is to discover certain image features that can discriminate text parts from non-text parts. For example, we examined two features, i.e., color uniformity and edgeness [6], because it is possible to assume that the same color is used for printing a letter (or even a word) and each letter is separable from its background by a sharp edge contour. In [6], it was found that edgeness is better than color uniformity in detection accuracy.

Another approach is the so-called multiple hypothesis, where multiple features and detectors are used and the multiple detection results are then finally combined into a single detection result. This approach is reasonable because there is neither an "almighty" feature nor a detector that can deal with huge variations of scene texts. Even if a text is not detected by color uniformity, it will be rescued by other features, such as edgeness, and vice versa [7, 8]. Since this approach is very simple, it is possible to extend it in various directions. In particular, it is possible to use various methodologies for combining multiple results. In [8], the combination using global optimization is proposed and achieves top-level detection performance.

An important but overlooked concept of scene text detection is the "context" of scene text. Simply speaking, context is the surroundings of scene text and it gives a prior probability that text is inside of it. For example, since no text is in the sky, the probability of scene text is almost zero around a sky region. In this example, "sky" is the context giving a lower prior probability. "Tree" is also a context for a lower probability whereas "signboard" is a context for a higher probability. Consequently, image-based scene understanding, or semantic segmentation, is very important for scene text detection, although research on semantic segmentation seems rather independent of scene text detection. In [9, 10], the usefulness of context in scene text detection is experimentally proved.

Visual saliency is also a good clue for detecting scene text. It is natural to assume that scene text is salient because the role of scene text is to give some textual message to the reader and this role is not fulfilled unless it catches the reader's eyes by the appearance of scene text. This assumption is positively supported by a large-scale experiment using various types of visual saliency [11, 12]. This fact allows us to use the value of visual saliency as prior to scene text like the context. The saliency assumed in [11, 12] is Itti's saliency, which is a computational model of general human visual psychology, and thus the result proves that scene context is also salient not only for computers but also for human beings. Note that several methods of evaluating visual saliency specialized for scene text have been proposed. The saliency according to these methods is very different from the original idea of saliency for visual psychology research.

7.3.1.2 Part-Based Methods for Scene Text Detection Recognition

Part-based methods are widely used for visual object recognition. The concept is to describe an entire image by a set of local regions. Information on each local region is encoded in a certain way and the encoded results of all local regions are aggregated into a single representation. Bag-of-Features (BoF) is the most famous part-based method. From an entire image, keypoints are first detected and the small local region around individual keypoint is then represented as a feature vector, such as SIFT and SURF. Roughly speaking, a keypoint is often detected around a corner or a region with complex texture and the feature vector captures some direction of the texture in the local region. Each feature vector is quantized and then voted into a histogram. This histogram-based aggregation of votes from all local regions is BoF. An advantage of BoF is its robustness against global deformation. This is because a visual object is represented as a set of its local regions in BoF and the global structure of the object is thus no longer preserved.

Part-based methods have rarely been utilized for character recognition. One possible reason is that any character is comprised of a single or multiple lines and its local structure cannot represent character class information. In other words, global structure is far more important than local structure for character recognition and it is thus anticipated that no part-based method can achieve reasonable recognition accuracy.

In spite of this negative anticipation, we were able to prove that handwritten digits can be recognized with more than 95% accuracy by a part-based method [13]. Our method is based on majority voting. Specifically, it recognizes individual parts by referring to a part dictionary with the nearest-neighbor approach. If we have 50 parts from a digit image, we will have 50 (local) recognition results. Then, the class that becomes the most frequent recognition class among the 50 results is determined as the final recognition result.

The high recognition accuracy is achieved by the nature of majority voting. Imagine the recognition accuracy of individual parts is very low, say 30%. For a digit image of class "6," 30% of the votes go to "6" and the remaining 70% of the votes (by misrecognition) go to other classes. If misrecognition occurs randomly, each class (except for "6") will get 70/9 = 7.8% of the entire votes and this is far less than 30%. This means that the correct class "6" will be selected as the class with the largest votes regardless of the low accuracy of 30%. This example suggests that the image of "6" will be misrecognized only in the case that "0" (or another class) could have more than 30% of the votes, and it is not so easy to incorporate so many votes into one wrong class.

Since it is proved that part-based methods are applicable to character recognition, we can now exploit their advantages. For example, we can recognize characters even if their global structure is severely destroyed by partial occlusion and decoration [13]. In addition, part-based methods will make the text detection process easier. Even if a character is detected incompletely, it still has a chance of correct recognition.

7.3.1.3 Character Recognition Under Low Image Resolution

Scene text is often very small in a camera-captured image. In fact, if a text is captured by a distant camera, its size in the photo tends to be small. Such small-sized text images are difficult to recognize without special treatment. Super-resolution is a possible remedy for this problem. As another remedy, we proved that the mutual subspace method can improve recognition performance dramatically [14]. This paper also shows that enhancement of the difference between resembling classes can improve recognition performance.

7.3.1.4 Character Recognition with a Larger Dataset

In visual object recognition research, the power of using a large dataset has been proved so far. A larger dataset requires larger computation resources and often human efforts in attaching the ground truth. Recently, the former point is relaxed by commercial GPGPUs and the latter point, by crowd sourcing. The larger a dataset becomes, the more precisely it can grasp the real distribution of patterns. Consequently, even the simple 1-nearest-neighbor method can achieve very high recognition accuracy with a large dataset.

A large dataset is, of course, very beneficial for character recognition. We have prepared about 1 million patterns of handwritten digits and machine-printed digits and then analyzed how they are distributed in a feature space and how the dataset size affects recognition performance. The results show that we need 10 times more reference patterns to halve misrecognitions of handwritten digits. Moreover, we performed a network analysis of the large dataset and found that machine-printed digits have a dense-clustered distribution and that handwritten digits have a confusing (i.e., non-unimodal) distribution [15]. It is also possible to detect wrongly labeled patterns by using anomaly detection methods, if we have a sufficient number of data [16].

7.3.2 Construction of a Large-Scale Scene Character Dataset

In the history of pattern recognition research, datasets have played important roles. For example, in the research on Japanese offline handwritten character recognition, the ETL Character Database (http://etlcdb.db.aist.go.jp/) consisting of ETL-1 to ETL-9 [17] played important roles. However, due to the large cost of constructing a dataset, available public datasets were of small scale. Hence, as summarized in Table 7.1, we constructed five new datasets. So as to encourage character recognition research, we plan to make them publicly available unless this causes any copyright or privacy issues. The rest of the section is dedicated to introducing an overview of the datasets expected (1) in Table 7.1.

(1) Document image
This dataset was constructed by downloading PDF files available on the Internet so as to test the scalability of a camera-based document image retrieval method called locally likely arrangement hashing (LLAH) [18]. The downloaded PDF files were converted to produce their document images without any image distortion and stored in a database. LLAH was tested by using queries obtained by capturing printed version of the downloaded PDF files.

(2) Text in a camera-captured document
As shown in Fig. 7.3, document images captured with a camera suffer from perspective distortion, illumination change, blur, and so on. Since avoiding such degradation is difficult, recognition accuracy of characters and words in camera-captured document images has been far from satisfactory. A feasible solution is to collect many distorted real character and word images and use them to train a classifier. Though the solution requires ground truth of the collected images, manual groundtruthing requires laborious work and high cost.

Table 7.1 Constructed datasets and their scale

Contents	Scale
(1) Document image	100,000,000 pages
(2) Text in camera-captured document	1,000,000 words
(3) Scene text in still image	4,000 images, 25,000 words
(4) Scene text in video	55 videos, 500,000 words
(5) Scene text in video in Japan captured with omnidirectional camera	780,000 images, 790,000 words, 2,760,000 characters

Fig. 7.3 Degraded labeled word images obtained from camera-captured document images

Hence, we propose an automatic groudtruthing method that enables us to construct a dataset by just flipping the pages of documents [19]. It utilizes LLAH, which makes it possible to find the page region corresponding to the captured document image from a large-scale document image dataset. This functionality can match a word in the captured document image with one in a PDF file. Thus, words in camera-captured document images can be groundtruthed based on text information contained in the corresponding PDF files. We have confirmed that the proposed method automatically groundtruthed 1 million word images with an accuracy of 99.98%.

(3) Scene text in a still image

In scene text recognition, datasets provided by the series of ICDAR Robust Reading Competitions [2, 3, 20–22] are used as the de facto standard. The Street View Text Dataset [23, 24] that collected text regions from Google StreetView is also often used. In such datasets, it is common that text regions of groundtruth are represented by bounding boxes of texts. This means that the bounding boxes contain not only text regions but also backgrounds, and they are not suitable for evaluating pixel-level character segmentation methods.

Thus, we created pixel-level groundtruth for the dataset of the ICDAR2003 Robust Reading Competition [20] and Street View Text Dataset [23, 24]. In addition, an original dataset consisting of 3,018 text images downloaded from Flickr was constructed with pixel-level groundtruth. They can be used not only for evaluating text detection and recognition methods but also for estimating the statistics of character pixels and background pixels [25]. Among these datasets, the ICDAR2003 Robust Reading Competition dataset was used in the ICDAR2013 Robust Reading Competition [2].

(4) Scene text in video

Conventionally, scene text recognition research treated scene texts in still images. Toward realization of human-harmonized information environment, however, we cannot ignore scene texts in videos recorded with wearable cameras and mobile devices. Thus, we constructed the first dataset of scene texts in video in collaboration with researchers at the Computer Vision Center (CVC) in Spain. The dataset consisted of 55 videos containing about 500,000 words regions in English, French, and Spanish. The constructed dataset was used in a new challenge dedicated to scene text detection and recognition in videos in the ICDAR2013 and 2015 Robust Reading Competition [2, 3].

(5) Scene text in video in Japan captured with an omnidirectional camera
Most publicly available large-scale datasets only contain numerals and Latin characters. On the other hand, there was no dataset of Japanese characters including Chinese characters (kanji). Hence, in order to encourage development of detection and recognition methods for Japanese text, we constructed a large-scale Japanese scene text dataset [26]. In constructing the dataset, Point Grey Research Ladybug3, which is an omnidirectional camera equipped with six cameras, was used to capture movies of a scene of downtown Osaka. Among 780,000 images extracted from the captured videos, 31,000 images were manually groundtruthed. As a result, 910,000 text regions containing 790,000 words and 2,760,000 characters were obtained. The numbers of words and characters were almost four times those of the Street View House Numbers Dataset, known as the largest public dataset, consisting of 630,000 characters of 10 digits [27], while the unique numbers of words and characters were much fewer because they were extracted from consecutive images of videos. Since the images were extracted from videos, the constructed dataset can also be regarded as a dataset about "scene text in video" like the dataset explained in (4) above.

In addition to the constructed datasets mentioned above, we introduce two attempts.

- Automatic groundtruthing
  As available data are expected to increase and larger datasets are demanded, it is important to develop labor-saving ways of groundtruthing. Hence, we attempted automatic groundtruthing of scene texts [28]. First, a classifier was trained with a limited number of labeled data. Using the classifier, data without labels were groundtruthed. Then, the groundtruthed data were used to further train the classifier. Repeating the process, more labeled data and a better classifier were expected to be obtained. We confirmed that it worked at least for a small dataset.
- Data synthesis by font generation
  Since shapes of scene texts are diverse, training a classifier using various fonts is effective in improving character recognition performance. However, collecting many characters in various fonts is not easy. Thus, we propose an automatic font generation method that estimates the character shapes of unknown fonts. This is described in the next section.

7.3.3 Automatic Generation of Fonts

There are two main reasons for generating various kinds of fonts. One is to utilize impression of or additional information on the font. We see characters written in various fonts in our daily life. The impression we receive or the amount of information differs according to the font. An appropriate font should be chosen considering situation, purpose, circumstance, etc. A typical example is the usage of "universal fonts." Universal fonts are designed to be recognized by various persons and in any environment. Many fonts used in our daily life have been replaced by universal fonts. However, designing a universal font is steady and hard work that requires enormous time and cost.

The other is the contribution to the improvement of character recognition accuracy. Any method for character recognition is fundamentally based on pattern-matching technology, and having various font data directly leads to improvement of character recognition accuracy. However, collecting various fonts requires enormous time and effort. If automatic generation of fonts is available, it will become possible to generate a large number of various character patterns.

For these reasons, if a character font can be generated automatically, it is expected to contribute to both improving communication of man and machine and the performance of machines. However, as far as we know, there are few researches on automatic generation of fonts, and there is no system or software for designing fonts automatically.

In this section, we introduce an attempt to generate fonts automatically using the technique of rearranging patches [29]. Given a small number of sample fonts, all the character images are generated. This method applies the patch transform [30]. The patch transform breaks an image into small patches and generates a modified image by rearranging them under a certain constraint. The target of this method is a natural image. The arrangement is defined as an optimization problem considering that there is no unnaturalness or inconsistency as an image.

Based on this idea, the proposed method generates a character image by breaking the given font patterns into small patches and rearranging them. Since character images are binary, there is a problem whereby the continuity of an image is lost near the boundary of patches and it easily becomes unnatural, an issue that should be resolved.

Figure 7.4 gives an outline of the proposed method. First of all, some character images of a specific font are given as sample patterns. Then, skeleton data of characters that should be generated are given. Character patterns are generated by rearranging the patches obtained from the sample patterns along the skeleton data. In the example of Fig. 7.4, in order to make the character image of "E," the images of "T" and "F" are chosen, and the image of "E" is generated with two patches of "T" and 33 patches of "F." Along with the skeleton of "E," appropriate patches are placed in order to cover the skeleton with the black pixels of patches. Considering the global structure of a character, the patches with similar shape context [31] features are arranged. All these conditions and the similarities between the adjacent patches are represented by a cost function, and the optimal solution is obtained by the belief propagation.

Figure 7.5 displays examples of the fonts generated automatically by the proposed method. Figure 7.5a shows the original font, and Fig. 7.5b shows the generated character images. We used 26 capital alphabetical letters. To generate a character image, five characters except for the target character are randomly selected from the original

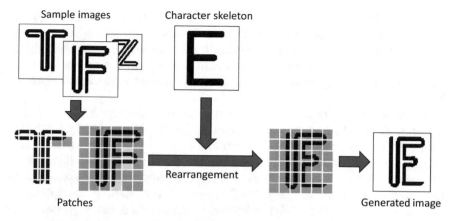

Fig. 7.4 Generation of fonts by rearranging patches

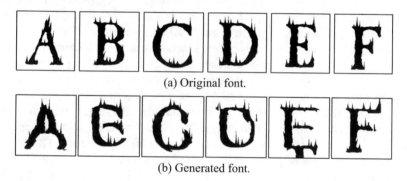

(a) Original font.

(b) Generated font.

Fig. 7.5 Example of generated fonts

font images. This figure shows that it is possible to generate character patterns that have the characteristics of the original character font only by breaking the images into patches and rearranging them. However, there are many unnatural portions and there is a room for improvement.

7.3.4 Real-Time Character Recognition

For a human-harmonized information environment, a machine is required to understand human intention and provide necessary information in a timely fashion. Hence, a machine should be able to recognize things as quickly as humans do. However, in the history of character recognition research, while people were interested in the processing time required for recognition with regard to convenience for practical use, it has never been explicitly aimed to realize real-time processing of recognition.

One reason is that recognition accuracy is considered to be more important than processing time. In general, processing time and recognition accuracy are in a trade-off relationship. Hence, reducing processing time means nothing other than reducing recognition accuracy. However, if we can reduce a long processing time with minimal reduction in recognition accuracy, such a character recognition technique will be very useful.

We propose two real-time character recognition methods. One is for recognizing alphabetical characters and numerals, and the other, for recognizing Japanese characters. Both were realized in the lazy learning framework; features extracted from training data were stored in the database in advance, and then recognition was performed by a fast similarity search that obtained features from the database similar to those extracted from the query. The fast search was realized by an approximate nearest-neighbor search (ANNS) technique, where ANNS does not guarantee that search errors do not happen so as to greatly reduce the computational time. Performance of ANNS methods is evaluated by search accuracy, processing time, and memory consumption. We propose a practically fastest ANNS method to realize certain accuracy, at least as of the time the paper was submitted [32].

The recognition method for alphabetical letters and numerals assumes that character regions are segmented by an established way such as binarization by a threshold, and segmented characters are recognized quickly in a way robust against perspective distortion [33]. As a recognition method robust against geometric transformation such as perspective transformation, geometric hashing [34] is known well. Letting N be the number of features in an image, the method requires computational cost of $O(N^4)$ so as to make the method robust against affine distortion. On the other hand, the proposed method greatly reduces the computational cost down to $O(N^2)$ by using geometric invariants in a different way from usual. As a result, we succeeded in running a camera-based character recognition method on a laptop computer in real time (more than 10 frames per second). The advantage of the method is that accuracy and recognition speed are not affected by change of layout of characters, character size, or camera angle; it works on images taken even from an elevation angle of 45°. So as to improve the method, a spell checker is integrated [35]. Use of the spell checker is effective in recognizing word images taken from an elevation angle of 20°; recognition accuracy of some words has been increased from 40 to 98%.

The recognition method for Japanese characters can recognize characters freely laid out on a complex background as shown in Fig. 7.6 [36]. The method uses local features such as SIFT (scale-invariant feature transform) [37] extracted from character images, as is often used in object recognition, to detect and recognize characters. The method is good at recognizing complex characters including Chinese characters; an experimental result shows that recall of 97% and precision of 98% are achieved. It runs on a laptop computer at about one frame per second. Since a large part of computational time is occupied by extraction of SIFT, to avoid this burden for speeding it up, we have changed it to an anytime algorithm [38]. The anytime algorithm is an algorithm that can output a calculation result at any time and a better result can be obtained as more time is spent. Introducing the feature of the anytime algo-

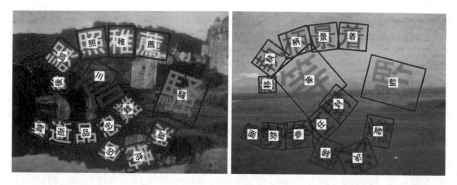

Fig. 7.6 Recognition result of the character recognition method for Japanese characters. The *red rectangles* represent the detected regions of characters and character images put in the rectangles recognition results

rithm makes it possible to realize flexible recognition where the recognition results of easier characters to recognize are obtained earlier and those of difficult characters, later. Figure 7.7 shows a comparison of the conventional method (not an anytime algorithm) and the proposed method (an anytime algorithm) with regard to recognition accuracy and processing time. Though the conventional method outputs the recognition result only all at once, the proposed method outputs it four times and more characters are recognized at each output. As a result, the proposed method can recognize 11 out of 14 characters earlier than the conventional method, though the processing time required for obtaining all the results increases. The proposed method has also been improved to cope with the problem of inaccurate estimation of the pose of the character of interest in the case that fewer local features are extracted from

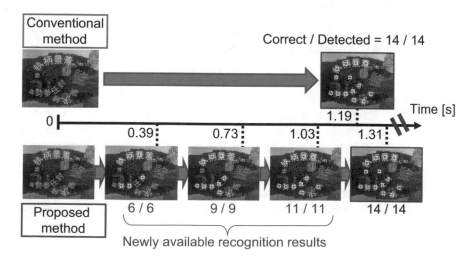

Fig. 7.7 Anytime algorithm of the Japanese scene text recognition method

a character region. The problem mainly arises when recognizing simpler characters such as hiragana and katakana. To avoid this problem, we propose a novel method that allows a robust estimation of the affine transformation matrix [39].

7.3.5 Omnidirectional Character Recognition

Omnidirectional character recognition is a process of recognizing all the characters in a 360-degree scene image. Unlike most of the existing methods assuming that the text areas are roughly detected or texts are included in the image, the purpose of omnidirectional recognition is to realize recognition without pointing. This technique enables us to support the discovery and offering of information that the user needs or the user has overlooked, supporting visually impaired persons, etc.

An omnidirectional image is obtained by an omnidirectional camera. Omnidirectional cameras are roughly classified into two types: using a spherical mirror and using multiple cameras. We selected the latter type considering the resolution of the acquired images. We used the camera called Ladybug3 of Point Grey Research. This camera includes five cameras arranged horizontally and one camera for the upper direction. All of the cameras are progressive-scan CCDs that can acquire 1600 by 1200 pixels at 15 frames per second.

An image acquired by an omnidirectional camera has a large number of pixels. On the other hand, the size of each character tends to be small. Therefore, in general, text detection requires time and the recognition accuracy is low. Moreover, since it operates outdoors, not only real-time processing but also robustness is required. In order to develop a system that offers the information necessary for a user, it must operate in real time and recognition accuracy must be high. To fulfill these conditions, methods based on template matching and edge detection are examined.

7.3.5.1 Template-Matching-Based Method

This method is based on the case-based method using the template-matching technique. In omnidirectional recognition, since the capturing environment is uncontrollable, it is important to cope with deteriorated character images. Therefore, two methods for low-resolution character recognition are considered. One is a template-matching method for recognizing low-resolution character images using high-resolution template images. The other is a technique of creating high-resolution images from many low-resolution images. In addition, we attempt to develop local features that are effective for low-resolution images. As a result, it was verified that character recognition can be achieved if the font is known and there is no geometrical distortion.

7.3.5.2   Edge Detection-Based Method

For detecting texts from scene images, it is known that edge information and binarization using color and intensity play complementary roles [40]. However, in the omnidirectional recognition task, rapidity of processing is important and the binarization process takes much time. We analyzed the processing time for each process and developed a fast detection method. First, edges are extracted from the acquired image. Then, candidate text areas are detected using the knowledge that the edges in text areas are strong, dense, and have various directions [40]. Then, binarization and labeling in the candidate area are performed to detect texts. Figure 7.8 shows an example of text areas detected by an omnidirectional camera. We constructed a system that deals with several frames per second without using special processors such as GPUs.

The detected characters are usually too small to be recognized by ordinary character recognition methods. Therefore, we developed a method based on the subspace method using the whole image of each character [14]. Exploiting the images obtained from multiple frames, a subspace that represents a character is constructed. The character is recognized by the similarities between the subspace and the subspaces constructed from training data. Figure 7.9 displays an example of character recognition.

7.3.6   Real-Time Document Image Retrieval

Document image retrieval is the task of retrieving the corresponding document image from the database in response to a query given as a document image. The query is often produced by using a camera, and it undergoes geometric distortion, blur, and

Fig. 7.8 Text detection by an omnidirectional camera

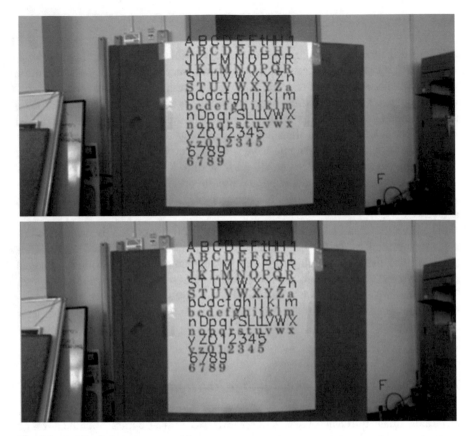

Fig. 7.9 Result of character recognition

variation of illumination. As a result, it is very different from the images stored in the database. Thus, the retrieval method should be capable of handling such distortions.

One may say that it is less meaningful to retrieve document images because documents are at hand when queries are captured. However, we have many applications such as provision of services that are associated with a specific part of a document image. For example, augmented reality is an easy-to-understand application of this technology.

Figure 7.10 illustrates an overview of this technology. On the left, a camera-captured query is shown. On the right of the figure, the retrieved document image is shown. The retrieval is based on the word-to-word matching indicated by the straight lines between two images. The technology is called locally likely arrangement hashing (LLAH) [19], which is still known as a state-of-the-art method in terms of robustness, accuracy, speed, scalability, and applicability. This technology is applicable to any script because it is independent of language and script. It just takes into account the distribution of centroids of connected components. It enables

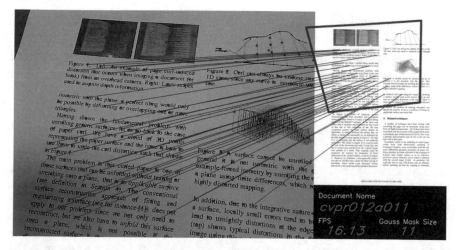

Fig. 7.10 Document image retrieval by LLAH

us to search a database of 100 million pages with an accuracy of 98.7% in 26.8 ms/query.

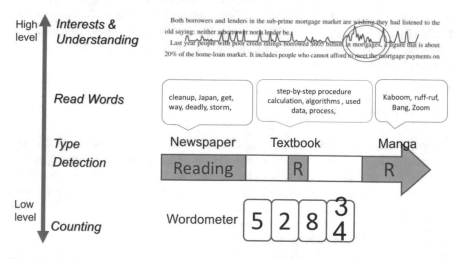

Fig. 7.11 Reading-life log for documents

7.4 Reading-Life Logs

In this section, we introduce various reading-life logs implemented by using the fundamental technologies.

7.4.1 Reading-Life Log for Documents

We have various functions that fall into this category of reading-life log. Figure 7.11 shows its overview that is characterized by what is to be measured: quantity is shown in the lower part of the figure and quality, in the higher part of the figure.

The simplest case is to measure purely the quantity of reading in terms of the number of read words. It is called a "wordometer" named after the pedometer. As compared to the pedometer, which measures the physical activity of the user, the wordometer quantifies the cognitive activity of the user. Another simple case is to measure the quantity of reading in terms of time. The function called reading detection detects reading activities among daily activities of the user. To be precise, it can output from when to when the user has read. A more content-oriented implementation of the reading-life log is "document type recognition," which classifies what type of document the user is reading. We also have the functionality of logging all read words, as well as logging the level of understanding and proficiency in the language as the highest (quality) level of the reading-life log. To implement the above functions, we employed the various devices shown in Fig. 7.2. In the following, details of each function will be explained.

7.4.1.1 Wordometer [41]

The wordometer has been implemented in many different ways. The simplest is just to measure the time taken to read a text. By multiplying his/her average speed of reading, the number of read words can be estimated. A better estimation can be obtained by combining document image retrieval LLAH and a wearable eye-tracker. The scene image captured by the eye-tracker is used as a query for LLAH to find which document the user is reading. This allows him/her to know the average number of words per text line. In addition, by analyzing the eye-tracking data as shown in Fig. 7.12, a long regression can be detected as a line break that can be used to estimate the number of read lines. By multiplying the average number of words per line and the number of read lines, we can estimate the number of read words. An even better estimation can be obtained by using a more sophisticated estimation. In our method, support vector regression is used to estimate the number of words, from eye-tracking data and the average number of words per line.

Another version of the wordometer using J!NS MEME EOG glasses is implemented. This will be described in the next Sect. 7.4.2 including more details about other implementations of the wordometer.

7.4.1.2   Reading Detection

Reading detection is the task of distinguishing reading activities from other activities. Head motion and blink frequency can be used for this purpose [42], because when reading, we blink much less with a specific head motion. Image features and eye-tracking data [43], as well as EEG signals [44] can also be used for reading detection. These are also based on the specificity of reading in terms of eye-tracking data and EEG signals.

7.4.1.3   Document Type Recognition

Document type recognition is to classify a document read into one of the predetermined classes of documents such as textbook, newspaper, novel, fashion magazine, or manga. By using this functionality, we are able to summarize reading activities

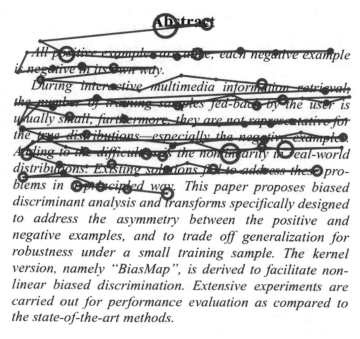

Fig. 7.12 Wordometer with an eye-tracker

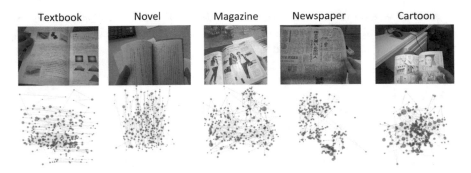

Fig. 7.13 Document type recognition based on the distribution of fixations and saccades

for each class of documents, for example, how many pages of a textbook you have read in a day.

Similar to other functions such as reading detection, we are able to recognize document types in many different ways. For example, recognizing document types is insignificant if document image retrieval is applicable. In the case that it is unavailable, we are still able to tackle this problem.

One way is to apply an object recognition technology. The Bag-of-Words representation of local features allows us to capture visual differences of document categories and thus to recognize the type [45]. Another way is to use eye gaze data [46]: the distribution of fixations and saccades. They definitely reflect the document layout as shown in Fig. 7.13 and can thus be employed for recognition. Surprisingly, an accuracy of 99% can be achieved by user-dependent training. An interesting counterexample of this approach is that if a document is not read in a typical way, it can be misclassified. For example, we asked subjects to read a fashion magazine and, for some male students, their gaze data are confused to be "textbook" because they really "read" the fashion magazine like reading a textbook. For other subjects with successful classification, their typical way of reading it was to browse the contents by skimming the text and looking at the pictures. We also attempted to use EEG signals for the recognition [44]. It is also possible to achieve similar accuracy as the case of eye gaze data. It is surprising that, by only looking at the EEG signals, we are able to recognize which type of document the user is reading.

7.4.1.4   Recording of Read Words

In addition to recognizing document types, we are able to log reading activities in more detail if we can record what the user has read. For this function of "recording of read words," it is necessary to associate eye gaze data with the contents of the document. Broadly speaking, there are two possible ways to realize this: retrieval-based and recognition-based methods.

The retrieval-based method associates eye gaze data with electronic contents of a document using the coordinates of fixations. When using stationary eye-trackers, the screen coordinates of fixations can be associated with the displayed contents. For the case of mobile eye-trackers, on the other hand, it is necessary to employ document image retrieval to achieve the association.

If there is no error in the eye gaze data, it is possible to know which word the user is looking at. However, in many cases, we are not able to avoid error. Even after careful calibration, a vertical error of about a few lines and a horizontal error of a few characters are unavoidable. Thus, what we can do is to estimate possible read words assuming that the error distribution is, for example, Gaussian. Based on this way of estimating possible read words, we are able to build a log in the form of Bag-of-Words (BoW) for a certain period of time [47]. Figure 7.14 represents a tag cloud representation of such BoWs. Another representation would be to build read paragraphs or read pages, which are with much fewer errors because of their larger area.

The recognition-based method is to obtain word information by applying character recognition to the images obtained by a scene camera. Although this approach is more error-prone compared to the retrieval-based approach, it allows us to log all word information not only on documents but also other scene text. This will be explained later in Sect. 7.4.3.

7.4.1.5   Estimating the Level of Understanding and Language Proficiency

Estimating the level of understanding and language proficiency is at the highest (quality) level of reading-life log for documents. Generally speaking, estimating how much a user understands is not an easy task because we do not have any means to evaluate the level of understanding. In order to make the task tractable, we limit the application field to an English standardized test called TOEIC (Test of English for International Communication). TOEIC is widely used in Asian countries including Japan as well as some Western countries. The test consists of two sections: listening and reading. We focus here on the reading section. In particular, we employ questions for Part 7 (reading comprehension) of the reading section. Based on the TOEIC test, we define the level of understanding as the number of correct answers to the questions in Part 7. In general, four questions are associated with a single long text. Thus, the number of correct answers ranges from zero to four. On the other hand, the language proficiency is estimated as the TOEIC score, which ranges from 10 to 990.

To estimate the number of correct answers, we employed fNIRS as the sensor. We measured the distribution of oxyhemoglobin on the forehead of subjects and analyzed its change while reading text. We attempt to solve this problem as a three-class problem, in which the following three classes are defined: (1) all four questions are correctly answered; (2) three questions are correctly answered; or (3) two or fewer questions are correctly answered. After training in a user-independent way, we have achieved an accuracy of 80%.

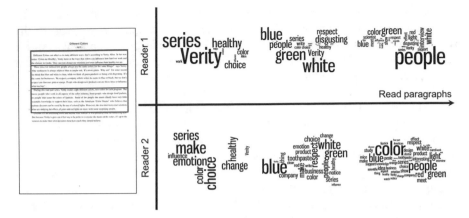

Fig. 7.14 Tag clouds generated from readers' reading behavior. As the number of read paragraphs increases, tag clouds become richer. It is also interesting to know the difference in tag clouds from different readers

To estimate language proficiency, we used SMI eye-trackers RED250 (250 Hz) and ETG (eye-tracking glasses) to analyze the behavior of reading text [48]. The first trial estimated English proficiency by analyzing eye gaze data when reading text [49]. We defined the task as three-class problem about TOEIC scores: (1) 400 or less; (2) more than 400 and less than 600; or (3) more than 600. By using a classifier trained in a user-independent way, we have achieved an accuracy of 91%. The second trial estimated the TOEIC score directly from eye gaze. We used ETG to obtain eye gaze data not only for the reading text part, but also for questions, and eye movement between text and question parts. As a result of applying trained regression, we were able to estimate the TOEIC score with an average error of 36 points after obtaining eye gaze data for 10 documents [50].

7.4.2 Smart Eyewear

To implement the reading-life log, we explored many different possibilities and used different systems from stationary setups towards wearable devices. Yet, regarding any life log, body-worn devices are a natural fit, as the user carries them. They can sense and recognize the environment from a first-person view of the user. This holds in particular for head-worn appliances, as humans perceive most of the world by sensing situated on the head. Therefore, the head seems to be a natural position for the reading-life log as well as cognitive assistance systems in general.

There are many interesting brain-sensing technologies like functional near-infrared spectroscopy (fNIRS) that can help to understand cognitive activities beneficial for the reading-life log, from cognitive load to indication of concentration and comprehension.

However, early head-mounted sensing devices are rather bulky, expensive, and socially stigmatizing. Recent commercial smart eyewear devices, such as Google Glass and PUPIL eye-trackers, lay the foundations for "eyewear computing." Fig. 7.15 shows the development from brain sensing and optical eye tracking to head-mounted computers (e.g., Google Glass) and smart glasses (e.g., J!NS MEME).

Regarding the social impact of reading-life log technologies, we wondered how to make them more attractive to the general public. For the first prototypes, we started collaborating with J!NS on J!NS MEME. MEME is lightweight and looks like ordinary glasses. Our main issue in implementing reading-life log technologies is that we are lacking cameras (egocentric as well as eye-tracking) as their setup is still too bulky. They require heavier processing and battery power. It is still not possible to equip easy-to-wear smart eyewear with such cameras. MEME focuses on electrooculography for eye movement tracking. As the eye is a dipole, we can use electrodes to recognize eye movements. Using this technique, we can recognize reading behavior in everyday scenarios [51]. As MEME shows (see Fig. 7.16), the electrodes can be unobtrusively embedded in glasses. For these reasons, we focus on reading detection and other reading habit-related research using these unobtrusive smart glasses.

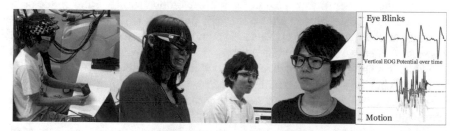

Fig. 7.15 From brain sensing, through eye-tracking glasses, to unobtrusive smart eyewear

Fig. 7.16 NS MEME, smart eyewear using electrooculography and motion sensors

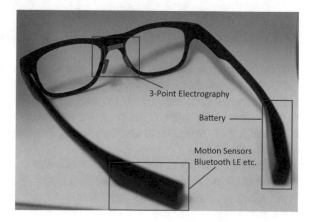

7.4.2.1 The Wordometer—Counting How Many Words You Read

Although reading is very well explored in the cognitive sciences and psychology, we still know very little about healthy reading habits. There are only few researchers tackling reading in real-life circumstances. Increased reading volume is associated with greater vocabulary skills and higher general knowledge as well as improved critical thinking. Smart eye-glasses are perfect for detecting reading activity and also quantify how many words a person reads.

As a first goal, we set out to just detect reading or not reading utilizing eye movement analysis.

Using optical eye tracking (SMI mobile glasses 2.0) we can recognize reading with very high accuracy (over 95%) in semi-controlled setups with around 30 users (Japanese students, age 20–27) [41, 51]. Porting a similar reading algorithm to J!NS MEME, we remain at around 85% accuracy for semi-controlled setups [52].

Not only can we detect when a user is reading but also the approximate amount. The idea behind the recognition is simple. Reading is detectable because of a relatively steady head position and repetitive forward-backward (or up-down) eye movements. These eye movements also include backwards saccades due to line breaks. We detect these backward saccades and get over their approximate length and their frequency the number of words a user read. The wordometer algorithm on the optical tracker now works with an error rate of 9% (std. 3%). On J!NS MEME, we are currently at 20% (std. 5%) [51]. There is room for improvement, yet comparing it to a step counter, we are in a similar accuracy range as the wrist-worn step counters available. It is still difficult to define what good reading habits are, yet the first tools for quantifying the amount of reading can help with this.

Also, for other reading-life log technologies, the wordometer provides useful information (e.g., distinguishing whether a user has actually read a sign or piece of text as opposed to just glancing over it). Yet, more important are the implications of the wordometer regarding the reading habits explored in the next section.

7.4.2.2 Quantifying Reading Habits with Smart Eyewear

Although we are increasingly aware of how important reading is for learning, it is difficult to get people to read more, especially as other types of more easily digestible content increase (e.g., videos). As tracking physical activities (e.g., step counts) can motivate users to be more active, we believe this also applies to reading. However, it is still difficult to define what healthy reading habits are, as we are lacking methods to quantify reading.

So tracking the words people read can not only motivate them to read more and improve their vocabulary and critical thinking skills, but also give initial insights into healthy reading habits. Having a measurement for speed, timing, and reading volume is a first step to exploring the cognitive life of users with the ultimate goal of improving learning.

7.4.3 Reading-Life Log for Scene Text

In our daily life, we read not only texts on paper documents but also scene texts, such as texts on signboards, price tags in supermarkets, labels on bottles and boxes, menus in restaurants, traffic signs, texts on displays, etc. Similar to the reading-life log for documents, it is possible to realize another reading-life log system for scene texts. If we can make a log of texts that we read in a scene, it will provide the reading-life log with another value. As suggested by the above examples, scene texts are often related to some object or location or activity, whereas document texts are not. Consequently, the reading-life log for scene texts will be a record of our activity and interaction with various objects, rather than a knowledge log.

To realize the reading-life log for scene texts, we can no longer fully rely on document retrieval techniques. This is simply because it is not practical to register all scene texts into the system. In particular, scene texts are often not static, that is, they are changeable dynamically. Therefore, we need to take the most straightforward solution: the development of an accurate scene text detector and recognizer.

We also encounter the practical problem of choosing a video camera for the system. (Note that it should not be a still camera but a video camera because the purpose of the reading-life log is unconscious and continuous capture of textual information, like typical life-logs.) There are many requirements of the video camera of the reading-life log system for scene texts. The camera should be compact and light, since we need to carry it attached to the body. In addition, it needs to have high resolution to capture each character with a reasonable size (say, more than 5050 pixels) without approaching the target text with the camera, high shutter speed to avoid motion blur, and an auto-focus function or deeper focus to deal with texts at various distances.

Since the target text is captured into multiple frames by a video camera, it is necessary to unify the same text in multiple frames. There are two approaches to this unification. The first approach is so-called video mosaicing, or video stitching, that combines video frames into a large single image while dealing with overlapping parts among the frames. A scene text detector and recognizer is then applied to the large image. The second and more practical approach is text-level integration. In this approach, a scene text detector and recognizer is applied to individual frames and text recognition results are then integrated while unifying the same text in different frames [53]. Figure 7.17 shows the result of this second approach. Text in the captured video is moved by scrolling but the system can achieve a unified result with good success.

7.4.4 Document Annotations

As a way of analyzing contents based on reading activities, we focus here on document annotations. Documents are annotated manually or automatically based on the

(a) A frame capturing texts on a smartphone display.

(b) Integration result of text recognition results on multiple frames.

Fig. 7.17 Reading-life log for scene texts

user's reading activities and possible services to be provided. We would like to show one example of each type of annotation. We also show an example of a simple way of showing annotation by using a mobile eye-tracker and a head-mounted display. An example of manual annotation is a system based on document image retrieval. As devices for annotation, we employ mobile phones and Google Glasses as shown in Fig. 7.18. Taking as input a picture of a document, the corresponding document is searched in the database. Various annotations such as text, image, highlight, voice, and video are supported to be put on a document. When using a mobile phone, a part

Capture the poster with Google Glass

Add a comment

Watch a demo video

Add an audio note

Download the paper file

Fig. 7.18 Putting and displaying annotations by using Google Glass

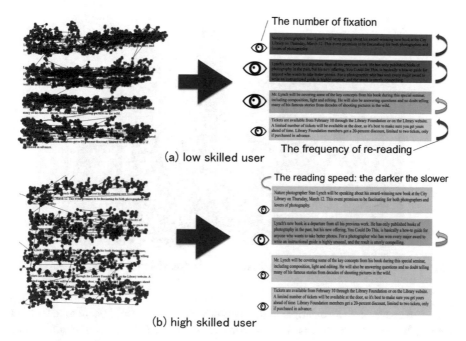

Fig. 7.19 Automated annotation by using eye gaze information

of a document at which the annotation is put can be specified by dragging that part. Retrieval of annotation is straightforward; as soon as the device captures a document, it can be used as a query and display retrieved annotations if they exist. If there is no corresponding entry of document in the database, the camera-captured document can be stored as a new entry at which the user can put annotations.

As an example of automatic annotation, we introduce here a visualization of the user's behavior while reading a document. For learners of foreign languages, it is useful to know which parts of a textbook are difficult to understand. For teachers, it is fruitful to know who is having trouble at what location in a textbook, and which parts in general learners have trouble with. In order to obtain clues for the above information, we focus here on the reading speed, the number of re-readings, and the number of fixations [54]. The parts that are read slowly, with many re-readings and fixations, indicate parts that the reader has difficulty understanding. An example of visualization is shown in Fig. 7.19. Figure 7.19a represents the behaviors of a novice learner, while Fig. 7.19b shows those of a skillful learner. In the figure, the slower the reading speed is, the darker a paragraph is. Similarly, the higher the number of re-readings is, the darker the arrow is. The number of fixations is displayed as the size of the eye icon. From the figure, it is easy to see that there is a clear difference between novice and skillful learners. For novice learners, not only by reviewing their performance visualized in this way, but also by comparing their behavior with other, more skillful learners allows them to motivate themselves to keep learning.

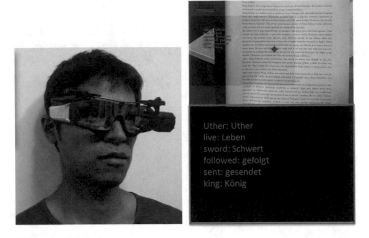

Fig. 7.20 Display of annotation by using a mobile eye-tracker and a head-mounted display

Let us move on to an example of displaying annotations. A representative method for displaying annotations is the research called Text 2.0 [55]. This method is to replay manually annotated contents based upon the reader's reading activities. A concrete use case is as follows. The reader is reading a document on a display with an eye-tracker. When the reader is reading a specific part with which a service is associated, it is provided. Examples of such service are sound effects and dictionary lookup. A more advanced method we developed along this line will be described in Sect. 7.4.6. One disadvantage of Text 2.0 is that the service is provided only on the displayed document. This problem can be solved by using a mobile eye-tracker with a head-mounted display [56]. A camera-captured document with the reader's eye gaze is given to the document image retrieval LLAH, in order to obtain information about the part of the document the reader is reading. After that, a mechanism similar to Text 2.0 is employed. Figure 7.20 shows the overall system and an example of dictionary lookup based upon the reader's eye gaze.

7.4.5 AffectiveWear

In addition to straightforward annotations related to eye movements (saccade speed, fixation count), which can give some indication of reader proficiency and interest [54], we can also record facial expressions with the text [57]. For this purpose, we implemented AffectiveWear, smart glasses that detect the distance of the skin from the glass frame using proximity sensors. With this technology, we can detect up to eight different facial expressions. Figure 7.21 gives a brief overview of the system and the types of facial expressions it can detect.

This system and similar approaches can give indications about the emotional state of the reader. Authors can get feedback regarding whether a specific text evokes the intended effect. One can get classifications about especially funny, sad etc. paragraphs and so on.

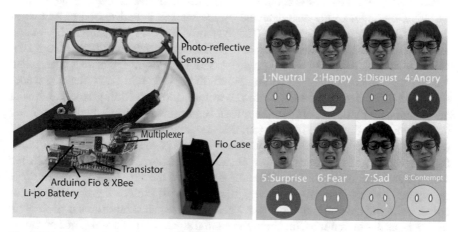

Fig. 7.21 AffectiveWear, detecting facial expressions using distance sensors between the skin and glasses frame

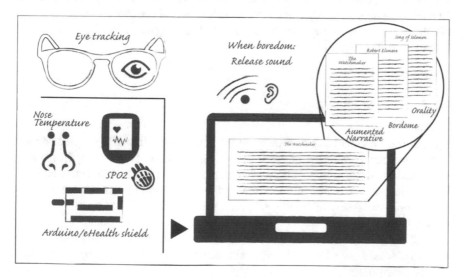

Fig. 7.22 Augmented narrative: using physiological signals as feedback mechanism for books triggering audio and haptic interactions

7.4.6 Augmented Narrative

Augmented narrative uses bio-feedback (nose temperature, eye blink, eye movement, heart rate) in a text-body interaction for a more immersive experience [58]. Figure 7.22 gives an overview about the augmented narrative concept. In augmented narrative, the input of the data detected by the sensors is understood to be that of the mental workload of the reader. The system is then set to distinguish whether the reader is bored, frustrated, or misunderstanding the story or whether the reader is in a state of flow and therefore engaged with the storyline. For example, when reading the story of Little Red Riding Hood, the system will know that the reader should be immersed in the story's climax when Little Red Riding Hood arrives at her grandmother's house, not realizing that, in her grandmother's bed, lies not her grandmother but the wolf. If the system finds no input of engagement when reading through this climatic part of the story, meaning there is no stimulation, then it infers that the reader needs extra-textual content and will release a sound, for example, the wolf's claws scratching the bed. Overall, augmented narrative intends to reconcile orality and literacy bringing them together in order to present the transmission of culture with the best of both worlds, by giving the reader a multimodal perception of events, as in oral cultures, that help the mental simulation of a story, in a narration whose meaning is conveyed in writing.

With a first prototype of the augmented narrative, we showed that we are able to detect engagement in a story using nose temperature and eye movements and that, in a further step, we can increase engagement by giving haptic and audio stimuli when the user loses interest [58].

7.4.7 Future Directions

In the future we would like to extend our research toward the following directions.

A promising application of reading-life log for scene text is to help disabled people such as visually impaired people and people with dyslexia. The technologies of real-time scene text recognition allows us to read text in the environment to give those people the ability of "reading." The most difficult part for implementing this service is its interface: how to display the results of recognition. If the machine reads all text in the scene and display them as sounds, the information overflows and annoying. A goal directed and/or spatially separated display of recognized results must be incorporated.

Another important application of reading-life log for scene text is memory aid. Not only for dementia people but also for healthy people, it is not always easy to remember everything needed for their life. Our technology can amplify the memory by recording all of the read text with indexes of time, place and context. People can search what they have read to remember things. Combination of this technology with an intelligent interface of finding what to search enables us to augment the human memory. In other words, the user is connected to his/her reading-life.

The reading-life log for documents also has its future directions. One way is just to extend the current direction toward learning help. For the current target English as a foreign language, finding real problems of users and give them recommendations about what to do next are important task. We can also think of extending the application area from English to other subjects. We hope in the near future that the machine can help students to find their weak and strong points at each subject in order to motivate them to learn more.

An ultimate application of reading-life log for documents is to estimate the knowledge-level of users. One of the authors, Koichi Kise still remembers the comment made by the late Professor Naomi Miyake, who had been an advisor of our CREST. She told us that if we are able to record all what have been read, it is not necessary to have entrance examinations of universities. She thinks that the level of knowledge can be described by looking at his/her record of reading. Although such information is quite personal and may be problematic to record, it has a big impact of knowing people's abilities and interests. With a careful treatment of such information in terms of ELSI (Ethical, Legal and Social Issues), we believe that our life can be enriched, and our abilities can be extended by our technologies.

7.5 Conclusion

"You are what you have read." Based on the notion of this phrase discussed in the Introduction, we have implemented a variety of functions of the reading-life log using various sensors. Based on the implemented functions, readers are described in terms of the quantity and the quality of what they read. At the same time, documents and signboards are characterized by how they have been read and by whom. We do hope that this research will open a new field of research on readers and materials for reading.

We still have several things to do to make our technologies available to the public. One important aspect is to verify their effectiveness by conducting a larger user study. Another important point is how to use the reading-life log. A possible future direction would be to build an "actuator" to change a reader's behavior based on the facts found by the reading-life log.

References

1. K. Kise, S. Omachi, S. Uchida, M. Iwamura, A trial for development of fundamental technologies for new usage of character and document media. J. Inst. Electron. Inf. Commun. Eng. 98(4), 311–327 (2015)

2. D. Karatzas, F. Shafait, S. Uchida, M. Iwamura, L. Gomez, S.R. Mestre, J. Mas, D.F. Mota, J.A. Almazan, L.P. de las Heras, ICDAR 2013 robust reading competition, in *Proceedings of the 12th International Conference on Document Analysis and Recognition (ICDAR 2013)* (2013), pp. 1484–1493

3. D. Karatzas, L. Gomez, A. Nicolaou, S. Ghosh, A. Bagdanov, M. Iwamura, J. Matas, L. Neumann, V.R. Chandrasekhar, S. Lu, F. Shafait, S. Uchida, E. Valveny, ICDAR 2015 robust reading competition, in *Proceedings of the 13th International Conference on Document Analysis and Recognition (ICDAR 2015)* (2015), pp. 1156–1160

4. S. Uchida, *Text Localization and Recognition in Images and Video, Handbook of Document Image Processing and Recognition* (Springer, 2014)

5. Q. Ye, D. Doermann, Text detection and recognition in imagery: a survey. IEEE Trans. Pattern Anal. Mach. Intell. **37**(7), 1480–1500 (2015)

6. Y. Matsuda, S. Omachi, H. Aso, String detection from scene images by binarization and edge detection. IEICE Trans. Inf. Syst. (Japanese edition), **J93-D** (3), 336–344 (2010) (in Japanese)

7. R. Huang, P. Shivakumara, Y. Feng, S. Uchida, Scene character detection and recognition with cooperative multiple-hypothesis framework. IEICE Trans. Inf. Syst. **E96-D** (10), 2235–2244 (2013)

8. H. Takebe, S. Uchida, Scene character extraction by an optimal two-dimensional segmentation. IEICE Trans. Inf. Syst. (Japanese edition) (D), **J97-D** (3), 667–675 (2014) (in Japanese)

9. Y. Kunishige, Y. Feng, S. Uchida, Scenery character detection with environmental context, in *Proceedings of the 11th International Conference on Document Analysis and Recognition (ICDAR 2011)* (2011), pp. 1049–1053

10. A. Zhu, R. Gao, S. Uchida, Could scene context be beneficial for scene text detection?Pattern Recognit. **58**C, 204–215 (2016)

11. A. Shahab, F. Shafait, A. Dengel, S. Uchida, How salient is scene text? in *Proceedings of the 10th IAPR International Workshop on Document Analysis Systems (DAS2012)* (2012), pp. 317–321

12. R. Gao, S. Uchida, A. Shahab, F. Shafait, V. Frinken, Visual Saliency Models for Text Detection in Real World. PLoS one **9**(12), e114539 (2014)

13. S. Wang, S. Uchida, M. Liwicki, Y. Feng, Part-based methods for handwritten digit recognition. Front. Comput. Sci. **7**(4), 514–525 (2013)

14. S. Toba, H. Kudo, T. Miyazaki, Y. Sugaya, S. Omachi, Ultra-low resolution character recognition system with pruning mutual subspace method, in *Proceedings of the 2015 International Conference on Consumer Electronics—Taiwan (ICCE-TW)* (2015), pp. 284–285

15. M. Goto, R. Ishida, Y. Feng, S. Uchida, Analyzing the distribution of a large-scale character pattern set using relative neighborhood graph, in *Proceedings of the 12th International Conference on Document Analysis and Recognition (ICDAR 2013)* (2013), pp. 3–7

16. M. Goldstein, S. Uchida, A comparative study on outlier removal from a large-scale dataset using unsupervised anomaly detection, in *Proceedings of the 5th International Conference on Pattern Recognition Applications and Methods (ICPRAM2016)* (2016), pp. 263–269

17. T. Saito, H. Yamada, K. Yamamoto, On the data base ETL9 of handprinted characters in JIS Chinese characters and its analysis. IEICE Trans. Inf. Syst. (Japanese edition) (D), **J68-D**(4), 757–764 (1985) (in Japanese)

18. T. Nakai, K. Kise, M. Iwamura, Use of affine invariants in locally likely arrangement hashing for camera-based document image retrieval, in *Document Analysis Systems VII*, vol. 3872, Lecture Notes in Computer Science, (2006), pp. 541–552

19. S. Ahmed, K. Kise, M. Iwamura, M. Liwicki, A. Dengel, Automatic ground truth generation of camera captured documents using document image retrieval, in *Proceedings of the 12th International Conference on Document Analysis and Recognition (ICDAR 2013)* (2013), pp. 528–532

20. S.M. Lucas, A. Panaretos, L. Sosa, A. Tang, S. Wong, R. Young, K. Ashida, H. Nagai, M. Okamoto, H. Yamamoto, H. Miyao, J. Zhu, W. Ou, C. Wolf, J.-M. Jolion, L. Todoran, M. Worring, X. Lin, ICDAR 2003 robust reading competitions: entries, results and future directions. Int. J. Doc. Anal. Recognit. (IJDAR) **7**(2–3), 105–122 (2005)

21. S. Lucas, ICDAR 2005 text locating competition results, in *Proceedings of the 8th International Conference on Document Analysis and Recognition (ICDAR2005)*, **1**, (2005), pp. 80–84
22. A. Shahab, F. Shafait, A. Dengel, ICDAR 2011 robust reading competition challenge 2: reading text in scene images, in *Proceedings of the 11th International Conference on Document Analysis and Recognition (ICDAR 2011)* (2011), pp. 1491–1496
23. K. Wang, S. Belongie, Word spotting in the wild, in *Proceedings of the 11th European Conference on Computer Vision (ECCV2010), Part I* (2010), pp. 591–604
24. K. Wang, B. Babenko, S. Belongie, End-to-end scene text recognition, in *Proceedings of the 13th International Conference on Computer Vision (ICCV2011)* (2011), pp. 1457–1464
25. R. Gao, F. Shafait, S. Uchida, Y. Feng, A hierarchical visual saliency model for character detection in natural scenes. Camera-Based Document Analysis and Recognition, LNCS **8357**, 18–29 (2014)
26. M. Iwamura, T. Matsuda, N. Morimoto, H. Sato, Y. Ikeda, K. Kise, Downtown osaka scene text dataset, in *Proceedings of the 2nd International Workshop on Robust Reading (IWRR2016)* (2016) (in printing)
27. Y. Netzer, T. Wang, A. Coates, A. Bissacco, B. Wu, A.Y. Ng, Reading digits in natural images with unsupervised feature learning, in *Proceedings of the NIPS Workshop on Deep Learning and Unsupervised Feature Learning* (2011), p. 9
28. M. Iwamura, M. Tsukada, K. Kise, Automatic labeling for scene text database, in *Proceedings of the 12th International Conference on Document Analysis and Recognition (ICDAR 2013)* (2013), pp. 1397–1401
29. H. Saito, Y. Sugaya, S. Omachi, S. Uchida, M. Iwamura, K. Kise, Generation of character patterns from sample character images, in IEICE Technical Report, PRMU2010-287 (2011) (in Japanese)
30. T.S. Cho, S. Avidan, W.T. Freeman, The patch transform. IEEE Trans. Pattern Anal. Mach. Intell. **32**(8), 1489–1501 (2010)
31. S. Belongie, J. Malik, and J. Puzicha, Shape context: a new descriptor for shape matching and object recognition, in *Advances in Neural Information Processing Systems* (2000), pp. 831–837
32. M. Iwamura, T. Sato, K. Kise, What is the most efficient way to select nearest neighbor candidates for fast approximate nearest neighbor search? in *Proceedings of the 14th International Conference on Computer Vision (ICCV 2013)* (2013), pp. 3535–3542
33. M. Iwamura, T. Tsuji, K. Kise, Memory-based recognition of camera-captured characters, in *Proceedings of the 9th IAPR International Workshop on Document Analysis Systems (DAS2010)* (2010), pp. 89–96
34. Y. Lamdan, H.J. Wolfson, Geometric hashing: a general and efficient model-based recognition scheme, in *Proceedings of the 2nd International Conference on Computer Vision (ICCV1988)* (1988), pp. 238–249
35. N. Asada, M. Iwamura, K. Kise, Improvement of word recognition accuracy with spellchecker based on tendency of recognition error of characters, IEICE Technical Report, **110**(467), PRMU2010-268, pp. 183–188 (2011) (in Japanese)
36. M. Iwamura, T. Kobayashi, K. Kise, Recognition of multiple characters in a scene image using arrangement of local features, in *Proceedings of the 11th International Conference on Document Analysis and Recognition (ICDAR 2011)* (2011), pp. 1409–1413
37. D.G. Lowe, Object recognition from local scale-invariant features, in *Proceedings of the International Conference on Computer Vision* (1999), pp. 1150–1157
38. T. Kobayashi, M. Iwamura, T. Matsuda, K. Kise, An anytime algorithm for camera-based character recognition, in *Proceedings of the 12th International Conference on Document Analysis and Recognition (ICDAR 2013)* (2013), pp. 1172–1176
39. T. Matsuda, M. Iwamura, K. Kise, Performance improvement in local feature based camera-captured character recognition, in *Proceedings of the 11th IAPR International Workshop on Document Analysis Systems (DAS2014)* (2014), pp. 196–201
40. X. Liu, J. Samarabandu, An edge-based text region extraction algorithm for indoor mobile robot navigation, in *Proceedings of the 2005 IEEE International Conference on Mechatronics and Automation*, **2**, (2005), pp. 701–706

41. K. Kunze, H. Kawaichi, K. Kise, K. Yoshimura, The wordometer—estimating the number of words read using document image retrieval and mobile eye tracking, in *Proceedings of the 12th International Conference on Document Analysis and Recognition (ICDAR 2013)* (2013), pp. 25–29

42. S. Ishimaru, J. Weppner, K. Kunze, A. Bulling, K. Kise, A. Dengel, P. Lukowicz, In the blink of an eye—combining head motion and eye blink frequency for activity recognition with Google Glass, in *Proceedings of the 5th Augmented Human International Conference* (2014), pp. 150–153

43. Y. Shiga, T. Toyama, Y. Utsumi, A. Dengel, K. Kise, Daily activity recognition combining gaze motion and visual features, in *PETMEI 2014: 4th International Workshop on Pervasive Eye Tracking and Mobile Eye-based Interaction, Proceedings of the 16th International Conference on Ubiquitous Computing* (2014), pp. 1103–1111

44. K. Kunze, Y. Shiga, S. Ishimaru, K. Kise, Reading activity recognition using an off-the-shelf EEG—detecting reading activities and distinguishing genres of documents, in *Proceedings of the12th International Conference on Document Analysis and Recognition (ICDAR2013)* (2013), pp. 96–100

45. Y. Utsumi, Y. Shiga, M. Iwamura, K. Kunze, K. Kise, Document type classification toward understanding reading habits, in *Proceedings of the 20th Korea-Japan Joint Workshop on Frontiers of Computer Vision*, **3**, (2014), pp. 11–17

46. K. Kunze, Y. Utsumi, Y. Shiga, K. Kise, A. Bulling, I know what you are reading: recognition of document types using mobile eye tracking, in *Proceedings of the 17th Annual International Symposium on Wearable Computers* (2013), pp. 113–116

47. O. Augereau, K. Kise, K. Hoshika, A proposal of a document image reading-life log based on document image retrieval and eyetracking, in *Proceedings of the 13th International Conference on Document Analysis and Recognition (ICDAR2015)* (2015), pp. 246–250

48. K. Kunze, H. Kawaichi, K. Yoshimura, K. Kise, Towards inferring language expertise using eye tracking, in *CHI'13 Extended Abstracts on Human Factors in Computing Systems* (2013), p. 6

49. K. Yoshimura, K. Kunze, K. Kise, The eye as the window of the language ability: estimation of english skills by analyzing eye movement while reading documents, in *Proceedings of the 13th International Conference on Document Analysis and Recognition (ICDAR2015)* (2015), pp. 251–255

50. H. Fujiyoshi, K. Yoshimura, K. Kunze, K. Kise, A method of estimating English skills using eye gaze information of answering questions of English exercises, IEICE Technical Report, **115**(24), PRMU2015-10, pp. 49–54 (2015) (in Japanese)

51. K. Kunze, K. Masai, M. Inami, Ö. Sacakli, M. Liwicki, A. Dengel, S. Ishimaru, K. Kise, Quantifying reading habits: counting how many words you read, in *Presented at the UbiComp'15: Proceedings of the 2015 ACM International Joint Conference on Pervasive and Ubiquitous Computing* (2015), pp. 87–96

52. S. Ishimaru, K. Kunze, K. Tanaka, Y. Uema, K. Kise, M. Inami, Smart eyewear for interaction and activity recognition, in *Presented at the CHI EA'15: Proceedings of the 33rd Annual ACM Conference Extended Abstracts on Human Factors in Computing Systems* (2015), pp. 307–310

53. T. Kimura, R. Huang, S. Uchida, M. Iwamura, S. Omachi, K. Kise, The reading-life log—technologies to recognize texts that we read, in *Proceedings of the 12th International Conference on Document Analysis and Recognition (ICDAR 2013)* (2013), pp. 91–95

54. A. Okoso, K. Kunze, K. Kise, Implicit gaze based annotations to support second language learning, in *Proceedings of the 2014 ACM Conference on Pervasive and Ubiquitous Computing: Adjunct Publication (UbiComp2014)* (2014), pp. 143–146

55. R. Biedert, G. Buscher, S. Schwarz, J. Hees, A. Dengel, Text 2.0, in *Proceedings of the 28th ACM Conference on Human Factors in Computing Systems (CHI2011)* (2011)

56. T. Toyama, W. Suzuki, A. Dengel, K. Kise, User attention oriented augmented reality on documents with document dependent dynamic overlay, in *Proceedings of the IEEE International Symposium on Mixed and Augmented Reality (ISMAR2013)* (2013), pp. 299–300

57. K. Masai, Y. Sugiura, K. Suzuki, S. Shimamura, K. Kunze, M. Ogata, M. Inami, M. Sugimoto, AffectiveWear: towards recognizing affect in real life, in *Presented at the UbiComp/ISWC'15 Adjunct: Adjunct Proceedings of the 2015 ACM International Joint Conference on Pervasive and Ubiquitous Computing and Proceedings of the 2015 ACM International Symposium on Wearable Computers* (2015), pp. 357–360
58. S. Sanchez, T. Dingler, H. Gu, K. Kunze, Embodied reading: a multisensory experience, in *Presented at the CHI EA'16: Proceedings of the 2016 CHI Conference Extended Abstracts on Human Factors in Computing Systems* (2016), pp. 1459–1466

Chapter 8
Pedagogical Machine: Studies Towards a Machine that Teaches Humans

Kazuo Hiraki

Abstract This project aimed to better understand the possibilities and limitations of an artificial pedagogical agent. For example, could an agent be programmed into a robot or a computer to teach? If so, how should such an agent be designed? To answer these questions, we used an approach that integrated developmental cognitive science, information technology, and field studies in educational setting. This chapter discusses the results of our research to date and the outlook for the future development of pedagogical machines.

Keywords Pedagogical machines · Education · Developmental cognitive science · Mother-child interaction

8.1 Introduction

Teaching is an ability seen universally in humans. On the one hand, it has long been considered a special ability that only humans possess, because ostensive teaching behaviors for general knowledge have not been observed even in chimpanzees, which are considered phylogenetically closest to humans. In westernized societies, there is a tendency to assume that school education accounts for all "teaching," but there are many places in the world where schools are underdeveloped or do not exist. However, parents and people around small children can universally be seen teaching them the names of things and their usage regardless of place or ethnic group. Teaching is not limited to school education settings.

Just as with the ability to teach, the ability to be taught (to learn) is also universal to human beings. Recent research in developmental cognitive science has shown that infants from an early developmental stage are sensitive to ostensive cues and perform a specific process when others (mainly adults in the surroundings) point, use motherese, gaze or make facial expressions at them, or contingently react to them.

K. Hiraki (✉)
Department of General Systems Studies and Center for Evolutionary Cognitive Sciences,
The University of Tokyo, 3-8-1 Komaba, Meguro-ku, Tokyo 153-8902, Japan
e-mail: khiraki@idea.c.u-tokyo.ac.jp

© Springer Japan KK 2017
T. Nishida (ed.), *Human-Harmonized Information Technology, Volume 2*,
DOI 10.1007/978-4-431-56535-2_8

These facts show that teaching and being taught in human societies are indispensable abilities for the transmission of new knowledge and the passing on of culture. In other words, this suggests that the reciprocal relationship of teaching and being taught and the basic ability to build and maintain that relationship—Natural Pedagogy—universally exists in human societies and in the human beings that constitute them [1].

Before discussing the topic of pedagogical machines—teaching artifacts—from the perspective of cognitive science, we would like to discuss what teaching is in the first place. Caro and Hauser [2] have defined the criteria for teaching in ethology as follows [2]:

1. The behavior is shown by individual A only in the presence of a naïve individual B.
2. The behavior is without direct benefit or incurs some kind of cost for individual A.
3. As a result of A's behavior B is able to acquire knowledge or learn a skill more easily or earlier in its development, or without A's behavior B would not have been able to acquire knowledge or learn a skill at all.

These three criteria may seem too obvious to be meaningful for (cognitive scientific) research on teaching. However, it is also important to understand teaching in as broad a meaning as possible as a starting point for discussion in order to avoid being caught up in trivial problems related to individual cases.

Although the above criteria are extremely broad and flexible, are there any non-human animals that meet them all? Teaching has long been considered a special ability possessed only by humans, but exciting discoveries have been made recently in ethology. For example, adult meerkats (Suricata suricatta), in the presence of young individuals inept at catching food, catch prey for them alive or leave it for them dead according to the ages of the younger individuals to provide circumstances in which they can practice the skills necessary to capture their own prey [3]. This behavior is only seen when an adult is with a younger individual (criterion 1). For the adult meerkat, there is no immediate benefit (criterion 2). Further, it is likely that the younger individual's skills for catching prey are enhanced by the experience accumulated through the circumstances provided by the adult (criterion 3). Outside of meerkats, behaviors (partially) meeting the above criteria have also been discovered in babblers (a type of songbird) and ants. Thus, if one uses the above criteria of Caro and Hauser [2], teaching is not likely to be an ability unique to man.

However, Csibra [3] would argue that teaching in these nonhuman animals is limited to episodic settings and does not extend to generalizable knowledge as taught by humans [4]. The behavior observed in meerkats resembles the process of "scaffolding" used in human pedagogical situation, but meerkats are not directly teaching a "method" to catch prey. Young meerkats need to learn that independently based on the circumstances that have been set up for them. Csibra and Gergely [1] argue that, in man, teaching is inseparable from communication (both linguistic and non-linguistic). In addition, they hypothesize that human communication has evolved to efficiently transmit opaque knowledge from generation to generation through the creation and use of complex tools [1].

The arguments of Csibra et al. that suggest the importance of the mutual give and take of communication in teaching provide a clue as to why Caro and Hauser's [2] previously presented criteria for teaching could be advanced as "cognitive science" criteria. Is it then possible for the artifact we would like to discuss to serve as a pedagogical agent? Much educational content has already been developed mainly using the internet and digital processing technologies. However, many of these do not go beyond the level of so-called "teaching materials." The majority are limited simply to the presentation of digitized texts and videos. As a relatively new type of venture, educational content referred to as "serious games" and "edutainment" leverages the entertainment value of games. Even in Japan, the adoption of digital textbooks is being considered for the near future. However, these all continue to fall under the category of teaching materials and it may be safe to say that artifacts that can teach or be taught are not being seriously considered.

As we discussed in the above teaching and learning has presupposed the existence of two parties (individuals) as agents. This assumption has a significant impact on learning strategies for learners. There is a significant difference between only teaching materials being available and a (teaching) agent being present. Learning from another requires that there be at least two individuals, a teacher and a learner. A recent tendency in schools has been to prioritize learners' independence through, for example, independent study and active learning. However, to resolve many of the potential problems in learning and education, the character of the two individuals who are teaching and being taught (teacher and student, or student and student) is important, along with improving the relationship between them. To simply narrow the focus to only the learner's side risks neglecting learning strategies that are specifically human.

The roles of individuality and (humans as) agents are also important in (the learning situations of) early human development. The presence or absence of an agent has an effect even in infants less than a year old. For example, research on phonetic discrimination in infants has shown that infants exposed multiple times to speakers of a foreign language (adults) speaking within their sight were able to distinguish sounds unique to the foreign language. However, infants shown audiovisual or audio-only recordings of the same scenarios were unable to distinguish any sounds [5]. This both exposes the limitations of unidirectional instruction and suggests the importance of interactive instruction.

In order to make a teaching artifact a reality, it appears that the key will be to figure out what makes an individual a teaching agent. In addition, how would such an agent be designed?

Currently, in the fields of information technology and communication engineering, the underlying technologies are rapidly developing and we believe the groundwork exists to take the first step toward creating a teaching artifact. Specifically, the technologies for speaker identification from speech, the tracking of facial information from images, and motion tracking can be run at set levels of accuracy and speed on cheap notebook PCs, small digital cameras, and TV game sensors, such as Kinect.

However, there is a continued and unfortunate dearth of ideas regarding how to leverage these underlying technologies. In this context, one can expect that the integration of individual digital processing technologies as the components for the development of a pedagogical machine would suggest that a research orientation is needed that includes both information technology and cognitive science.

In the following sections, our research project that began in 2012 is explained from three different approaches: a cognitive science approach, an information technology approach, and a field study approach.

8.2 Cognitive Science Approach to Pedagogical Machines

Could an agent be programmed into a robot or a computer to teach humans? If so, how should such an agent be designed? One plausible approach for a first step toward these questions is to study human teaching and learning behaviors and clarify the essential part of them. Because human can be seen the only agent who can teach through communication, we need to understand the human pedagogical communication in order to create a pedagogical machine.

The vast majority of developmental psychology literature suggests that human learning is influenced by social interaction. The ability to socially interact with others begins very early [6] and is thought to be crucial for learning general knowledge [1, 7] and language [8, 9]. Children under 3 years of age learn less from screen media than from engaging in live social interaction with adults [5, 10]; a phenomenon called the video-deficit effect [11].

Evidence of previous studies suggested that interaction between children as learners and adults as demonstrators can play an important role in children's learning [12–15]. While the cause of video deficit is not yet fully understood, several studies have found that providing live social interaction through screen media mitigates the effect [14, 16]. For example, Nielsen et al. [14] found that 24-month-old children who observed demonstrator teaching behaviours during live interaction exhibited better imitation performance with novel toys than children taught via pre-recorded videos. It is a possibility that a disruption of temporal contingency of demonstrators' responses in video condition interfered with children's imitation learning from videos [14].

Further more recent evidence suggests that temporal regulation, or temporal contingency, influences language learning. For example, Goldstein et al. [13] demonstrated that the immediate reactions of mothers to infant vocalizations or gestures facilitate speech production from infants. Therefore, our project focused on temporal aspects—contingency, contiguity—between the learner and teacher.

8.2.1 Double TV Environment:

In order to investigate the temporal aspect of the teaching/learning behaviors in communication, we created an experimental environment called Double TV environment.

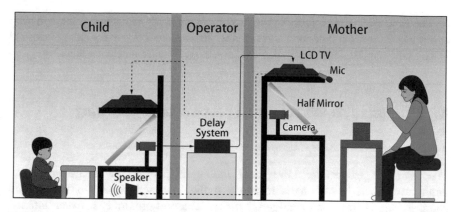

Fig. 8.1 Double TV environment for mother-child interaction study [50]

The environment consists of two adjacent rooms connected by a double liquid-crystal color television system, as shown in Fig. 8.1. Mothers' (demonstrators') images and voices recorded by a camera and microphone were presented to a monitor located in front of children. Children's (learner's) images were presented to a monitor located in front of their mothers (demonstrators). To prevent mothers from hearing their own delayed voices, sounds in the children's room (including children's voices) were not presented to mothers.

In the mothers' room, a 32-inch color television monitor was set facing down on a steel frame located in front of mothers. The image presented on the monitor was reflected by a one-way mirror that was placed at a 45° inclination on a steel deck, presented at an average eye level for females. A digital video camera was placed behind the mirror and recorded mothers' upper body and face. In the children's room, the height of the apparatuses was adjusted to the average eye level for 24-month children; that is, a 32-inch color television monitor was set on a steel frame and a one-way mirror and digital video camera was placed on a steel deck. The camera in the mothers' room was directly connected to the monitor in the children's room, whereas the camera in the children's room was connected to the monitor in the mothers' room via an audiovisual delay device (EDS-3306, FOR-A YEM Eletex), used to insert a temporal delay in visual information presentation. The video data (30 fps) for front views of children and mothers that were placed behind each mirror were synchronously recorded for data analysis. An additional digital video camera was placed diagonally behind children to record their responses and imitation behaviors.

Adding the closed circuit TV system, we adopted a 3D motion capture system with 10 infrared high-speed cameras (Oqus 3+, Qualisys, Sweden) operated by Qualisys Track Manager 2.7 (Qualysis, Sweden). Using the system, we can evaluate both mothers and children's motions. The motion capture system had an accuracy of better than 1 mm, with a temporal resolution of 120 Hz.

The following section describes an experimental study focusing on the temporal contiguity between mother and child. Using the Double-TV environment, we could clarify how temporal delays among mother-child interaction affect a learning.

8.2.2   Subtle Temporal Delays Affect Imitation Learning

Aim

In pedagogical perspective, a key issue is whether infants and children are sensitive to temporal characteristic of others' responses to their own actions. One of the temporal characteristic is "temporal contiguity" that is temporal proximity between infants' actions and subsequent adult responses [17]. It can be argued that the temporal contiguity of others' responses may be useful for infants because it enables to judge whether effective interaction was established between himself/herself and others.

There are a few previous studies that demonstrated the importance of temporal contiguity on social cognition of infants. Striano et al. [18] examined the role of temporal contiguity in social interaction by observing live and delayed face-to-face interaction between 6-month-old infants and their mothers [18]. The infants and mothers in the live condition could interact with each other in real time, whereas infants and mothers in the delayed condition experienced a subtle 1-second time lag between infants' and mothers' behaviors. Striano et al. [18] discovered that the infants in the live condition watched their mothers' images much more than the infants in the delayed condition. The results suggested that infants appear to use temporal contiguity as a cue to judge whether mothers' responses are directed toward their own action, and whether their interaction is established. However, the contribution of temporal contiguity to cognitive aspects such as learning has yet to be fully understood.

There were several unresolved problems in the previous studies concerning the temporal contiguity of interactive learning. First, the previous study has not controlled the temporal contiguity of demonstrators' responses because of comparing live interaction with pre-recorded videos. Therefore, it is still unknown whether the temporal contiguity of demonstrators' responses directly impact children's learning performances. Second problem is that the previous study did not evaluate change in the demonstrators' responses in the interaction with children. A previous study demonstrated that mothers modify child-directed actions based on children's actions in order to maintain children's attention and promote learning [19]. Thus, there is a possibility that adults' demonstrations in the previous study were modified based on a slight change of children's action and then their modified demonstrations affected children's learning performances.

In present study, we examined the role of temporal contiguity of mothers' responses to their children's actions on children's imitation learning using the double-TV environment [50]. There were two experimental conditions—live and delayed condition—in our study. In the live condition, children received demonstrators' prompt responses without a time lag between them; that is, children could interact with their mothers as usual. In the delayed condition, there was a one second time lag between children and mothers; that is, children received mothers' one-second delayed responses more than usual.

Participants

Eighteen mother-child dyads (9 girls and 9 boys) separately participated in this study. Mean child age was 26.72 months ($SD = 2.47$) and mean mother age was 35.21 years ($SD = 4.56$). Additional dyads were tested but excluded because of technical problems ($n = 2$) or because children could not tolerate separation from their mothers ($n = 4$). All child-mother dyads were recruited through birth records at city hall branch offices. After the mothers had been given a description of the study, written informed consent was obtained in accordance with the Declaration of Helsinki. The Ethics Committee of the University of Tokyo (No. 246-4) approved the experiment reported here.

Method and Procedure

The experiment was conducted in two adjacent rooms connected by a double television system, as shown in Fig. 8.1. Two toys were specifically constructed in our laboratory for this study: a wooden tower and a treasure box. Each toy was designed to have two different action sequences corresponding to different end goals. Each action sequence consisted of three target actions. These toys were fully novel to both mothers and children (See Fig. 8.2).

Mothers were asked to demonstrate four types of action sequences (two toys × two action sequences) toward their own children over the double-TV system in a pre-determined teaching context, and they were provided with verbal and written instructions for teaching purposes.

For each action sequence, a set of attention-getting and manipulation phases was repeated three times, with an interval time of approximately 10 s. During the interval

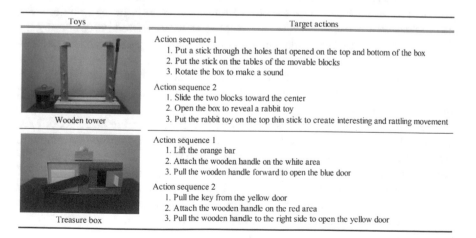

Toys	Target actions
Wooden tower	Action sequence 1 1. Put a stick through the holes that opened on the top and bottom of the box 2. Put the stick on the tables of the movable blocks 3. Rotate the box to make a sound Action sequence 2 1. Slide the two blocks toward the center 2. Open the box to reveal a rabbit toy 3. Put the rabbit toy on the top thin stick to create interesting and rattling movement
Treasure box	Action sequence 1 1. Lift the orange bar 2. Attach the wooden handle on the white area 3. Pull the wooden handle forward to open the blue door Action sequence 2 1. Pull the key from the yellow door 2. Attach the wooden handle on the red area 3. Pull the wooden handle to the right side to open the yellow door

Fig. 8.2 Toys and action sequences used in the study [50]

time, monitors were turned off. Before demonstration of all action sequences, mothers viewed movies that depicted how to perform each action sequence. Each movie showed an experimenter performing each 15 s action sequence in which her face was digitally blurred. Mothers were then given a few minutes to practice until they felt comfortable and natural in their demonstrations. To avoid biasing mothers' behaviors, we specifically did not mention that there were live and delayed conditions, and informed mothers that the goal of the study was to investigate how children could imitate mothers' behaviors.

After a brief warm-up session where each pair of mothers and children had an opportunity to acclimate to the environment and experimenters, they were asked to sit in front of each table in different rooms. One experimenter sat on the right side of the mothers and another on the right side of the children, to give instructions and encouragement. At first, only the children participated in a baseline session, and then both mothers and children participated in a short interaction session. Shortly afterward, an imitation test session including four trials corresponding to each action sequence was conducted.

The baseline session was included to assess the likelihood that three target actions involving the two toys would occur in children's spontaneous behaviors, irrespective of mothers' demonstrations. During this session, the mothers waited in the other room without being able to watch the children.

To habituate the children and mothers to the double television system, dyads were given the opportunity to interact with each other in real time over the system. The mothers were instructed to talk freely to their children on the monitor. They were allowed to interact with each other for 15 s, at which time an ending sound was presented and the images disappeared.

After the short interaction session, the dyads participated in an imitation test session that included four trials corresponding to each of four action sequences. A single trial consisted of a mothers' demonstration and a subsequent imitation test. In the demonstration, the children observed mothers' demonstrations of one of four types of action sequences over the double television system. In the imitation test, the children were presented with a toy that the children viewed before during the mothers' demonstrations in order to assess their imitation performances, and they were allowed to play with each toy for 30 s from when they first touched it. During the play interval, children and mothers could not watch each other. The four trials were separated by an intertrial interval of a few minutes in which the mothers prepared for the next demonstration.

One of the toys was always assigned to both of the live and delayed conditions; namely, one of two action sequences of each object was used in the live condition and the other was used in the delayed condition. The only difference between the live and delayed conditions was the 1 s delay of the children's images. The order of action sequences and two conditions were determined pseudorandomly across the dyads. At the end of the session, the mothers were asked to answer the question "Did you note a temporal delay on the children's images during your demonstration?" by saying "yes" or "no".

Fig. 8.3 The imitation score in live and delayed condition [51]

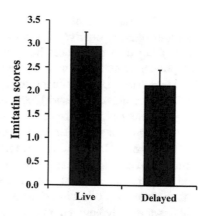

Results

Figure 8.3 shows imitation scores in the live and delayed conditions. Overall, children in both conditions showed increased (above chance) imitation performance, confirmed using one-sample-tests in the live condition ($t(17) = 9.26$, $p < 0.001$) and the delayed condition ($t(17) = 6.01$, $p < 0.001$). A paired t-test showed that imitation scores in the delayed condition ($M = 2.94$, $SD = 1.31$) were significantly lower than those in the live condition ($M = 2.11$, $SD = 1.45$) ($t(17) = 2.73$, $p < 0.05$). In addition, children watched on average 95.94% ($SD = 1.06$) of the toy manipulations in the live condition and 96.82% ($SD = 1.42$) of those in the delayed condition. No condition difference was found here ($t(17) = 0.62$, $p > 0.05$). No mothers noticed a temporal delay for the children's images.

8.2.3   Why the Temporal Contiguity Is so Important in a Pedagogical Situation?

As shown in the above experiment, temporal contiguity plays an important role in children's imitation learning. Two-years-old children are capable of imitating mothers' toy manipulations over a double television system. Additionally, partially consistent with our hypothesis, a disruption in temporal contiguity between children's and their mothers' responses impaired imitation performance, although this manipulation had no effect on children's looking times.

Why did disrupted temporal contiguity have such a significant effect on imitation performance? First, the effects of temporal contiguity can potentially be explained by differences in mothers' demonstrations between the conditions. Caregivers do attempt to provide useful behavioral cues such as changes in speech, pauses, and a trajectory of motion based on their children's responses [19, 20]. In the present study, if the mothers had detected the disrupted temporal contiguity, they could have adjusted their behaviors during the demonstrations. However, no mother perceived the 1-second delay, and in fact their behaviors did not differ between conditions.

Another plausible interpretation was that the children simply watched the demonstrations more in the live than in the delayed condition [18]. However, there were no looking time differences between conditions. This suggests that disruption of temporal contiguity had no effects on children's visual attention.

It therefore seems reasonable to explain the effects of temporal disruption in terms of decreased importance and directionality of mothers' behaviors. Miyazaki & Hiraki [21] demonstrated that 3-years-old children who watched 2-s delayed self-images on a TV monitor show less self-directed behavior than children who watched 1-sec delay images [21]. Children seem able to judge relationships between self-performed actions and external visual events on the basis of temporal contiguity (see also, [22] and [23]), presumably because such temporal characteristics convey the importance and directionality of mothers' behaviors throughout daily interaction. Although it is unknown exactly how temporal contiguity of mothers' responses affects children's cognitive processes and ultimately their imitation performance, our findings highlight the importance of temporal contiguity of demonstrators' teaching behaviors from a pedagogical perspective.

8.3 Machine Intelligence Approach to Pedagogical Machines

As shown in the previous section, one of the advantages of the cognitive science approach is to provide clear understanding of the essential part of teaching-learning interaction through experiments. However, the experiments only with humans are not enough to design a pedagogical machine. The key issue is that how to implement the essential part of human-human interaction into human-machine interaction.

The following section describes two systems as examples for machine intelligence approach to pedagogical machines. The first system is called PAGI (a Pedagogical Agent with Gaze Interaction). The PAGI is an experimental animated pedagogical agent designed to teach Korean words to Japanese students. It is a three-dimensional male cartoon character voiced by a male Korean-Japanese bilingual speaker, lip-synced to the voice using predefined visages. The second system aimed to create a pedagogical robot that can learn from humans. The system is still at preliminary stage. So, as a first step, we started to observe and analyze through case studies the characteristic behavior of a human teacher and the effectiveness of the behavior designed for the robot.

8.3.1 PAGI: Pedagogical Agent with Gaze Interaction

Facilitating social interaction has been one of the central topics in pedagogical agent literature [24]. However, the approach has been largely concentrated on the animation quality of agents, such as liveliness of agent's gesture [25, 26] and voice [27].

As we discussed in the previous section, social interaction holds a distinct feature: temporal contingency and/or temporal contiguity. Indeed, human social cues involve a high level of temporal regulation. When humans communicate, gestures [28] and eye movements [29] become temporally coupled. Therefore, we focused on temporal contingency between the student and pedagogical agent.

Gaze is one of the most well-described social cues [30], can be easily measured and be added to virtual characters with relative ease. Also, previous research from the field of developmental psychology indicates that gaze interaction is critical for the early stage of language learning [31–33]. For experimental purposes, we simplified gaze interaction into three key elements, mutual gaze, joint attention and gaze following, which are thought to play crucial roles in learning [31–35].

For learning material, we used foreign language vocabulary. While it is not a suitable teaching material for pedagogical agents to establish superiority over traditional teaching formats (e.g. books), we wanted to start with a material that adds less complication to experiment design. Adopting features for more advanced materials would propose another research topic, as we have to consider how to adopt each feature to fit the materials. In summary, our aim is to test the feature—temporal contingency—of the pedagogical agent and examine its effect per se as much as possible. To do so we started with a simple learning material, foreign language words.

This study is theoretically based on previous findings related to infants or children, but targets adults. Although it is necessary to note the differences between adult learning and child learning, learning unfamiliar words poses relatively similar demands to both children and to adults. Moreover, why the video deficit effect diminishes with age is under debate, and it would be interesting to see whether factors facilitating screen-media-learning in children could potentially impact adult learners.

In this study, we tested the hypothesis that the temporally contingent gaze interaction of animated pedagogical agents would enhance word learning. We developed an animated pedagogical agent capable of temporal contingent gaze interaction, called a Pedagogical Agent with Gaze Interaction (PAGI) [51]. PAGI simulates mutual gaze, gaze following, and joint attention with students while teaching foreign language words.

PAGI started with an opening narration, explaining that he will be teaching Korean words, while gazing at participant's eyes, initiating eye contact (Fig. 8.4). After the narration, PAGI initiated the word learning phase. First, two pictures were presented (stage 1). PAGI waited for an eye contact and then shifted his gaze to the target picture. He then waited for the participant to follow his gaze and fixate on the target picture, and form joint attention. After joint attention was formed, PAGI returned his gaze to the participant and spoke a frame sentence (the first portion of the sentence leading to a target word, e.g. 'this is' or 'next is' in Japanese (stage 2)). Finally, PAGI spoke the target Korean word twice (stage 3). PAGI repeated stages 1–3 for each word.

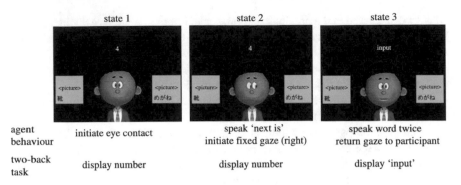

Fig. 8.4 The sequence of the experiment with PAGI [51]

In Stage 2, if the participant did not form the joint attention within 3 s time limit, PAGI looked at the participant and delivered attention-redirecting dialogue ('Please follow my lead') in Japanese. This was to mimic the behaviour of human tutor delivering attention-redirecting dialogue and to prevent the live group participants from taking advantage of the system and taking too much time to memorize each word.

8.3.1.1   Experiment with PAGI

Participants

Thirty participants (seven women) were recruited from a subject pool at the University of Tokyo. Their mean age was 20.19 (s.d. = 1.47) years. Participants were all native Japanese without Korean language experience. An additional five participants were not included in the sample owing to the failure of the eye-tracking system during the experiment, which caused the agent to malfunction. Participants were randomly assigned to either live ($n = 15$; women $= 4$; meanage $= 20.0$) or recorded ($n = 15$; women $= 3$; meanage $= 20.4$) group.

Experimental Design

A between-subjects yoked-condition design was used, in which participants learned Korean words with the temporally contingent agent (live group) or the recorded agent (recorded group). The live group was paired with the live-interacting pedagogical agent, and the recorded group with the agent replaying behaviour sequence recorded during live group sessions. Thus, the recorded group was provided with the same agent exhibiting the same behaviours in the exact sequence as the live group, except without temporal contingency.

All dialogues except target words were presented in Japanese. Korean nouns with less than four syllables were used for the lesson. Each word was presented with a corresponding picture and written Japanese word (Fig. 8.4). The word list was identical for all participants and was presented in the same sequence. The words

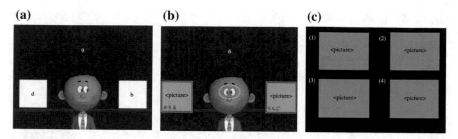

Fig. 8.5 The example of the target (**a**) and distracter picture (**b**). **c** is the example of the testing phase [51]

were selected by a Korean-Japanese bilingual based on two criteria, low resemblance between the pair and familiarity to the general population.

A distracter picture was presented with each target picture to force gaze following. If only the target picture was presented, gaze following would be unnecessary. To avoid this, a random picture from the word list was simultaneously presented as a non-target word. As a result, to obtain the correct meaning of the word, participants needed to watch and follow PAGI's gaze. The target and distracter picture pairs were presented randomly to the left or right of PAGI (Fig. 8.5). Participants learned 60 words, which were divided into two blocks of 30 words, with a 1 min rest between the blocks.

As the task was simple and repetitive, a pre-test revealed a ceiling effect, and participants reported that the difference between two conditions was too minor to be noticed. To solve these two problems, we employed a dual-task design using a digit span two-back task. A single-digit number appeared above PAGI and then was replaced by 'input', thus forcing participants to take their eye away from PAGI from time to time. This enabled participants to notice whether PAGI was responding to them or not. Participants were instructed to input the digit using a keyboard numpad while the two-back sign was showing 'input'. When the answer was inputted during the input time window, the sign changed to blank to inform participants that their input was handled, regardless of its correctness. Key inputs made when the sign showed otherwise (a number or blank) were ignored. The two-back task was temporally synced to the word learning task; started and ended at the same time as each word (Fig. 8.4).

The eye-tracker (Tobii, Sweden) was integrated with a 17 in. LCD monitor, on which stimuli were displayed. A nine-point calibration was administered at the start of every block. A webcam placed under the eye-tracker focused on the participant's eyes to monitor the gaze interaction. For the test phase, a 17 in. CRT monitor was used. Sound stimuli were presented through two speakers (BOSE Media Mate II).

The test phase was carried out immediately after the learning phase. Four pictures were presented on the screen and a Korean word was verbally given (Fig. 8.5c). Participants were instructed to pick the picture that corresponded to the word. Participants used number keys 1–4 on a keyboard during the test to choose the picture.

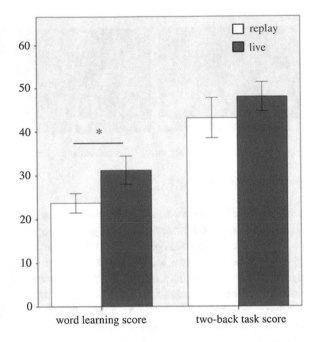

Fig. 8.6 The result of word learning task and two-back task [51]

Participants were informed that there was no time limit during the test phase. The entire experiment lasted 25–30 min.

8.3.1.2 Result with PAGI

The test score was composed of the number of correct answers. Participants from both groups scored higher than the chance level; 15 words as the test phase consisted of 64 choice questions (live group: $t14 = 10.193$, $p < 0.001$; recorded group: $t14 = 7.572$, $p < 0.001$, one-sample t-test). The mean test scores differed significantly between the two groups ($t28 = 3.372$, $p = 0.002$, $d = 1.24$; See Fig. 8.6).

The live group also performed better on the two-back task, with marginal significance ($t28 = 3.046$, $p = 0.095$). This was expected as the two-back task was temporally synced to the word learning task, thus was also under temporal contingency effect, albeit less explicit than the main task.

As the experiment used dual-task design, the difference of attention allocation on two tasks may have affected the result (i.e. the live group assigned a larger proportion of cognitive resource on the word learning task). The difference could not be compared between the two groups, however, as both tasks were affected by temporal contingency. Nonetheless, analysis on each group showed no significant correlations between the test scores and two-back scores. Also, group difference of test scores cannot be explained by attention allocation as the live group scored better on both tasks.

Generally, memory task performance increases when participants are given more time, and the time spent on the learning phase was not controlled in our experiment. To assess the influence of the time spent on learning, we examined the relationship between participants' learning time and test scores. The duration of the learning phase did not differ significantly between the two groups (live group: $M = 368.7$ s, recorded group: $M = 352.8$ s; $t28 = 1.391$, $p > 0.1$). There was no significant correlation between learning phase duration and test scores. These analyses revealed that time spent on learning did not significantly affect the test scores.

8.3.1.3   Why Gaze Contingency Enhances Human Learning?

The above study demonstrated that temporally contingent gaze interaction improves the word learning with animated pedagogical agents. Our study supports the importance of live social interaction on human learning and extends this to computer-based education.

Because the attention-redirecting dialogue was presented only for the live group, we initially suspected that the dialogue might have influenced the result. However, our auxiliary analysis suggests that the influence was negligible. This seems at a glance to contradict with previous finding of D'Mello et al. [36], who reported that the use of attention-redirecting dialogue improved learning of high school biology. However, they also reported that the effect was confined to deep reasoning, and the effect was not found in overall learning, especially in directly transferred knowledge. As attention-redirecting dialogue is strongly related to boredom or drift of attention, its effect is understandably influenced by complexity of learning material and the length of lesson. The facts that the learning material of our experiment was relatively simple and short should have minimized the effect of the attention-redirecting dialogues, as shown in our result.

If the attention-redirecting dialogue did not improve learning, it remains unclear why the temporal contingency of gaze interaction had such a significant effect. One possible explanation is that lack of temporal contingency induced larger cognitive load by inflicting the need for more frequent visual search; the replay group participants had to constantly check for the agent's cues whereas the live group participants could progress on their own terms. The analysis of the fixation duration average showed that the live group was more likely than the replay group to have fixation average inside the time window of 400–700 ms which was linked to higher test scores, and the replay group was more likely to have shorter fixation average. While fixation duration cannot always be directly linked to cognitive processes, in regard to our experimental task, shorter fixation durations can be linked to greater devotion towards visual search. Therefore, it can be assumed that temporal contingency reduced extraneous cognitive load, contributing to less burden for visual search.

The most important topic deferred for future work is 'follow- and lead-in' of joint attention and its effect on learning. In this study, joint attention was initiated by the pedagogical agent, which put participants in a follow-in position. While the interaction still proved beneficial, previous studies indicate that lead-in joint attention may be favourable to follow-in joint attention. Schilbach et al. [37] found that lead-in gaze interaction activates the brain area related to the reward system, which implies having learners lead gaze interaction could enhance motivational outcomes. In addition, evidence from developmental psychology suggests that lead-in joint attention has more benefits than follow-in joint attention in early language development [38]. Therefore, adding lead-in joint attention to the agent may lead to enhanced learning outcomes.

This study also proposes the merit of using artificial agents in the field of developmental psychology as a tool for assessing human-machine interactions. The merits of using virtual environments in psychological experiments has been discussed [39] and has been successfully implemented in social neuropsychology [37]. In this study, by using an artificial agent, we had strict control over the temporal contingency, which would have been difficult for a human experimenter. Therefore, we believe artificial agents have potential as experimental tools. For example, one construct that can benefit forthwith from using artificial agents is the video deficit effect. Currently, the most common practice when examining the video deficit effect is to use human experimenters as a counterpart to video stimuli [15, 40, 41]. There are two limitations to this experimental design. First, strict control over variables cannot be ensured. Second, the granularity of the experiment is limited by the precision of human perception. For example, the latency of mutual gaze cannot be controlled in milliseconds. We believe artificial agents open new possibilities for assessing subtle human behaviours, precisely and cost-efficiently.

In conclusion, our experiment has led us to conclude that temporal contingency of gaze interaction is a key feature in the improvement of the effectiveness of animated pedagogical agents. Our data suggest that temporal contingency should be considered when designing animated pedagogical agents. Furthermore, our methodology proposes the merit of using artificial agents in the field of developmental psychology to overcome the limits of previous experimental methods involving human experimenters.

8.3.2 Can a Robot Learn from Humans?

Our final goal is to establish between an agent (or a robot) and person the pedagogical relationship that naturally occurs among people. The PAGI shown in the above section focused on the temporal aspect of teaching. However, the pedagogical relationship sometimes varies, that is the position of teacher and learner changes depending on a situation. This section describes our first attempt to design a robot that can learn from a person [52].

When a person teaches something to a robot, the latter needs to correctly recognize the behavior of the human teacher, learn what the teacher is teaching, and react appropriately. For this purpose, the behavior of the person that the robot should recognize needs to be clarified. If the characteristic behavior of the person teaching the robot is clarified, the robot might be able to recognize the person's behavior correctly. If such clarification can be realized, a robot that can behave appropriately in accordance with the human teacher's behavior, namely, a robot that can establish the pedagogical relationship, can be developed.

The aim of this study is to investigate the characteristic behavior of the human teacher and the behavior necessary for the learner robot in order to develop the pedagogical relationship. Both the person's teaching behavior and robot's learning behavior are analyzed through tasks where the person teaches the robot face-to-face. For the study we considered that, if the person's dialogue is included in his/her teaching behavior, the technology implementation and experiments might become complicated. Therefore, we first focus on a case study where a person teaches a robot a game on a tablet device, and observe and analyze the direction of the person's attention and motion of his/her hands.

8.3.2.1 Prototype System

We first attempted to develop a relationship between a person and robot using a game in order to study the person's teaching behavior in the pedagogical relationship. The task is to teach the robot a game of magnifying or reducing a figure shown on a tablet device through touch operation, and fitting the figure onto another. The person's teaching behavior is analyzed based on the position and size of the figures.

The system consists of a game task, task procedure, and robot that performs the game task with a person (Fig. 8.7). By performing some demonstration, the person shows the robot how the game can be played. After the person teaches the robot, the latter attempts to play the game according to what it learns from the person.

8.3.2.2 Preliminary Case Study

A case study was conducted to investigate the person's teaching behavior and the behavior required from the robot.

Participants

Three students from our laboratory (all male, average age 21.7) participated as subjects in the preliminary case study. They were not involved in our project or other humanoid robot studies.

Experimental Design

When the subject plays the game with the robot, he/she sits facing the robot, and the tablet is placed between them. For this case study, three trials of the game task were performed, and the position and size of the star were recorded at every frame when the subject controlled the star.

The case study was video-recorded in order to analyze the voice sound, gaze direction, and hand motion of the subjects. The analysis was made every time the subject taught the robot, and the difference, if any, between the trials was examined.

Fig. 8.7 The robot that performs the game task with a person [52]

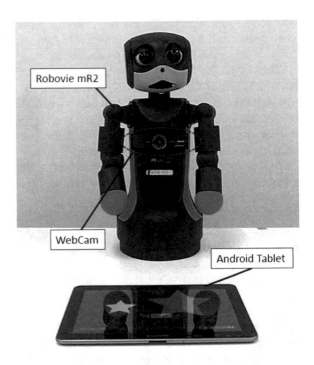

In addition, we interviewed the subjects after the case study with regard to their perception of actually having taught the robot to perform the task.

Results

Table 8.1 lists the behavior differences in the subjects in the preliminary case study.

In the experiment, the subjects simply played the game while watching the tablet screen, rather than attempt to teach the robot, and hence did not attempt to communicate with the robot. This might have occurred because the subjects believed that the robot could only recognize the touch coordinates on the tablet screen. For example, they seemed to consider that the robot could not understand what they said, even when they attempted to speak and communicate with it. Therefore, a function where the robot responds when a person talks to it is necessary.

8.3.2.3   A Case Study with Wizard-of-Oz

Based on the knowledge obtained from the preliminary case study, actions for providing some type of feedback to the subject when he/she teaches the robot were implemented. In order to form a case study with the Wizard-of-Oz method, a GUI was used for the robot to output voices manually when the subject is teaching it.

Table 8.1 Characteristic behavior of subjects in preliminary case study [52]

Subject	Trial	Tablet operation	Communication with robot
Subject A	1st, 3rd	Magnifying/reducing and moving straight the white star	Only staring at the tablet screen
	2nd	Magnifying/reducing and moving straight the white star to fit it on the gray star. Finally magnifying/reducing the white star again	
Subject B	1st to 3rd	Magnifying/reducing and moving straight the white star	Only staring at the tablet screen
Subject C	1st, 2nd	Magnifying/reducing and moving straight the white star	Only staring at the tablet screen
	3rd	Magnifying/reducing the white star, and moving along a roundabout path to the gray star	

The following two hypotheses were formed for this case study:

- Hypothesis 1: As in the preliminary case study, the hypothesis is that, because the robot wrongly understands repeatedly what is taught, the person might emphasize his/her behavior.
- Hypothesis 2: When a person teaches a robot under the pedagogical relationship, he/she might change his/her behavior depending on the robot's learning behavior, similar to his/her changes when in conversation with other people.

Participants

Three students from our laboratory, not those who participated in the preliminary case study, (all male, average age 23.7) participated in the case study. They were not involved in our project or other humanoid robot studies.

Design

As in the preliminary case study, when the subject plays the game with the robot, he/she sits facing the robot, and the tablet is placed between them (Fig. 8.7). Prior to starting the session, the subject is explained how to successfully finish the game, and allowed a certain period to practice the game. The subject is also told that the robot cannot finish the game if he/she does not teach it, but can improve its skills in playing the game as the subject teaches the robot how to play. For this case study, the game tasks were repeated five times. By considering that the subjects might make more attempts to teach the robot if they are allowed more opportunities for teaching it, we conducted more game tasks than for the preliminary case study. The position and size of the white star were recorded at every frame when the subject controlled the star. When the robot controlled the white star, the average of the recorded values over each session was reflected in order to determine the position and size of the star. In addition, the Wizard-of-Oz method was used for the robot to form dialogues under the operation of the experimenter with a GUI.

Result

Table 8.2 lists the behavior differences from the subjects in the case study.

In the case study where the teaching behavior of the subjects was investigated, it was found that they attempted to carefully teach the robot. For example, it was observed that the subjects attempted to move the white star slowly while paying attention to or talking to the robot in order to allow the robot to understand the importance of controlling the star. It was also found from the answers to a question that the subjects intentionally executed these behaviors in order to promote the robot's understanding. This is consistent with Hypothesis 1 of the case study. According to the knowledge obtained in this study, in order to establish the pedagogical relationship between people and robot, it is necessary to implement a mechanism where the robot turns into a learning state when it recognizes a slowly emphasized behavior from the person teaching it. Such mechanism should be designed so that, in the learning state, the robot can learn from the behavior or dialogue made by the teaching person, and can respond appropriately. In the future, additional experiments will be performed for the quantitative analysis of the teaching behavior of a person, and after the analysis, the knowledge obtained from the experiments will be implemented into a robot in order to realize autonomous robots that can establish a pedagogical relationship with people.

Table 8.2 Characteristic behavior of subjects in case study [52]

Subject	Trial	Tablet operation	Communication with robot
Subject D	1st	Moving straight and magnifying/reducing the white star	Staring at the robot immediately before magnifying/reducing the star
	2nd, 3rd	Moving straight and magnifying/reducing the white star	Only staring at the tablet screen
	4th	Magnifying/reducing and moving straight the white star	Staring at the robot immediately before magnifying/reducing the star
	5th	Magnifying/reducing and moving straight the white star. Finally, magnifying/reducing it again	Only staring at the tablet screen

(continued)

Table 8.2 (continued)

Subject	Trial	Tablet operation	Communication with robot
Subject E	1st, 2nd	Moving straight and magnifying/reducing the white star	Only staring at the tablet screen
	3rd	Carefully moving straight and magnifying/reducing the white star	Staring at the robot when moving the star
	4th	• Carefully moving straight the white star • Magnifying/reducing the white star after the robot said that it understood	• Staring at the robot after moving the star • Nodding after the robot said that it understood
	5th	• Carefully moving straight the white star • Moving the white star away from the gray star and moving it again closer to the gray star, after the robot said that it did not understand • Magnifying/reducing the star after the robot said that it understood	• Staring at the robot when moving the star away and moving it closer to the gray star again • Moving the star repeatedly after the robot said that it did not understand.
Subject F	1st, 2nd	Moving straight and magnifying/reducing the white star	Operating the tablet while speaking about how to move the star
	3rd	Moving straight and magnifying/reducing the white star	Staring at the robot when moving the star
	4th	• Carefully moving straight the white star • Moving the white star away from the gray star and moving it again closer to the gray star, after the robot said that it did not understand • Magnifying/Reducing the star after the robot said that it understood	• Staring at the robot when moving the star away and moving it closer to the gray star again • Moving the star repeatedly after the robot said that it did not understand
	5th	Moving straight and magnifying/reducing the white star	Staring at the robot when handling the star

In addition, it was observed that the subjects changed the way of teaching when they received feedback from the robot about what it learned. When they found that the robot behaved as though it understood what it was taught, they confirmed the robot's understanding and proceeded to the next step. On the other hand, when the subjects found that the robot behaved as though it could not understand, they considered that the robot did not understand what they taught and repeated the teaching behavior. This is consistent with Hypothesis 2 of the case study. From the above, it is found that the subjects' way of teaching changes depending on the robot's behavior with regard to what it is taught, and that a pedagogical relationship can be established not only between people, but also between people and robot.

8.4   Field Studies in an Educational Setting

Experimental studies such as those shown in the previous sections could be advantageous in clarifying the essential part of the human teaching-learning relationship and could be used for designing pedagogical machines. However, pedagogical relationships vary widely depending on the situation; for example, in schools and/or in kindergartens, there are complicated relationships not only between the teacher and children but also among children. Therefore, laboratory studies might lack some important information that is required to completely understand the variety of pedagogical relationships that exist. This section attempts to clarify two issues that exist in more complex educational environments but that cannot be found in a laboratory.

8.4.1   Can a Robot Teach a Foreign Language?

Aims and Method

As robots are expected to become more commonly used in our societies, and as they will then have to interact with humans in everyday life activities, their role should become particularly preponderant as pedagogical tools. Compared to other media, robots represent an ideal platform for teaching owing to their embodied and multimodal nature. Several studies have demonstrated the benefits of using robots to support education in many contexts: to develop problem-solving abilities, learn computer programming, learn mathematics or physics, etc. [42–44]. Robots have been also used in classroom environments to create natural interactions with children [45–47]. However, only a few studies have explored the possibility of using robots to teach a foreign language [47].

The present study was inspired by a work of Kuhl et al. [5], where infants naturally learnt foreign language sounds after several sessions of storytelling with a human; however, they were not able to learn after televised storytelling sessions. In our experiment, the human was replaced by a robot; the robot told a story in French ("The three little pigs") to Japanese children for ten minutes. During the storytelling, the robot frequently repeated three words (20 repetitions of the word "pig"; 21 repetitions of the words "wolf," and 22 repetitions of the word "house"); these words were used afterwards to test the children's word-learning performance. To evaluate the children's learning, a preferential looking procedure (PLP) using eye-tracking technology was chosen because of its ease of implementation, its robustness in language learning tasks and its suitability for a wide range of age groups. The PLP refers to a procedure presenting a linguistic stimulus and pictures to children while recording their visual fixations, and the linguistic stimulus matched only one of the pictures shown on the screen. For children old enough to understand the task, responses that included pointing were also recorded.

The aim of this experiment was two-fold: to know (a) if children can learn during a natural interaction with a robot such as short storytelling, and (b) if the robot has enough basic social skills to be a good teacher. As mentioned in Sect. 8.2, several studies have demonstrated the important role of social interactions for learning. It has also been demonstrated that in child-robot experiments, children used socials cues such as gaze combined with verbalizations that were provided by a robot to learn [35]. For these reasons, we have implemented social behaviors during the robot's storytelling to create an "illusion of life." The purpose was to create a rich natural learning environment for the children that was comparable to a social interaction with another human being.

The robot used as a platform in this study was Nao, a small humanoid robot developed by Aldebaran Robotics (see Fig. 8.8). It had 25 degrees of freedom, and it was equipped with two cameras, full color RGB LED eyes, and several sensors. Nao was previously shown to have a positive impact on child-robot interaction [47]. Additionally, four cameras were used to record the children's reactions during storytelling and the learning test was also recorded to obtain the children's pointing behaviors.

The experiment was conducted in a kindergarten at the Tokyo Gakugei University. The atmosphere of the kindergarten is that of a typical Japanese child-care institution and is a very natural environment for the children. Informed consent was obtained from the parents prior to participants' involvement in the study. Eighty-two children participated in the experiment (35 males, 47 females; mean age 5, 17 years, range: 3–9 years). Twenty-six children were excluded from the behavioral pointing analysis because they did not complete the pointing task (at least 50% of the trials). Twenty-seven children were excluded from the eye-tracking analysis because of the lack of gaze data (at least 50% of gaze) and/or their lack of concentration or refusal to participate during the task.

Procedure

A group of 4 to 5 children participated in a ten-minute session of storytelling in French by the robot Nao. Visual stimuli depicting the story were presented simultaneously on a television (see Fig. 8.8a). After this session, the children were tested individually

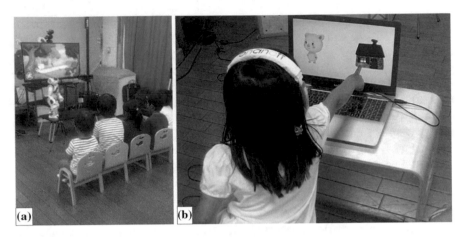

Fig. 8.8 The storytelling phase (**a**) and testing phase (**b**)

using the PLP on a laptop equipped with a portable Tobii eye-tracker (X2-30 compact) for the purpose of gaze analysis (Fig. 8.8b).

The PLP has been designed using Tobii studio software and includes 13 stimuli divided into four conditions for the testing of children's learning on the three words to which they were exposed during the storytelling (pig, wolf, and house). In conditions 1 and 2, the children heard a word taught during storytelling (i.e., "cochon", which is "pig" in French) and they had to choose between two visual stimuli presented simultaneously (another taught stimulus for condition 1 and a new stimulus for condition 2; see Fig. 8.9). In conditions 3 and 4, the children heard pseudowords that were aurally close to the words taught during the storytelling exposure time (i.e.,

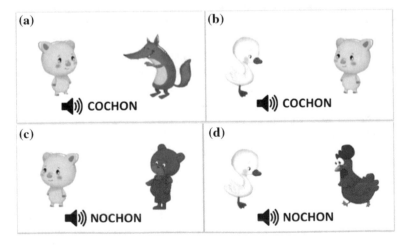

Fig. 8.9 Four testing conditions

Table 8.3 Results and statistical analysis of pointing responses for each condition of the PLP

Condition	% of answers			Binomial test	
	Target	Non target	No answer	Proportion test	p-value
Condition 1	60.56%	23.89 %	15.56 %	0.50	0.00000003
Condition 2	63.69 %	30.95 %	7.14 %	0.50	0.00000408
Condition 3	63.69 %	29.17 %	7.14 %	0.50	0.00000110
	Picture 1	Picture 2	No answer		
Condition 4	45.24 %	44.05 %	10.71 %	0.50	0.06418274

"nochon", which has been created by replacing the first consonant of "cochon") and they had to choose between two visual stimuli (a new one and a previously taught stimulus for condition 3; two new stimuli for condition 4, which is used as control condition). The order of presentation of the stimuli had been randomized.

Results

PLP Behavioral Pointing Responses

The pointing responses were extracted from the videos recorded during the PLP task. Each child's answers were recorded as 0 for a correct answer and 1 for an incorrect answer to obtain the percentages for each condition. For each condition, a binomial test was used to analyze whether the number of correct answers from the subject was greater than the chance level. The results are reported in Table 8.3.

As illustrated in Table 8.3, the number of correct answers for the target stimuli was significantly different from the chance level for conditions 1, 2, and 3 ($p < 0.001$), whereas there was no significant difference for condition 4. The behavioral pointing results demonstrated that the children have learnt the three words to which they were exposed during the storytelling exercise (see Fig. 8.10).

PLP Eye-tracking Data

For each stimulus used during the PLP, two areas of interest (AOIs) were created to match each visual stimulus, and the looking time (total visit duration in seconds) was extracted for each AOI. Paired-sample T-tests were conducted on the eye-tracker data to evaluate the difference in number of the gaze observations between the target and non-target AOIs. The results, reported in Table 8.4, showed that children looked at the target stimuli (a picture matching the word for conditions 1 and 2, or a new stimulus when they heard a pseudoword in condition 3) for a longer duration, in accordance with classically observed results with PLP during the language learning tasks.

Both the behavioral pointing and eye-tracking results indicated that children are able to learn the words of a foreign language with a robot teacher after only 10 min of exposure to French, during a simple and natural interaction such as storytelling. The basic social behaviors demonstrated by the robot seem sufficient to create a social interaction to facilitate language learning.

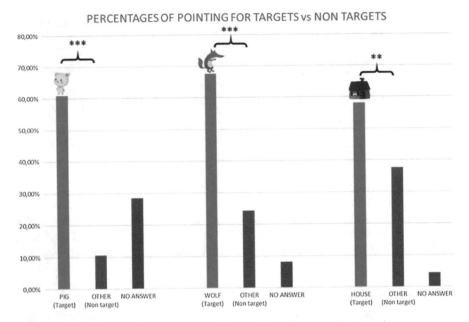

Fig. 8.10 Pointing results for the three words learnt during the storytelling exercise

Table 8.4 Results and statistical analysis of AOIs for each condition of the PLP

Condition	Total visit duration sec				Paired-sample T-tests (two-tailed)		
	Target AOI		Non target AOI		ddl	T-value	p-value
	M	SD	M	SD			
Condition 1	1.38	1.34	0.93	0.88	204	3.74	0.000237849
Condition 2	1.31	1.31	0.88	0.98	152	3.05	0.00269502
Condition 3	1.43	1.39	0.99	0.97	154	3.05	0.002690585
	AOI1		AOI2				
Condition 4	1.09	1.06	1.03	1.01	152	0.52	0.598785433

8.4.2 Do Children Help a Clumsy Robot in Their Natural Environment?

Because a pedagogical agent has to induce an active stance in people to build a teacher-learner relationship with them, we conducted an experiment to investigate what design factors are important for encouraging young children to behave altruistically and help a robot in an educational setting.

Altruistic behavior is related to pedagogy because a learner needs to take an active stance to acquire knowledge from a teacher. We found that learners follow important social signals and that the pedagogical agent must inevitably use these signals at appropriate times during the interaction to induce altruistic behavior. Thus, these

Fig. 8.11 Experimental environment: kinect sensor monitors positions of robot (NAO), ball, and children

signals need to be understood to better design pedagogical agents. We assumed that the theories for designing a pedagogical agent and an agent that induces altruistic behaviors are related. Through an experiment, we aim to investigate what insights the design for an agent that induces altruistic behavior provides for the design of a pedagogical agent.

We conducted an experiment (at the same kindergarten where the study described in the Sect. 8.4.1) to determine whether or not a robot can induce altruistic behaviors from children aged three to five, what social signals the robot has to show when failing at a task, and when it is appropriate to show the signal. Figure 8.11 shows the experimental environment. We used NAO as mentioned in the above section. In addition to the setup in Sect. 8.4.1, we set up a Kinect sensor because NAO's camera has a narrow field of view. Nao and the Kinect sensor tracked the locations of the children and the ball used in the experimental task.

NAO's task was to pick up the ball and throw it into a trashcan. NAO failed to pick up or throw the ball and displayed social signals designed for inducing altruistic behavior.

We prepared four types of social signals as key elements to induce altruistic behavior on the basis of Worneken's experiment [49]:

i. Responding to changes in the surrounding environment

NAO responded to a change as soon as possible when its camera or the Kinect sensor detected the change. This responsive behavior gave participants a feeling of sharing the same environment as NAO.

Fig. 8.12 Child picks ball up for NAO

ii. Representing NAO's intention

If NAO intended to pick up a ball, NAO needed to show this intention through embodied expressions. An inappropriate behavioral design causes a person to misunderstand a robot even if the robot succeeds in achieving its goal. The participants could understand NAO's intention on the basis of its representation.

iii. Opening a communication channel with a person

NAO made eye-contact with a participant to communicate when NAO needed to induce altruistic behavior.

iv. Expressing regret when NAO failed to achieve the goal

The expression of regret informed the participants of NAO's emotional state.

Figure 8.12 shows an example of a child behaving altruistically in the experiment. The child picked up the ball instead of NAO after watching NAO's behavior, which was based on all the four signals. On the other hand, the children did not react if NAO did not behave on the basis of any of the four principles, as shown in Fig. 8.13. Although we have to analyze the children's behaviors in more detail to determine the effect of the four design principles, we collected several pieces of evidence of the children behaving altruistically to help NAO to achieve the goal.

8.4.3 Merits of Field Studies in Natural Setting

Although the above two studies are still on-going and the results obtained are preliminary, the experimental results obtained in a natural environment such as a kinder-

Fig. 8.13 All children watch NAO attempt a task without helping

garten should have some information that cannot be found in a laboratory. First, we found several interactions among the children and the interactions seem to affect each child's learning Sect. 8.4.1 and altruistic behaviors Sect. 8.4.2. In a natural environment, a condition with only one teacher and one learner is unlikely to exist. There are so many people who are involved in pedagogical relations in a natural teaching-learning environment, and the peer-to-peer relationship might be rare. To design a pedagogical machine that can be used in a home or classroom, we must consider the relationships that exist among learners and teachers as well.

8.5   Current and Future Direction for Pedagogical Machines

This chapter described our project on a pedagogical machine from three different viewpoints: developmental cognitive science, machine intelligence, and field studies in an educational environment. It is apparent that these are strongly related and we recognized that collaboration with different research fields is valuable. Although it is very hard to predict the nature of future educational environments, we must continue this collaborative work for the future of children.

Through this project we found that two features—nowness and responsiveness—are very important for the design of a pedagogical machine. As described in Sect. 8.2, we found that infants are very sensitive to temporal contiguity during interaction with their mothers. The temporal contiguity of others' responses may be useful for the learning process of infants because it enables the infant to judge whether nowness and responsiveness were established between himself/herself and others. PAGI described in the Sect. 8.3 also revealed that even adults are implicitly affected by nowness and responsiveness during word learning with artificial agents.

For the future development of pedagogical machines, we need to expand and add more approaches such as neuroscience. Recent developments in social neuroscience suggest the need for a more reciprocal approach, suggesting that social cognition may be fundamentally different when individuals are interacting with others rather than merely observing [20, 21]. For example, Redcay et al. [22] showed that live interaction with a human experimenter, compared with viewing video recordings of the interaction, displayed greater activation in brain regions involved in social cognition and reward. In addition, Schilbach et al. [23] demonstrated that forming joint attention with a virtual character stimulates areas of the brain associated with social cognition, while avoiding joint attention recruited areas related to control of attention and eye movements. These results suggested that neuroscientific studies are now ready to contribute to the design of pedagogical machines.

The advances in sensing technology should also be taken into consideration to create a more intelligent pedagogical machine. There are many special sensing devices, such as gyro sensors, wearable eye-gaze tracker, and marker-based motion capturing devices. However, these sensors sometimes have serious side effects on the interaction analysis; for example, it could prevent the participants from behaving naturally.

Fig. 8.14 The example of the automatic annotation system

Moreover, the majority of existing devices do not focus on the interaction between the human and the object in the scene. For example, to detect joint-attention, we prepare another device to measure its position in advance.

To overcome the aforementioned problem, we are creating a system with fixed RGB-D cameras to measure both the human and objects in the scene (see Fig. 8.14). This is a real-time annotation system. Once the system detects the face of each participant, the 3D shape and colors of the head are reconstructed as a 3D model in real-time using GPU. The 3D motion of the head is estimated by fitting the 3D shape and colors model onto the captured color and depth images. This scheme enables the robust 3D estimation of the head direction from not only frontal views but also profile views of the participant. Using this system, we are now creating an automatic annotation system that can be used in the field of developmental psychology. We hope that such an endeavor can help in future research on pedagogical machines.

Acknowledgements This research was supported by CREST, JST. I would like to thank all children and mothers who participated in our experimental studies. This project has been conducted with the following members, Michita Imai (Keio University), Akiko Hayashi (Tokyo Gakugei University), Shinta Kimura (Animo).

References

1. G. Csibra, G. Gergely, Natural pedagogy. Trends Cognit. Sci. **13**, 148–153 (2009)
2. T.M. Caro, M.D. Hauser, Is there teaching in nonhumananimals? Quart. Rev. Biol. **67**, 151–174 (1992)
3. A. Thornton, K. McAuliffe, Teaching in wild meerkats. Science **313**, 227–229 (2006)
4. G. Csibra, Teachers in the wild. Trends Cogn. Sci. **11**, 95–96 (2007)
5. P.K. Kuhl, F. Tsao, H. Liu, Foreign-language experience in infancy: effects of short-term exposure and social interaction on phonetic learning. Proc. Natl. Acad. Sci. **100**, 9096–9101 (2003). USA
6. T. Grossmann, M.H. Johnson, The development of the social brain in human infancy. Eur. J. Neurosci. **25**, 909–919 (2007). doi:10.1111/j.1460-9568.2007.05379.x
7. M. Tomasello, M. Carpenter, J. Call, T. Behne, H. Moll, Understanding and sharing intentions: the origins of cultural cognition. Behav. Brain Sci. **28**, 675–735 (2005). doi:10.1017/s0140525x05000129
8. M. Morales, P. Mundy, C.E.F. Delgado, M. Yale, D. Messinger, R. Neal, H.K. Schwartz, Responding to joint attention across the 6-through 24-month age period and early language acquisition. J. Appl. Dev. Psychol. **21**, 283–298 (2000). doi:10.1016/s0193-3973(99)00040-4
9. M. Tomasello, The social bases of language acquisition. Soc. Dev. **1**(1), 67–87 (1992)
10. M. Krcmar, B. Grela, K. Lin, Can toddlers learn vocabulary from television? An experimental approach. Media Psychol. **10**, 41–63 (2007). doi:10.1080/15213260701375652
11. D.R. Anderson, T.A. Pempek, Television and very young children. Am. Behav. Sci. **48**, 505–522 (2005). doi:10.1177/0002764204271506
12. S. Shimada, K. Hiraki, Infant's brain responses to live and televised action. Neuroimage **32**(2), 930–939 (2006)
13. M.H. Goldstein, J.A. Schwade, Social feedback to infants' babbling facilitates rapid phonological learning. Psychol. Sci. **19**(5), 515–523 (2008)

14. M. Nielsen, G. Simcock, L. Jenkins, The effect of social engagement on 24-month-olds' imitation from live and televised models. Dev. Sci. **11**, 722–731 (2008). doi:10.1111/j.1467-7687.2008.00722.x
15. S. Roseberry, K. Hirsh-Pasek, R.M. Golinkoff, Skype me! socially contingent interactions help toddlers learn language. Child Dev. **85**(3), 956–970 (2014)
16. G.L. Troseth, M.M. Saylor, A.H. Archer, Young children's use of video as a source of socially relevant information. Child Dev. **77**, 786–799 (2006)
17. C.S. Tamis-LeMonda, Y. Kuchirko, L. Song, Why is infant language learning facilitated by parental responsiveness? Curr. Dir. Psychol. Sci. **23**(2), 121–126 (2014)
18. T. Striano, A. Henning, D. Stahl, Sensitivity to interpersonal timing at 3 and 6 months of age. Interact. Stud. **7**(2), 251–271 (2006)
19. N.A. Smith, L.J. Trainor, Infant-directed speech is modulated by infant feedback. Infancy **13**(4), 410–420 (2008)
20. R.J. Brand, D.A. Baldwin, L.A. Ashburn, Evidence for 'motionese': modifications in mothers' infant-directed action. Dev. Sci. **5**(1), 72–83 (2002)
21. M. Miyazaki, K. Hiraki, Delayed intermodal contingency affects young children's recognition of their current self. Child Dev. **77**(3), 736–750 (2006)
22. W.S. Millar, J.S. Watson, Effect of delayed feedback on infant learning reexamined. Child Dev. **50**(3), 747–751 (1979)
23. L.E. Bahrick, J.S. Watson, Detection of intermodal proprioceptive visual contingency as a potential basis of self-perception in infancy. Dev. Psychol. **21**(6), 963–973 (1985)
24. R. Moreno, R.E. Mayer, H.A. Spires, J.C. Lester, The case for social agency in computer-based teaching: do students learn more deeply when they interact with animated pedagogical agents? Cogn. Instr. **19**, 177–213 (2001)
25. A.L. Baylor, S. Kim, Designing nonverbal communication for pedagogical agents: when less is more. Comput. Hum. Behav. **25**, 450–457 (2009)
26. R.E. Mayer, C.S. DaPra, An embodiment e ect in computer-based learning with animated pedagogical agents. J. Exp. Psychol. Appl. **18**, 239–252 (2012)
27. R.K. Atkinson, R.E. Mayer, M.M. Merrill, Fostering social agency in multimedia learning: examining the impact of an animated agent's voice. Contemp. Educ. Psychol. **30**, 117–139 (2005). doi:10.1016/j.cedpsych.2004.07.001
28. K. Shockley, M.V. Santana, C.A. Fowler, Mutual interpersonal postural constraints are involved in cooperative conversation. J. Exp. Psychol. **29**, 326–332 (2003)
29. D.C. Richardson, R. Dale, N.Z. Kirkham, The art of conversation is coordination-common ground and the coupling of eye movements during dialogue. Psychol. Sci. **18**, 407–413 (2007)
30. N.J. Emery, The eyes have it: the neuroethology, function and evolution of social gaze. Neurosci. Biobehav. Rev. **24**, 581–604 (2000)
31. M. Morales, P. Mundy, C.E.F. Delgado, M. Yale, D. Messinger, R. Neal, H.K. Schwartz, Responding to joint attention across the 6-through 24-month age period and early language acquisition. J. Appl. Dev. Psychol. **21**, 283–298 (2000)
32. R. Brooks, A.N. Meltzoff, The development of gaze following and its relation to language. Dev. Sci. **8**, 535–543 (2005)
33. T. Striano, X. Chen, A. Cleveland, S. Bradshaw, Joint attention social cues influence infant learning. Eur. J. Dev. Psychol. **3**, 289–299 (2006)
34. A. Senju, G. Csibra, Gaze following in human infants depends on communicative signals. Curr. Biol. **18**, 239–252 (2008)
35. Y. Okumura, Y. Kanakogi, T. Kanda, H. Ishiguro, S. Itakura, The power of human gaze on infant learning. Cognition **128**, 127–133 (2013)
36. S. D'Mello, A. Olney, C. Williams, P. Hays, Gaze tutor: a gaze-reactive intelligent tutoring system. Int. J. Hum. Comput. Stud. **70**, 377–398 (2012)
37. L. Schilbach, M. Wilms, S.B. Eickho, S. Romanzetti, R. Tepest, G. Bente, N.J. Shah, G.R. Fink, K. Vogeley, Minds made for sharing: initiating joint attention recruits reward-related neurocircuitry. J. Cogn. Neurosci. **22**, 2702–2715 (2010)

38. M. Tomasello, M.J. Farrar, Joint attention and early language. Child Dev. **57**, 1454–1463 (1986)
39. J. Blascovich, J. Loomis, A.C. Beall, K.R. Swinth, C.L. Hoyt, J.N. Bailenson, Immersive virtual environment technology as a methodological tool for social psychology. Psychol. Inq. **13**, 103–124 (2002)
40. M. Krcmar, B. Grela, K. Lin, Can toddlers learn vocabulary from television? an experimental approach. Media Psychol. **10**, 41–63 (2007)
41. M. Krcmar, Can social meaningfulness and repeat exposure help infants and toddlers overcome the video de cit? Media Psychol. **13**, 31–53 (2010)
42. K.W. Lau, H.K. Tan, B.T. Erwin, P. Petrovic, Creative learning in school with LEGO (R) programmable robotics products, in *29th Annual 1999 FIE'99 Frontiers in Education Conference*, vol. 2, pp. 12D4-26 (1999)
43. P. Mosley, R. Kline, Engaging students: a framework using LEGO robotics to teach problem solving. J. Inf. Technol. Learn. Perform. **24**(1), 39 (2006)
44. M. Cooper, D. Keating, W. Harwin, K. Dautenhahn, Robots in the classroom: tools for accessible education, in *Assistive Technology on the Threshold of the New Millennium*, ed. by C. Buhler, H. Knops (IOS Press, Amsterdam, 1999), pp. 448–452
45. F. Tanaka, J.R. Movellan, B. Fortenberry, K. Aisaka, Daily HRI evaluation at a classroom environment: reports from dance interaction experiments, in *Proceedings of the 1st ACM SIGCHI/SIGART conference on Human-robot interaction*, ACM, pp. 3–9 March 2006
46. F. Tanaka, A. Cicourel, J.R. Movellan, Socialization between toddlers and robots at an early childhood education center. Proc. Natl. Acad. Sci. **104**(46), 17954–17958 (2007)
47. M. Fridin, Storytelling by a kindergarten social assistive robot: a tool for constructive learning in preschool education. Comput. Educ. **70**, 53–64 (2014)
48. C.W. Chang, J.H. Lee, P.Y. Chao, C.Y. Wang, G.D. Chen, Exploring the possibility of using humanoid robots as instructional tools for teaching a second language in primary school. Educ. Technol. Soc. **13**(2), 13–24 (2010)
49. F. Warneken, M. Tomasello, Altruistic helping in human infants and young chimpanzees. Science **311**, 1301–1303 (2006)
50. E. Yamamoto, G. Matsuda, K. Nagata, D. Naoko, K. Hiraki, Subtle temporal delays on mothers' responses affect imitation learning in children: mother-child interaction study. (submitted)
51. H. Lee, Y. Kanakogi, K. Hiraki, Building a responsive teacher: how temporally contingent gaze interaction influences word learning with virtual tutors. R. Soc. Open Sci. **2**, 140361 (2015)
52. H. Okazaki, Y. Kanai, M. Ogata, K. Hasegawa, K. Ishii, M. Imai, Toward understanding pedagogical relationship in human-robot interaction. J. Robot. Mechatron. **28**(1), 69–78 (2016)

Chapter 9
Epilog

Toyoaki Nishida

Abstract Human-harmonized information technology is intended to establish basic technologies to achieve harmony between human beings and the information environment by integrating element technologies encompassing real-space communication, human interface, and media processing. It promotes a transdisciplinary approach featuring (1) the recognition and comprehension of human behaviors and real-space contexts by utilizing sensor networks and ubiquitous computing, (2) technologies for facilitating man–machine communication utilizing robots and ubiquitous networks, and (3) content technologies for analyzing, mining, integrating, and structuring multimedia data including those in text, voice, music, and images. It ranges from scientific research on the cognitive aspects of human-harmonized information processes to social implementations that may lead to breakthroughs in the harmonious interactions of human and information environments. In this chapter, I give an overview of achievements over the past eight years, remarking on insights as well as limitations. I also discuss future perspectives, singling out promising approaches.

Keywords Changing world · Computer and communication technology · Convivial society · Human and social potential · Human-harmonized information technology

9.1 A Brief History of Research on Human-Harmonized Information Technology

Our long and exciting journey was launched eight years ago by the late Professor Yoh'ichi Tohkura, based on a five-stage model, in which progress in the history of information in human society is conceptualized as consisting of the stages of

T. Nishida (✉)
Graduate School of Informatics, Kyoto University, Kyoto, Japan
e-mail: nishida@i.kyoto-u.ac.jp

T. Nishida
JST-CREST Research Area on Creation of Human-Harmonized
Information Technology for Convivial Society, Tokyo, Japan

© Springer Japan KK 2017
T. Nishida (ed.), *Human-Harmonized Information Technology, Volume 2*,
DOI 10.1007/978-4-431-56535-2_9

- the hunter–gatherer society, where information is used for creating and sharing knowledge about hunting to find food while avoiding dangers;
- the agricultural society, where information is used for sharing knowledge about growing and harvesting crops;
- the industrial society, where information is used for living to achieve material affluence;
- the information society, where information plays a central role in society, supporting our life; and
- the (prospective) convivial society, where information will be used to achieve harmony and enable creativity.

The present stands at the transition between the information society and the convivial society called the AI-supported society, in which people are surrounded by numerous autonomous intelligent agents that mediate between people and services.

AI-supported society may bring with it new problems, and an AI-supported society might eventually release human beings from the duties of supporting mankind on the planet. The transition phase from an information society to a convivial society may be painful. In the transition, people will need to find new areas of self-actualization. We will need to harmonize relationships between human beings and technology, not just by inventing human-friendly technology but also by making technology explore new forms of perception, activity, and creativity.

We consider human and social potential to be a central issue. Human potential is the power of an individual that enables her or him to actively sustain an endeavor to achieve a goal in maintaining a social relationship with other people. It involves vision, activity, sustainability, empathy, ethics, humor, and an esthetic sense. Vision permits one to initiate long-term coherent activity. Social potential is the power that a society of people possesses as a whole. It encompasses generosity, support, conviviality, diversity, connectedness, and innovativeness.

Human-harmonized information technology (IT) is intended for a convivial society, featuring perceptual information processing to harmonically interface between human beings and the information environment, featuring

- the recognition and comprehension of human behaviors and real-space contexts, utilizing sensor networks and ubiquitous computing;
- technologies for facilitating man–machine communication, utilizing robots and ubiquitous networks; and
- content technologies related to analyzing, mining, integrating, and structuring multi-media information processing.[1]

Supported by a research grant from the Japan Science and Technology Agency (JST),[2] seventeen research teams were selected, each of which was funded for slightly more than five years.

This work is now approaching its conclusion. Table 9.1 summarizes the current status of the projects. More than two-thirds have already been concluded, nine of

---

[1]http://www.jst.go.jp/kisoken/crest/en/research_area/ongoing/areah21-1.html.
[2]http://www.jst.go.jp/EN/index.html.

Table 9.1 Teams of the JST-CREST research area on Creation of Human-Harmonized Information Technology for convivial society

Duration	ID	Team
FY2009–2014	P1	*Life Log Infrastructure for Food (PI: Kiyoharu Aizawa)
	P2	*Dynamic Information Space based on High-speed Sensor Technology (PI: Masatoshi Ishikawa) ⇒ ACCEL Feasibility Study (2015) / ACCEL (FY2016–)
	P3	*Developing a communication environment by decoding and controlling implicit interpersonal information (PI: Makio Kashino)
	P4	*Smart seminar room based on multi-modal recognition of verbal and non-verbal information (PI: Tatsuya Kawahara)
	P5	*Elucidation of perceptual illusion and development of secse-centered human interface (PI: Yasuharu Koike)
	P6	*Sensing and controlling human gaze in daily living space for human-harmonized information environments (PI: Yoichi Sato)
	P7	*Modeling and detecting overtrust from behavior signals (PI: Kazuya Takeda)
	P8	*Construction and Utilization of Human-harmonized "Tangible" Information Environment (PI: Susumu Tachi) ⇒ ACCEL: Embodied Media Project (2014)
FY2010–2014	P9	*Studies on cellphone-type teleoperated androids transmitting human presence (PI: Hiroshi Ishiguro) ⇒ ERATO: Ishiguro Symbiotic Human-Robot Interaction Project (FY2014–)
FY2010–2015	P10	Development of a sound field sharing system for creating and exchanging music (PI: Shiro Ise)
	P11	Enabling a mobile social robot to adapt to a public space in a city (PI: Takayuki Kanda)
	P12	Development of Fundamental Technologies for Innovative Use of Character/Document Media and Their Application to Creating Human Harmonized Information Environment (PI: Koichi Kise)
	P13	Behavior Understanding based on Intention-Gait Model (PI: Yasushi Yagi)
FY2011–2016	P14	Building a Similarity-aware Information Environment for a Content-Symbiotic Society (PI: Masataka Goto) ⇒ ACCEL (FY2016–)
	P15	Pedagogical Machine: Developmental cognitive science approach to create teaching/teachable machines (PI: Kazuo Hiraki)
	P16	User Generated Dialogue Systems: uDialogue (PI: Keiichi Tokuda)
	P17	Harmonized Inter-Personal Display Based on Position and Direction Control (PI: Takeshi Naemura)

*: in the previous volume

which were reported in the previous volume and the remaining eight of which are presented in the preceding chapters in this volume. It is extraordinary that four teams have been upgraded, as one ERATO and three ACCEL projects supported by JST[3] have been launched, based on their achievements in the CREST research area.

In this chapter, I will summarize what has been achieved and examine its implications. I review the vision that I presented in our previous volume and discuss technical challenges and opportunities from a contemporary point of view.

9.2 What Has Been Achieved

Table 9.2 provides us with a bird's eye view of the entire contribution. This is an updated version of the one I presented in the previous volume. In this section, I will focus on achievements newly added since the previous volume.

9.2.1 Platform Research Level

The platform research level is a technical core of the human-harmonized IT. Our focus was interaction at the perceptual level.

In the previous volume, Tachi and his colleagues presented a rather comprehensive suite of platforms for a tangible information environment [21], including a number of haptic information displays, an introductory haptic toolkit, a vision-based thermal sensor, a telexistence avatar robot system that can provide the experience of an extended body schema, a retro-reflective projection technology (RPT)-based full-parallax autostereoscopic 3D that can generate vertical and horizontal motion parallax, and an autostereoscopic display that can produce a 3D image in mid-air with a view of 180 degrees.

Ishikawa and his colleagues presented four technologies: high-speed 3D vision for insensible dynamics sensing, a high-speed resistor network proximity sensor array for detecting nearby objects, non-contact low-latency haptic feedback, and high-speed display of visual information toward creating a dynamic information space that could harmonize the human perception system, recognition system, and motor system [9]. They also demonstrated how a system of a dynamic information space could be developed by using these four technologies. Their demonstration included an AR typing interface for mobile devices and a high-speed gaze controller for high-speed computer-human interactions, as well as more integrated systems, such as VibroTracker, a vibrotactile sensor for tracking objects, and AIRR Tablet, a floating display with a high-speed gesture user interface.

Sato and his colleagues described a suite of techniques to sense and control human gazes not only in a laboratory environment but also in a living space [19]. They intro-

---

[3]https://www.jst.go.jp/kisoken/accel/en/index.html and https://www.jst.go.jp/erato/en/index.html.

Table 9.2 A bird's eye view of the Human-Harmonized Information Technology in this volume

Category and features

Social implementation

- *Field studies on *sonzaikan* media: eldery care and education support [8]
- *Field studies with FoodLog Web and app [1]
- *Public installation at Miraikan
- Field trials of robot services at public space [10]
- Public installation at Nagoya Institute of Technology and Handa City [23]

Application

- *A suite of *sonzaikan* media: Telenoid, Hugvie, and Elfoid [8]
- music-sync applications using Songle Widget, TextAlive and many other web services [5]
- SHelective, Inter-Personal Browsing, PVLC projector, EnchanTable, MiragePrinter, and fVisiOn [16]
- *FoodLog Web with image processing for food-balance estimation and FoodLog app for assisting food recording by image retrieval [1]

Platform

- *Tangible information environment encompassing haptic information display, Telexistence avatar robot system: TELESAR V, RPT-based full-parallax autostereoscopic 3D: RePro3D, and an autostereoscopic display for seamless interaction with the real environment mixed together: HaptoMIRAGE [21]
- *Dynamic information space based on integrated high-speed 3D vision for insensible dynamics sensing, high-speed resistor network proximity sensor array for detecting nearby object, noncontact low-latency haptic feedback, and high-speed display of visual information [9]
- Intention-Gait model [26]
- Human-robot symbiosis technology based on high precision pedestrian sensing and modeling [10]
- *Technology for sensing and controlling human gaze in daily living space [19]
- Reading-life log [13]
- Songle and Songle Widget, geared by musical similarity and typicality estimation technologies [5]
- MMDAgent [23]
- Sound cask [7]
- *Smart Posterboard for archiving poster conversation [12]

Basic science

- Finding of sensitivity to temporal contiguity in pedagogical interaction [6]
- *Cognitive model of excessive trust [22]
- *Sonzai* and *sonzaikan*: cognitive model of sense of presence [8]
- *Implicit interpersonal information in communication [11]
- *Haptic primary color model [21]
- *Conceptual model of sense-centered human interface based on illusions in perceived heaviness [14]
- *Multi-modal corpus for poster conversation [12]

*: in the previous volume

duced and implemented an appearance-based gaze-sensing method with adaptive linear regression (ALR), which can make an optimal selection of a sparse set of training samples for gaze estimation, a new approach to the auto-calibration of gaze sensing from a user's natural viewing behavior, which was predicted with a computational model of visual saliency, and (3) user-independent single-shot gaze estimation. They also studied a subtle modulation of visual stimuli based on visual saliency models and the use of a robot's nonverbal behaviors in human–robot interaction.

Kawahara and his colleagues gave useful insights into the prediction of turn-taking, speaker dialization, hot-spot detection, and the prediction of interest and comprehension levels by analyzing multi-modal conversations using the Smart Poster-board they developed [12]. For example, it was found that about 70% of next speakers in turn-taking events could be predicted by combining eye-gaze objects, joint eye-gaze events, duration, and backchannels. It was also found that interest levels could be predicted by using the occurrence of questions and prominent tokens and comprehension levels could be estimated from question types.

In this volume, Yagi and his colleagues focused on the varieties of gait a person has to determine the relation between gait variation and inertial states, i.e., attention (gaze direction), human relations (group segmentation), and cognitive level (assessment of dementia) [26]. For attention estimation, they conducted numerous experiments studying the relationship between gaze and whole-body behaviors. They found that there is a similar eye–head coordination in different conditions, which suggests that head orientation is directly related to visual perception; the distribution of the eye position varies systematically with head orientation; the angles of the gaze, head, and chest have linear relationships, under non-walking and walking conditions; not only the head but also the arm and leg movements are related to the gaze locations; etc. They also propose a method for determining whether two people belong to the same group, combining motion trajectory, chest orientation, and gesture. Researching dual-task analysis for cognitive level estimation, they conducted data collection at an elderly-care facility and at the National Museum of Emerging Science and Innovation, or Miraikan, in Tokyo. The data obtained from the latter are immense, with more than 95,000 participants. The analysis of these data is in progress.

Kanda and his colleagues presented a project intended to enable a mobile social robot to adapt to an open public space in a city [10]. To harmonize mobile social robots in daily human contexts, they address common-sense problems in the domain of open public spaces, such as shopping mall corridors, where pedestrians do not just walk but stop to interact, stop to observe, slow down to look, and leave uninterested. They built a comprehensive pedestrian model for human–robot symbiosis. This includes collision avoidance and task-oriented HRI, encompassing such activities as shopping and observation. It can predict the behavior of people in low-density situations (less than 0.25 person/m^2). They also introduced high-level harmonized HRI features to avoid collision, prevent congestion, and escape "robot abuse"—the nasty treatment of robots, by children in particular. They conducted several field studies and found that they were able to harmonize mobile robots in daily human contexts and encouraged people to acquire information from them.

Kise and his colleagues presented reading-life log technology to help people live with characters [13]. Their technology is comprehensive, including real-time character recognition for alpha-numeric and Japanese characters, omnidirectional character recognition that allows the recognition of all characters in a 360-degree scene image, and real-time document-image retrieval based on basic character detectors and recognizers, a large-scale character dataset, and an automatic font generator. The reading-life log allows not only the construction of a record of one's reading life, including the time spent on, amount of, and attitude toward reading activities, but also the analysis of the content of the reading to support the user's intellectual activities. Using reading-life log technology, they prototyped applications such as Wordometer, which counts the number of words one reads to diagnose one's reading life, a scene-text detector and generator, an automated text annotator, a system for recording texts together with the facial expressions of the reader, and an augmented narrative that uses bio-feedback in a text–body interaction.

Goto and his colleagues presented a suite of technologies for building a similarity-aware information environment [5]. Songle is a web-based active music appreciation service that can automatically determine four types of musical descriptions: musical structure (chorus sections and repeated sections), hierarchical beat structure (musical beats and bar lines), melody line (fundamental frequency, f0 of the vocal melody), and chords (root note and chord type). Songle's web service permits anonymous users to correct errors in the musical archive, to cope with the incompleteness of the automated tool. Songle Widget is a web-based multimedia development framework that allows for the control of computer-graphic animation and physical devices such as robots in synchronization with music publicly available on the web.

Tokuda and his colleagues describe a framework for user-generated content creation [23]. They developed the MMDAgent toolkit to build speech-interaction systems for consumer-generated media (CGM). This allows the building of voice-interaction systems incorporating speech recognition, HMM-based flexible speech synthesis, embodied 3D agent rendering with simulated physics, and dialogue management based on a finite-state transducer. MMDAgent was released as an open-source software toolkit. Tokuda and colleagues have constructed the all-in-one Encyclopedia MMDAgent package, integrating a set of materials on the use of MMDAgent and the production of dialogue content, including guide books/tutorials, slides, reference manuals, and sample scripts.

Ise and his colleagues addressed 3D-sound-scene reproduction [7]. They have succeeded in the world's first implementation of an immersive auditory display, named the Sound Cask, which implements the principle of boundary surface control (BoSC), a theory of 3D-sound-field reproduction. BoSC features the ability to reproduce a sound field, not by points but in three dimensions. Sound Cask was designed to be a wooden output device based on BoSC theory, considering the reflection from the wooden frame, strong normal modes of the outer rectangular chamber, and the wooden distribution of loudspeakers. The system can provide high performance of spatial information reproduction, including sound localization and sound distance, even as the listener freely moves her or his head. A performance evaluation of the system is reported, which encompasses physical performance, localization, and the psychological and physiological evaluation of the feeling of reality in a 3D sound field. The Sound Cask system helps music professionals such as musicians, acoustic engineers, music educators, and music critics enhance their skills and further explore their creativity by providing them with the means to experience 3D sound in a telecommunications environment. Applications include a sound-field simulator, sound table tennis, and sound-field sharing. Sound Cask has been evaluated from various angles: physical performance, localization, and psychological and physiological aspects of feeling reality in a 3D field.

9.2.2 Basic Science Level

The basic science level of the human-harmonized IT addresses basic scientific issues for supporting the platform level. It involves human perception that underlies inter-human and human-agent interactions.

In the previous volume, Takeda and his colleagues presented a cognitive model of excessive trust in human cognition and behaviors [22]. They demonstrated that an integrated model of the gaze and vehicle operational behavior was effective for detecting risky lane changes. Ishiguro and his colleagues introduced sonzaikan[4] media, combining auditory and tactile sensations to represent the feeling of presence in the challenge to transmit human presence [8]. A minimal design approach was employed so that the user can project her or his own image of the communication partner on the terminal device. Kashino and his colleagues employed the idea of implicit interpersonal information (IIPI) to decode mental states, identify the cause of impaired communication in high-functioning autism spectrum disorder (ASD), improve the quality of communication, and elucidate neural mechanisms involved in the processing of IIPI [11]. Tachi and his colleagues proposed a haptic primary-color model to serve as the foundation for designing a haptic information display to recreate cutaneous sensation [21]. Their study draws on studies of how information is mapped between physical, physiological, and psychological spaces. Koike and his colleagues studied the illusion of perceived heaviness induced by the time offset between visual and haptic contact [14]. Their interesting findings included that an object was perceived to be heavier when force was applied earlier than visual contact and perceived to be lighter when it was applied later. They introduced the point of subjective simultaneity (PSS) and the point of subjective equality (PSE) to quantitatively measure the subjective evaluation of timing and weight perception.

In this volume, Hiraki and his colleagues addressed pedagogical machines that can teach and be taught, as teaching and learning behaviors are central to human intelligence. They took a three-fold approach: the development of cognitive science, machine intelligence, and field studies in an educational environment. In the first approach, they found that infants are very sensitive to temporal contiguity in interac-

---

[4]The sense of presence. It is present when its presence is recognized by a person. In contrast, an accompanying concept, sonzai refers to an objective presence.

tion with their mothers. In particular, it became clear that nowness and responsiveness are very important for the design of a pedagogical machine. They investigated temporal contiguity in pedagogical situations and found from a controlled experiment that a 1-second delay in presenting an image significantly deteriorated imitation scores. With the second approach, they developed a pedagogical agent with gaze interaction (PAGI) that is designed to teach Korean words to Japanese students, capable of simulating mutual gaze, gaze following, and joint attention. Experiments with PAGI revealed that even adults are implicitly affected by nowness and responsiveness during word learning with artificial agents. As a result of the third approach, several novel findings have been obtained, e.g., several interactions among children where the interactions seem to affect each child's learning and altruistic behaviors.

9.2.2.1 Application Level

In contrast to the basic science level, the application level of the human-harmonized IT is oriented toward building engineered artifacts to benefit society.

In the previous volume, Ishiguro and his colleagues presented a suite of *sonzaikan* media, consisting of Telenoid, Hugvie, and Elfoid. Telenoid was created as a testbed based on the minimal design of a human being. Hugvie is a human-shaped cushion phone. Human-likeness in visual and tactile information was emphasized in Telenoid's design to facilitate human–robot and mediated inter-human interactions. Hugvie focused on human voice and a human-like touch. Elfoid is a hand-held version of Telenoid. The cellular phone version can connect to a public cellular phone network and was designed to provoke stronger *sonzaikan* than normal cellular phones. The underlying technologies include motion generation through speech information and motion generation and emotional expression through visual stimuli.

Aizawa and his colleagues described FoodLog Web and an app. FoodLog Web is a system that not only allows the user to create a food log by simply taking a photograph of what they have eaten but also applies image processing to analyze the uploaded photograph to generate food-balance information to enable food assessment [1]. The FoodLog app runs on smart phones, allowing the use of photographs to easily add textual descriptions.

In this volume, Goto and his colleagues listed various music-sync applications using Songle Widget, which has been made open to the public [5]. They include a two-dimensional music-sync animation, three-dimensional animated dancing characters, music-sync lighting, a video-jockey web service, real-time control of music-syncro bot dancing, a music visualizer featuring three-dimensional music-sync animation, and a music-sync photo slideshow. Songrium is a music-browsing assistance service that allows the visualization and exploration of a large amount of user-generated music content. They also developed content-creation support technologies. TextAlive enables the creation of music-synchronized lyrics animation. This makes it easy to produce lyric animations based on online music and lyrics information. It supports creativity with intuitive interfaces and mechanisms that simplify the production of derivative work, and it enables the enhancement of effects and incorporation of editing features by web-based programming. It should be noted that Goto and colleagues have developed numerous other applications.

Naemura and his colleagues addressed the privacy control of display content to promote discussion in groups, projection-based control of physical objects for suppressing the incompatibility between the physical and digital worlds, and spatial imaging for augmented reality among people without wearable displays [16]. For privacy-control issues, they developed a privacy-control method called SHelective for sharing displays, and a group-work facilitation system called Inter-Personal Browsing for collaborative web search. For the projection-based augmentation issue, they propose the concept of a bit-data projection system called the Pixel-level Visible Light Communication (PVLC) Projector, and a chemical augmentation system called Hand-Rewriting for paper-based computing. These latter two are functional extensions of existing image projectors to realize a more advanced augmentation of the physical world. For spatial imaging, they propose EnchanTable, which can display a vertically standing mid-air image on a table surface using reflection, MiragePrinter for interactive fabrication on a 3D printer with a mid-air display, and fVisiOn for a glasses-free tabletop 3D display viewable from 360 degrees to augment ordinary tabletop communications.

9.2.3 Social Implementation and Field Study

The social implementation level of the human-harmonized IT addresses implementation of technology as a part of a social system. It includes public installations and field studies.

In the previous volume, we presented four long-term exhibitions at the National Museum of Emerging Science and Innovation (Miraikan)[5] by Naemura, Ishiguro, Tachi, Yagi, and their colleagues as a valuable outreach to society. The first exhibition, by Naemura and his colleagues, entitled "The Studio—Extend Your Real World—"[6] demonstrated display design in a mixed-reality environment, mounted for 164 days from July 3, 2013, to January 13, 2014. It attracted about 130,000 visitors. The second exhibition, by Ishiguro and his colleagues, has been sustained for over two and half years since June 25, 2014. The exhibition, entitled "Android: What is Human?"[7] demonstrating interaction with androids and a Telenoid, attracted enormous public attention. The estimated number of visitors before March 2014 was more than 500,000. The third exhibition, by Tachi and his colleagues, was open under the title "Touch the World, Feel the Future," from October 22, 2014, to May 11, 2015.[8] The installation includes a telexistence robot TELESAR V, a 3D-display HaptoMIRAGE, which allows the user to touch something that they see exactly as

---

[5]http://www.miraikan.jst.go.jp/en/.

[6]http://miraikan.jp/medialab/en/12.html.

[7]https://www.miraikan.jst.go.jp/en/exhibition/future/robot/android.html.

[8]http://miraikan.jp/medialab/en/14.html.

they see it, Haptic Broadcast, which can transfer tactile sensations through the activation of sport apparatus in synchronization with audio–visual information, Haptic Search, which allows searching for an object with the sense of touch similar to a given stimulus, the TECHTILE toolkit, which allows a user to design his or her own senses of touch easily, and GravityGrabber, which can produce normal and tangential forces on a fingertip. Around 140,000 people visited in the first half of the exhibition period. The fourth, launched by Yagi and his colleagues on July 15, 2015,[9] was about behavior understanding, based on an intention-gait model. The exhibition, originally planned to go until April 11, 2016, was extended to June 27. More than 95,000 people participated in the experiment in the installation.

We described field studies on *sonzaikan* media conducted by Ishiguro and his colleagues. Elder care with Telenoid, cultural differences toward Telenoid, and educational support with Telenoid were investigated in field studies. We also described the FoodLog web service[10] that Aizawa and his colleagues developed, which not only allows the user to create a food log simply by taking a photo of what she or he eats but also generates food-balance information through image analysis [1].

In this volume, the list of longitudinal public installations is extended. Numerous web services have been made available, as reported by Goto and his colleagues [5]. Tokuda and his colleagues demonstrated their uDialogue technology through a public installation. They developed a bidirectional voice-guidance digital signage system ("Mei-chan") using the MMDAgent toolkit and installed it in an open space just outside the main gate of Nagoya Institute of Technology. They also built an indoor digital signage system capable of bidirectional voice guidance, installing it at a tourist information office for public service in Handa city, Aichi, Japan [23]. Kanda conducted two field trials evaluating robot service in a public space. In the flyer distribution trial, they developed a detailed behavioral model of people in the flyer-distribution service, as well as analyzing successful behaviors. Thanks to these efforts, the success ratio of the robot distributor reached 87.9%, exceeding that of average human distributors (40.7%). In the direction-giving trial, 96.6% of visitors reported that the robot's service was good; people tended to listen to the robot and seemed happy during the interaction [10].

9.3 Present Situation

In the year since the previous volume, weak AI, or AI as an intelligent tool, has become even more popular in our living spaces, as seen in talking assistants, chatbots, and semi-autonomous vehicles using autopilot, in addition to epoch-making events, such as AlphaGo's win against Lee Sedol.

Strong AI, or AI as a conscious autonomous agent, is now visible on the horizon, though currently beyond implementation. Although strong AI appears solely in

---

[9]http://www.miraikan.jst.go.jp/en/exhibition/future/digital/medialabo.html.
[10]http://www.foodlog.jp/en.

science fiction, as an extrapolation of existing weak AIs, people perceive it rather concretely, either as it is written about in stories or depicted in movies.

The mixture of weak and strong AI has provoked social concerns. Some of these concerns are pressing, such as safety and controllability, for example in autonomous vehicles, for their behaviors are not completely predictable or continuous as a function of situations. Other concerns are imaginary but not innocent, as they provoke anxiety in society.

A pair of open letters from the Future of Life Institute (FLI) concisely represents social concern with the current status of artificial intelligence. The first open letter [4] openly proposes that AI research should not only focus on technological advances in artificial intelligence but also make maximal effort to ensure AI is beneficial to society. In the detailed version of a report published in AI Magazine [18], Russell et al. present a rather comprehensive list of research priorities for socializing artificial intelligence. They emphasize verification, validity, security, and control as computer-science research aspects of AI. The second open letter [3] claims that autonomous weapons using AI technology should be prevented for the sake of humanity. AI is even counted among the twelve risks that threaten human civilization [17].

Long-term issues have been discussed in different contexts. The report of the 2015 study panel on a 100-year study on artificial intelligence [20] takes the positive approach that there is "no cause for concern that AI is an imminent threat to humankind," whereas AI technologies have the "potential to be used for good or nefarious purposes." This motivates us to steer AI research and development so that it benefits society.

Machine ethics is the study of giving machines ethical principles or procedures for autonomously judging whether a given action is good [2]. So, long as machines are living with us, the more autonomy the machines have, the more ethical they need to be. Moor classifies ethical agents into four categories, namely normative agents that are not designed for ethical situations, ethical impact agents whose behavior may have an ethical impact regardless of their task, implicit ethical agents that have been programmed to either support ethical behaviors or avoid unethical behaviors, and explicit ethical agents that can calculate the best action in ethical dilemmas [15].

The influence of technology on mankind may be more implicit, quietly going on beneath the surface and hard to observe without insight and professional investigation. In her best-selling book Alone Together [25], Turkle analyzes digital culture from a psychoanalytic viewpoint. She focuses on robotic creatures and networked life. On the one hand, Turkle points out, digital creatures invoke a sense of companionship even though they do not understand the user. This may be regarded as moral complacency resulting from a non-authentic relationship with an artificial caregiver; as she wrote, "robots cannot pretend because it can only pretend."[11] With regard to other people, Turkle discusses the multi-tasking brought about by the digital network that may lead to getting "alone together" even if they physically live together. Technology always brings about negative effects as well as positive ones. Sometimes, the

---

[11]p. 124 in [25].

Fig. 9.1 Role of
human-harmonized
information technology

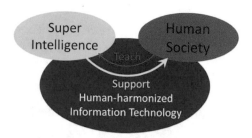

former silently spreads beneath the surface. People are vulnerable to loneliness and
hence to artificial togetherness.

We are convinced that movement toward human-harmonized IT is well-supported
and on the right track. We have to date only focused on the perception level. For the
next step, we will need to shed light on the higher level and aim for integrated services.
In addition to the treatment of semantic and contextual information, we will need to
address the huge amount of information on the net. Goto has made an initial attempt
in this direction in the Songrium project. Generalization is needed.

9.4 Potential Next Challenges

What are the next challenges? As we witness the rise of superintelligence accelerating
the shift from an information society to an AI society, more people are coming to share
the view that human society will benefit from superintelligence, through learning
(Fig. 9.1). The role of human-harmonized IT is realizing the intensive integration
between human society and super intelligence, so that human and social potential
may be maximized. In this chapter, we will draw a clear picture of integration and
identify technical challenges and opportunities to make the maximization happen.

9.4.1 Companion Agent

Among other potential contributions to human-harmonized IT, the most integrated
image of the target may be the companion agent (Fig. 9.2), which works with each
individual user by exploiting functions provided by the social platform geared by
superintelligence. The role of a companion agent is to provide a personalized comprehensive support for the user, not just by protecting her or him from potential
threats in the jungle of complex functions available from numerous services built on
the social platform, but also by enhancing her or his human potential to maximally
leverage and contribute to social potential.

The notion of companionship is much more subtle and sophisticated than assistance. Unlike an intelligent assistant, a companion agent involves numerous con-

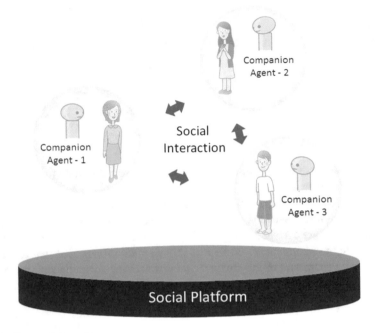

Fig. 9.2 Companion agents

ceptual challenges as well as technical ones. David Traum [24] suggested that a companion may be characterized by a long-term relationship such as unquestionable loyalty, second banana/sidekick, and interest in its prime or boss. Traum suggests that companions should be carefully distinguished from similar concepts such as servants, agents, leaders, and counselors as well as assistants and even romantic partners. Traum lists ten dos and don'ts for artificial companionship:

1. Do something useful!
2. Don't just do one thing!
3. Do understand the situation (as much as possible)!
4. Do what I want!
5. Be a good conversationalist!
6. Do revisit conversations appropriately!
7. Do understand what you are saying!
8. Don't be repetitive!
9. Do learn and customize!
10. Do maintain immersion!

Furthermore, ethical issues need to be addressed, even though companions are not explicitly at the ethical-agent level but implicitly at the ethical-agent level [15]. Ethical issues come in at various stages in scenes.

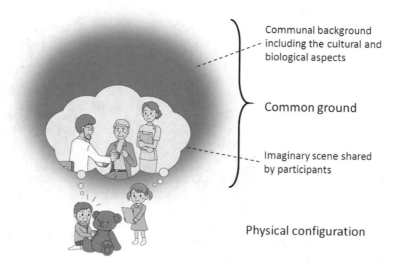

Communal background
including the cultural and
biological aspects

Common ground

Imaginary scene shared
by participants

Physical configuration

Fig. 9.3 Common ground

9.4.2 Common Ground

Common ground is the collection of knowledge, beliefs, and suppositions that are required that each participant in an interaction share prior to interaction. It ranges from communal background, including a cultural and biological basis, to an imaginary scene dynamically formed, shared, and updated as interaction proceeds (Fig. 9.3). Unless extensive common ground is shared, interactants must spend immense effort coordinating their actions and sharing ideas.

Common ground ranges from the perceptual to the story levels. The implicit nature of common ground makes its computation difficult. Even if immense amounts of data are available on the net and sensory data are measurable by advanced sensors, these are useless unless they are organized and associated with the given situation.

9.4.3 Robotic Apprentice

Building a robotic apprentice that can mimic a human instructor may be a promising approach to acquiring common ground regarding actions and interactions (Fig. 9.4). Humanoid robots may be employed to transfer human knowledge and expertise rooted in embodiment, ranging from daily activities to highly skilled behaviors. Humanoid robots with human-like perceptions are mandated for this task, as the apprentice needs to be able to capture the world and its tasks in a very similar fashion to human instructors. Put another way, robotic apprentices for such tasks

Fig. 9.4 Robotic apprentice   Human instructor   Robotic assistant

must possess common ground at a perceptual and motor level in addition to basic language-communication capabilities.

Robots with different levels of embodiment may be used in cases where we need to transfer task-related knowledge at a more abstract level. This setting is more challenging, as the robot must be able to transform the perceptions and behaviors of the user to a different embodiment of the robot.

In addition, a powerful machine-learning algorithm is necessary to generalize the robotic apprentice's experience into a more general form of knowledge for incorporation into a larger body of knowledge for reuse.

9.4.4 From Perception to Cognition

Both common-ground building and robotic apprentices require multiple levels of information to be integrated, because these tasks need a full range of communication with people. Two challenges arise. The first is addressing modalities other than speech and vision. People interact with the environment and each other not just through audio-visual channels but also through haptic, tangible, smell, taste, temperature, and other sensations. People use a rich vocabulary regarding these sensations, sometimes single and sometimes composite, to communicate their experiences. The second challenge is to create a solid link between perception and cognition where high-level issues such as understanding, storytelling, and memory organization matter. I believe that this will also benefit the machine ethics that should accompany practice in daily life.

9.4.5   Helping People Grasp Huge Information Space

A difficulty for the information society and its successors is the explosion of information, which makes it desperate for people to gain the sense of the "whole" space, which may lead people to ignorance or anxiety and significantly hinder creativity and other forms of human potential. An important challenge to human-harmonized IT is helping people gain the sense of the "whole" in the huge information space, so they are able to feel its benefits and risks. A less ambitious but still useful challenge is to produce a historical development of an idea in the information space, e.g., the history of artificial intelligence research, on demand. As human beings cannot spend an infinite amount of time answering a question, the ability to address such historical development questions would be a valuable function for a companion agent.

9.4.6   Gamification and Storytelling

In the convivial society, creativity will become a central concern of life. Gamification and storytelling are keys to creativity. Our companion agent must be able to help people gamify and tell stories. Both games and stories are great inventions of the humanity and are lots of fun to people. They are complementary to each other, shedding light on different aspects of reality. Games abstract the reality as interactions with rules, while stories allow people to capture it as relations. We can characterize the relationship between the reality, games and stories as in Fig. 9.5. Gamification is a process of abstracting the real world by eliciting the rules for competition, whereas storytelling is a process of organizing experiences, either real or gamified, into a structure. Conversely, the science of the artificial allows us to pave the world as we think in stories and games.

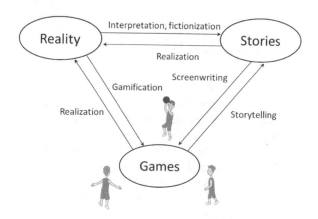

Fig. 9.5 Gamification and Storytelling

9.4.7 Longitudinal Companionship

The sharp difference between companionship and mere assistance is that companionship must be longitudinal by definition. For a valuable companion agent, one-time assistance is less critical than long-term sustaining support and underlying trust and emotional attachment. Even if a companion agent makes a mistake or an error, it can be repaired. However, social and emotional relationships matter. Any negative actions that may hurt a social or emotional relationship, such as betrayal or insults, may immediately lead to the breakdown of companionship. The challenge is how to build a long-term mutual trust, incorporating repair and resilience functions. Companionship must also be designed to retain human potential that may even lead to the break-up of companionship. Ethics must cope with such negative occurrences.

9.4.8 Practice and Social Implementation

It is always important for us to learn from people through practice. There are several issues for us in designing our research for social implementation. Apart from specialized subjects such as medical clinics, scientific research, and athletics, we need to choose subject domains carefully. We believe that daily-life support is not only demanded but also allows us to learn a great deal, though it is very challenging in the sense that the boundary is hard to find and information is unstructured and tacit.

Methods of evaluation and assessment are crucial for learning from feedback. In addition to standard means, such as brochures or physiological indices, it is instructive to explore new approaches, as, for instance, it was found that the measurement of neuroendocrine responses is useful for probing the effects of social interactions [8]. Further investigation is expected to greatly contribute to the evaluation and assessment of companion agents.

9.5 Conclusion

This chapter gave an overview to the JST-CREST research area on the creation of human-harmonized IT for a convivial society. I emphasized changing-world phenomena as a background and characterized our research area as a challenge for developing key technology for a convivial society in which humans and technology are in harmony. I referred to the late Professor Tohkura's grand conjecture concerning the five-stage shift in the role of information in society, and pointed out that we are at the stage of an information society and are moving toward an AI-supported society. I argued that a key idea in making a successful transition to a convivial society is through human and social potential. Human potential is the power of an individual that enables her or him to actively sustain an endeavor to achieve a goal in maintaining a social relationship with other people. It involves vision, activity, sustainability, empathy, ethics, humor, and esthetic sense. Social potential is the power that a society of people possesses as a whole. It encompasses generosity, support, conviviality, diversity, connectedness, and innovativeness. We believe that our research area contributes to the construction of technology that will enhance human and social potential. The outcomes from the first group encompass a suite of topics ranging from foundation to social implementation, covering novel subjects such as implicit interpersonal information, sense-centered human interfaces, excessive trust, and sense of presence (*sonzaikan*). Applications include FoodLog, which is a suite of *sonzaikan* media that has been socially implemented through field trials.

References

1. K. Aizawa, FoodLog: multimedia food recording tools for diverse applications (2016). (in volume 1)
2. M. Anderson, S.L. Anderson (eds.), *Machine Ethics* (Cambridge University Press, Cambridge, 2011)
3. Future of life institute. Autonomous weapons: an open letter from AI and robotics researchers (2015), http://futureoflife.org/open-letter-autonomous-weapons/
4. Future of life institute. Research priorities for robust and beneficial artificial intelligence (2015), http://futureoflife.org/ai-open-letter/
5. M. Goto, Building a similarity-aware information environment for a content-symbiotic society (2016). (in this volume)
6. K. Hiraki, Pedagogical machine: Developmental cognitive science approach to create teaching/teachable machines (2016). (in this volume)
7. S. Ise, Deelopment of a sound field sharing system for creating and exchanging music (2016). (in this volume)
8. H. Ishiguro, Transmitting human presence through portable teleoperated androids—a minimal design approach (2016). (in volume 1)
9. M. Ishikawa, I. Ishii, Y. Sakaguchi, M. Shimojo, H. Shinoda, H. Yamamoto, T. Komuro, H. Oku, Y. Nakajima, Y. Watanabe, Dynamic information space based on high-speed sensor technology (2016). (in volume 1)
10. T. Kanda, Enabling a mobile social robot to adapt to a public space in a city (2016). (in this volume)
11. M. Kashino, S. Shimojo, K. Watanabe, Critical roles of implicit interpersonal information in communication (2016). (in volume 1)
12. T. Kawahara, Smart posterboard: multi-modal sensing and analysis of poster conversations (2016). (in volume 1)
13. K. Kise, Reading-life log as a new paradigm of utilizing character and document media (2016). (in this volume)
14. Y. Koike, Elucidation of perceptual illusion and development of sense-centered human interface (2016). (in Volume 1)
15. J.H. Moor, The nature, importance, and difficulty of machine ethics, in *Machine Ethics*, ed. by M. Anderson, S.L. Anderson (Cambridge University Press, New York, 2011), pp. 13–20. Cambridge Books Online
16. T. Naemura, Inter-personal displays: augmenting the physical world where people get together (2016). (in this volume)
17. D. Pamlin, S. Armstrong, Global challenges: 12 risks that threaten human civilization (Global Challenges Foundation, Stockholm, 2015)

18. S. Russell, D. Dewey, M. Tegmark, Research priorities for robust and beneficial artificial intelligence. AI Mag. **36**(4), 105–114 (2014)
19. Y. Sato, Y. Sugano, A. Sugimoto, Y. Kuno, H. Koike, Sensing and controlling human gaze in daily living space for human-harmonized information environments (2016). (in volume 1)
20. P. Stone, R. Brooks, E. Brynjolfsson, R. Calo, O. Etzioni, G. Hager, J. Hirschberg, S. Kalyanakrishnan, E. Kamar, S. Kraus, K. Leyton-Brown, D. Parkes, W, Press, A. Saxenian, J. Shah, M. Tambe, A. Teller, Artificial intelligence and life in 2030, 2016. One hundred year study on artificial intelligence: report of the 2015-2016 Study Panel (Stanford University, Stanford, CA, September 2016), http://ai100.stanford.edu/2016-report. Accessed 1 Aug 2016
21. S. Tachi, Haptic Media: construction and utilization of haptic virtual reality and haptic telexistence (2016). (in volume 1)
22. K. Takeda, Modeling and detecting exceesive trust from behavior signals: Overview of research project and results (2016). (in volume 1)
23. K. Tokuda, User generated dialogue systems: uDialogue (2016). (in this volume)
24. D.R. Traum, Do's and don'ts for software companions. In *Proceedings of the International Workshop on Emotion Representations and Modelling for Companion Technologies*, ERM4CT '15 (ACM, New York, NY, USA, 2015), pp. 3–3
25. S. Turkle, *Alone Together: Why we expect more from technology and less from each other* (Basic Books, New York, 2011)
26. Y. Yagi, Behavior understanding based on intention-gait model (2016). (in this volume)

Index

© Springer Japan KK 2017
T. Nishida (ed.), *Human-Harmonized Information Technology, Volume 2,*
DOI 10.1007/978-4-431-56535-2

Printed in the United States
By Bookmasters